TRANSPERSONAL DEVELOPMENT

The Dimension Beyond Psychosynthesis

ROBERTO ASSAGIOLI, M.D.

Crucible
An Imprint of HarperCollins*Publishers*

Crucible
An Imprint of Grafton Books
A Division of HarperCollins*Publishers*
77-85 Fulham Palace Road,
Hammersmith, London W6 8JB

First published in Italy as *Sviluppo
Transpersonale* by Casa Editrice
Astrolabio, Rome, 1988
This edition published by
Crucible 1991
1 3 5 7 9 10 8 6 4 2
Copyright © Casa Editrice Astrolabio—
Ubaldini Editore, Roma, 1988
English Translation
© The Aquarian Press 1991

Roberto Assagioli asserts the moral
right to be identified as the author
of this work.

British Library Cataloguing in
Publication Data
Assagioli, Roberto
Transpersonal development.
1. Psychosynthesis. Theories
I. Title
II. Sviluppo transpersonale. *English*
158.9

ISBN 1-85274-062-0

Typeset by Harper Phototypesetters
Limited, Northampton, England
Printed in Great Britain by
Mackays, Chatham, Kent

CONTENTS

PART TWO
SPIRITUAL AWAKENING

PART THREE
SPIRITUALITY IN EVERYDAY LIFE

PREFACE

This book was produced 13 years after the author's death and takes the form of a collection of miscellaneous writings penned at different times and for different purposes: notes, essays, speeches and lectures. It will nevertheless prove an invaluable work for anyone seeking practical guidelines in the demanding task of self-knowledge and self-realization.

The title *Transpersonal Development* is certainly most appropriate for the scientific approach of Roberto Assagioli's Psychosynthesis, for he saw the inner search and realization of the Self as a valid means whereby, when psychical maturity permits, that latent dimension within each person is able to become active: this is precisely what transpersonality means—that which is 'beyond' the normal experience of phenomena. This is not to be understood as an exceptional gift reserved for the few, but as a reservoir of higher powers which, though recessive initially, are available to anyone who is willing to call them forth and develop them by a conscious effort and by the deliberate use of their own energies, using appropriate techniques and training.

As far as Psychosynthesis is concerned, the one and only certainty of the 'human phenomenon' is the Self, that focal point from which we cannot escape and from which it would be dangerous to move away. This does not of course mean evading the problems of personality and of the world; it simply means coming to terms with what is relative and what is permanent in the atomic structure of man, what is 'structurally' identical to that great energy which permeates the Universe. Looked at in this way, Psychosynthesis is able to put forward its theories and to make use of all the potential of this 'planet-man' who represents a microcosm in a continuous state of development, endued with the responsibility of the consciousness which animates his being.

In this sense Roberto Assagioli was truly a scientist of the spirit, devoting his life to the discovery of the reality of phenomena beyond the evidence of the facts presented. His thought may be rejected without consideration by those who adopt a dogmatically materialist approach, or it may be confused with some vague integrated psycho-existential system by those who look at it from the viewpoint of superficiality or cultural prejudice. But whenever it is carefully examined, its concept of man is seen to be unchallengeable, and the psychosynthetic approach to life is shown to have unlimited breadth. It is an 'open system' undergoing a continuous, infinite development, and allowing for an experimental approach, based on hypotheses which are shown to be incontestable and on tested psychodynamic techniques which have practical application in all areas of human activity.

The work of the doctor and psychiatrist Roberto Assagioli acquires even greater significance if it is placed in the historic context in which he lived and carried out his work of research and discovery.

His first writings date from 1906, even before he graduated in medicine at the age of 22 and went on to Zurich to specialize in psychiatry. As a close contemporary of Freud and Jung he quickly became aware of the interaction between biological structure and the emotional/mental substratum of the human make-up; this enabled him to establish the relationships between the two aspects and to put forward certain fundamental laws of psychodynamics. And this at a time when the official medical world was far from entertaining any psychosomatic approach.

As an outstanding humanist Assagioli was not content with these first achievements, but went on to push back the boundaries of psychology into the uncharted waters of spirituality. While Freud was sounding the depths of the mind and Jung was glimpsing the splendours of human destiny in the shadows of the past, he was setting out to discover the 'permanent atom' of man, describing its structure and pointing out the means of access, thus opening up a whole new area to that inner seeking after the divine. Psychosynthesis actually provided a new pathway for self-realization in keeping with the hypotheses and methods of the new science and based on action and direct responsibility: life passes through our hands and each of us takes control of it, accepting the present as the inevitable corollary of the past, and conscious of the fact that at any given moment we are shaping our own future.

The first part of this book is descriptive in nature and introduces the idea of the 'superconscious', i.e. that latent aspect of man's being in which his higher values are to be found. What comes across quite clearly is the author's intention of freeing the spiritual content from the historic confines to which it had been relegated: religions, philosophies and various occult ideologies. Siding with the psychological findings of such people as W. James, Bucke, Hall, Jung, Frankl, Maslow and other scholars of the time, Assagioli took up a position against the exclusion of the 'spiritual' from the domain of scientific research and, in the name of authentic humanist science, put forward a method of experimental enquiry which did not restrict its attention to quantitative aspects, but supplemented them with the qualitative value of experience.

This method provided tools and techniques suited to a type of research which shifts the focus of attention from the external world to the world within, at the same time retaining the essential factors of objectivity and of the reality of phenomena.

Such an exercise obviously involves the difficulty of making man a neutral observer of himself, a detached analyst of his own inner psychological reactions. But, as Assagioli emphasized, what matters here is 'good reasoning' and an openness to the experience of renewal without preconceived ideas or prejudices, as we receive the direct witness of that evolutionary process which is the fundamental law of the Universe, imposing an incessant transformation on everything that exists, by natural selection or by deliberate self-management.

The second part of the book focuses on the problems and difficulties which may be encountered along the spiritual path, and gives guidelines on the most appropriate ways of tackling and overcoming them. We see here the balanced perspective and personal involvement of Assagioli the man, who certainly travelled along this path himself and knew its hardships. Indeed he had the great advantage of being able to integrate three fundamental aspects of his existential experience: the cultural aspect, in that his great learning enabled him to draw together the most significant fruits of human knowledge from the earliest traditions up to his own day; the scientific aspect, in the sense that the profession of psychiatrist and psychotherapist gave him firsthand experience in dealing with 'man's problems'; and the human aspect, in the sense that his true vocation for self-realization enabled him to overcome the arduous trials of life with serenity and courage. This synthesis within Assagioli himself is very apparent and it shows itself in the form of an inner enlightenment and a love for humanity, characteristics that pervade his work. What strikes one most is his ability to side with man, and even when he is dealing with negative attributes he redeems him with his boundless faith in the future.

The third part of the book brings the earlier research into the modern world, pointing out the values of the spirit and the primary goals of our existence. Here too the words of Assagioli act as witness. Anyone who knew him will never forget the radiance of the person he was, expressing at one and the same time beauty, love, joy, goodwill and peace.

After reading these pages one comes away with the certainty that the waning of great suffering will give way to the birth from the depths of man's being of the bright dawning of divinity, in the glorious light of which suffering, attachments and passions will vanish as if by magic, transfigured by the exalting process of renewal. This is the catharsis which announces the birth of a new Humanity, a Humanity which Roberto Assagioli perceived and inhabited in his own consciousness. The works of Roberto Assagioli do not require a long preface: the clarity of his exposition, the fluency and coherence of his language, the continuous use of examples to explain concepts, the absence of any obscure references, and an absolute respect for semantic values make him a very special writer. Because he is always at pains to explain his thought processes, he is the ideal companion for anyone wishing to follow him in his inner discoveries.

As I see it, this is a book to be pondered over. It does not contain anything existentially new, it does not advocate exciting adventures of the mind, even less does it provide easy methods for entering into some illusory paradise. Rather it is a precious collection of gems of wisdom and of psychospiritual reflections, one which can be used as a useful tool for meditation by all those who seek truth in the depths of their being.

Sergio Bartoli

EDITOR'S INTRODUCTION

Roberto Assagioli was born in Venice on 27 February 1888 and died in Capolona, in the province of Arezzo, on 23 August 1974. He wrote three books: *Psicosintesi: per l'armonia della vita* [Psychosynthesis: for Harmony in Life] (Mediterranée, Rome, 1965); *Principi e metodi della psicosintesi terapeutica* [Principles and Methods of Therapeutic Psychosynthesis] (Astrolabio, Rome, 1973), and *L'atto di volonta* [The Act of Will] (Astrolabio, Rome, 1977). In addition he left behind an immense number of other writings which he produced over the years, for the most part unedited and most of them undated; in these the psychological system which he formulated and developed under the name Psychosynthesis is expounded in all its richness. In publishing the first volume of those writings on the centenary of the birth of its founder, it is the aim of the Institute of Psychosynthesis to highlight that richness.

Editing the writings brought foreseeable initial difficulties: the lack of a comprehensive catalogue, the heterogeneous nature of the material and the lack of dates. But to immerse oneself in the world of Assagioli's thought means that in addition to its vastness and richness, one comes away with a sense of coherence and unity: there is a thread which runs through the writings of the different periods and links together the ideas they contain. It is this quality which has lightened the task of dividing up and organizing the material.

In undertaking an in-depth reading of Assagioli's writings, one becomes aware that the bio-psychospiritual reality of man came to him in its entirety and that his thinking then developed and gave form to his initial intuition. As early as 1909, when he published his article 'The Psychology of Ideas-Forces and Psychagogy' in the *Rivista di Psicologia Applicata* [The Applied Psychology Review], Assagioli was putting forward a view of man and a psychological discipline which, as he himself recalled in 1971,[1] already contained the key points of psychosynthesis in embryo form. With the years and with experience that first insight was confirmed, the system of thought was developed, its tenets were enriched, various nuances were introduced, and the concept was expressed with depth and beauty.

To attempt a chronological arrangement of the various writings is difficult, and it is perhaps superfluous, more a matter of curiosity than necessity. Despite the varied nature of the material, Assagioli's thought, which developed with clarity and coherence over the years, is able to arrange itself. The editor has only to give outward expression to this implicit organization, the subject matter takes shape spontaneously—and here we have the first volume: *Transpersonal Development* is a melting pot for writings which may well have provided the substance of the book Assagioli was on the point of writing before his death. In it he was proposing to 'continue [his] treatment, in a more coordinated and systematic way' of the 'study and investigation' of the superconscious experiences that had occupied his mind 'for some decades' and on which the attention of transpersonal psychology was focused.

That these writings were to be brought together in a collection is also borne out by the grey sheet on which Assagioli himself, in his ornate nineteenth-century handwriting, had penned the words 'Volume of Spiritual Essays' in blue ink.

In one sense all Assagioli's writings are spiritual, but the attribute of spirituality applies more particularly to the part of his work which deals with that 'long and arduous adventure', that 'journey through alien lands' which describes the spiritual development of man (Chapter 10, page 116). This is the theme of the present volume. It is a theme of great human and scientific interest, and one which can be looked at from many aspects. The approach adopted by Assagioli the psychiatrist and psychotherapist is truly psychological—it is to emphasize this

[1] See R. Assagioli, *La psicologia e l'esistenza umana* [Psychology and Human Existence], the Institute of Psychosynthesis, Florence 1971.

fact that the adjective *transpersonal* has been used in the title, 'a term,' Assagioli observes, 'introduced above all by Maslow and by those of his school to refer to what is commonly called spiritual. Scientifically speaking, it is a better word; it is more precise and, in a certain sense, neutral in that it points to that which is beyond or above ordinary personality. Furthermore it avoids confusion with many things which are now called spiritual but which are actually pseudo-spiritual or para-psychological.' Throughout this book, however, in order to keep to the author's original wording, we have retained the term *spiritual*, which is used by Assagioli 'in its widest sense to include not only specifically religious experiences, but all states of consciousness, and all those functions and activities which have to do with values above the norm: ethical, aesthetic, heroic, humanitarian and altruistic values'.

As Assagioli himself saw it, then, the term *spiritual development* includes 'all experiences connected with awareness of the contents of the superconscious, which may or may not include experience of the Self'.[1]

The book is in three parts: the first part, in cognitive fashion, introduces the theme of the reality of the superconscious world; the second follows at close hand the stages and problems encountered in the process of spiritual development; and the third deals with the everyday application of its effects.

For 'every psychical process is made up of two aspects or moments which are inseparable and yet distinct; the first being consciousness and understanding, and the second being the application thereof',[2] and 'a spiritual appreciation of life and of its various manifestations, far from being theoretical and unpractical, is eminently revolutionary, dynamic and creative'.[3]

Maria Luisa Girelli

[1] See R. Assagioli, *Principi e Metodi della Psicosintesi Terapeutica* [Principles and Methods of Therapeutic Psychosynthesis], Astrolabio, Rome 1973, page 43.
[2] R. Assagioli, *Il valore pratico ed umano della cultura psichica* [The Practical and Human Value of Psychical Knowledge], The Institute of Knowledge and Psychical Therapy, Rome 1929.
[3] R. Assagioli, *Denaro e vita spirituale* [Money and Spiritual Life], page 181.

PART ONE

THE STUDY OF THE SUPERCONSCIOUS

THE AWAKENING AND DEVELOPMENT OF SPIRITUAL CONSCIOUSNESS

The superficial and unclear way in which the word 'spiritual' has been and is still often used has created a great deal of confusion and misunderstanding. It is our deliberate intention to avoid a definition, preferring instead a more scientific approach: starting with *facts* and experience, and then interpreting what has been observed and discovered. In this way the precise sense in which the word 'spiritual' is used here will become clear as this chapter proceeds.

The basic fact claiming our attention is *experience and spiritual consciousness*, and it may be expressed in this way: from the earliest times there have been human beings who have claimed to have experienced states of consciousness which differed greatly—in quality, intensity and effect—from those that normally project their images of light and dark on the screen of human consciousness. But they also make another claim: they maintain that these states of consciousness are the result of coming or being brought involuntarily into contact with a plane or sphere of Reality which is 'above' or 'beyond' those which are normally regarded as 'real'.

This Reality has often been called transcendent, but we will not use this word to refer to something abstract and remote. Those who have had fleeting glimpses of this Reality testify that it is perceived as something more real, lasting and substantial than the everyday world in which we live, as the true source and essence of being, and as 'life in greater abundance'.

The vast number of testimonies to such encounters with a greater, fuller, higher Reality is astounding. We come across such individuals in all ages and in all countries, and among their ranks are the cream of humanity.

Therefore any attempts that have been made to deny such experiences, any statements to the effect that they are nothing more than illusions or at best sublimations of our sexual instincts, are completely arbitrary and show the absence of the true scientific spirit. William James, whose book *The Varieties of Religious Experience* is a model for the impartial scientific investigation of this subject, was at pains to show the reality and value of the transcendent world. 'It seems to me that the extreme limits of our being,' he wrote, 'find their way into a dimension of existence which is completely different from the world of our senses and our natural understanding as generally perceived; one might call this a mystical region or a supernatural region.'

To the extent that our ideals have their origin in this region (and many of them do, for we find that they possess us in a way that cannot be expressed in words), we belong to that region far more intimately than we belong to the visible world, because we have a more intimate sense of belonging in the place where our ideals belong. Yet the invisible region we are talking about is not simply an idealized one because it produces effects in this world. When we enter into it our work is actually carried out at the level of our complete personality because we have become new men, and this means a way of behaving in the natural world which is in keeping with the regeneration we have undergone. But something which is able to produce effects within another reality must be regarded as a reality itself, thus it seems to me that there is no justification for calling the invisible or mystical world 'unreal'.

> The importance of this higher realm of experience and reality cannot be overvalued, and the mere possibility of its existence should stimulate scientists to devote an amount of energy, time and enthusiasm to their investigation of it, which is in keeping with its human value.

This statement by James is one which might well be accepted by any free individual, for it encourages him to adopt it as a valid basis for confidence as he prepares to engage in further research. This being so, what should our attitude be to this higher realm? Common sense tells us that we should treat it with the same degree of seriousness we are prepared to give to a statement by a group of explorers who tell us they have discovered, let us say, an unknown land rich in oil and precious metals. To ignore such a statement would be madness, because we would be running the risk of cheating ourselves of the opportunity to acquire immense new sources of wealth. Yet a disorganized foray into a new region without the right equipment, the right weapons and tools, would most certainly expose those involved to hazardous climatic conditions and even to wild beasts. At best such rash action would only be likely to succeed after overcoming great difficulties, and its only reward would be a handful of treasures awaiting only the most skilful, most alert and best-equipped explorers.

Reason and experience would suggest, of course, that a rational approach to the problem would be:

1. To carry out an in-depth study of any available information on the territory concerned.
2. To organize a proper expedition and to equip it in the best possible way.

This, then, is the method we will adopt as we examine and compare what the explorers of this little known 'territory' that we are considering have to tell us.

We are faced with considerable difficulties at the outset. In the first place, that central fact and point of agreement to which we have already referred has become overloaded with countless descriptive words which vary according to the point of view of the observer. That is to say, each of them has clothed his own account with words which imply serious discrepancies; his experience has produced different emotional reactions in him which he has interpreted in various, and at times contradictory, ways. To use James's own well-picked words, each individual adds to the original experience a series of inexact personal structures, structures to which he is often firmly attached, both mentally and emotionally. It is this diversity which has caused the confusion, wrong ideas and doubts that surround the subject we are discussing.

Yet the existence of such differences is not surprising and it should not in any way invalidate the fundamental reality of the experiences themselves. It is perfectly natural and, to a certain extent, inevitable, for two important reasons. The first is that no sphere of reality is a homogeneous, straightforward thing; rather it is a real, multi-faceted, varied 'world' abounding in fullness and life. It should not surprise us, therefore, when the many aspects of that Reality have produced such different perceptions of what has been seen. The second reason may be attributed to the vast dissimilarities which exist in the psycho-physical make-up of the observers, as well as in their mental development and their historic and cultural preparation for the experiences they have had. One and the same aspect of Reality may therefore be perceived, interpreted and related in very different ways.

The first conclusion to be drawn from what we have said so far is that spiritual consciousness should not in any way be limited by the type of experience and religious or mystical system of belief, nor should it be identified with them. The importance of this distinction is illustrated by the many misunderstandings and the countless conflicts that have taken place, and by the confusion and consternation that have resulted from its absence. There is a growing number of individuals today who, consciously or not, are in desperate need and are desperately searching for something more satisfying, more *real* than their normal, everyday lives. Many of them have a keen intellect and are realistically minded, unable to find what they need in traditional religion. Some of them feel a marked antagonism towards it, others are simply indifferent. The creeds, theology, hymns, rituals and emotional appeals to a personal God and even to the churches themselves belong, as far as they are concerned, to a bygone age, almost indeed to a different world.

However lamentable this may seem, it is an undeniable fact and it is all too apparent in the attitude of the younger generations. They want to discover things for themselves, to have direct experience of every aspect of life, and they will only accept what is offered to them objectively, in a well-substantiated, meaningful way: in other words, scientifically— in the best sense of the word.

THE SUPERCONSCIOUS

In our study of the psychological make-up of human beings the time has come to focus our attention on the higher part of the unconscious: the superconscious and the spiritual Self. We need, at the outset, to affirm the *reality* of the superconscious because it is not yet generally recognized, particularly in the area of science and psychology where it is an unknown quantity. (We will look at the reasons for this later.) The reality of the superconscious does not need to be demonstrated, however, it is an *experience* and, when we become aware of it, it can be seen as one of those 'facts of the consciousness', as Bergson so aptly described it, facts which contain their own evidence and proof within themselves. It is a direct experience such as that of a colour, a sound or a feeling. It is neither possible nor necessary for anyone to 'demonstrate' the sensation of redness or greenness, joy or pain: for those who experience such things they are a psychological reality.

We need, at this point, to dispel a possible misunderstanding and clarify a doubt. How can one talk of experience or awareness of things that are outside of or above one's consciousness? The answer is easy, and it is the same as the answer one might give for any other aspect or level of the unconscious. We are able to have a conscious experience of phenomena, activities and psychological processes which *normally* exist outside of our consciousness, when—at certain times and under certain conditions—they break through into our field of consciousness.

There is a continuous exchange—we might call it a process of osmosis—between the conscious mind and the unconscious.

There comes a point at which what was superconscious becomes conscious, remains in the conscious mind for a greater or lesser period of time, and then returns to the superconscious state. I would point out here that 'superconscious', 'unconscious' and 'conscious' are *adjectives*, that is to say they are temporary conditions of a psychological fact.

This breakthrough of the superconscious into the conscious mind can come about in two ways. The first, and most frequent, we might call 'descendant': this is the bursting in of superconscious elements into the conscious mind in the form of intuitive thoughts, sudden enlightenment or inspiration. Often these are spontaneous, unexpected occurrences, but sometimes they may come in response to an appeal or an earnest wish for an answer, whether we are aware of this or not. The second way may be called 'ascendant': this consists of raising our centre of consciousness, the self-conscious 'I', to levels above the ordinary, until we reach the sphere of the superconscious.

There are countless testimonies to experiences of the superconscious, from all times and all places, ancient and modern, from the East and from the West. They are of various types. First there are those which occur in the religious field, mystical experiences in particular. But it should be noted that these are not the only type: there are superconscious experiences which have other characteristics of a non-religious nature. If superconscious experiences are a fact, they must of course lend themselves to scientific inquiry, as do all other types of facts. Indeed a start has been made in this direction, but it is extremely limited given the great importance and the human and spiritual value of the superconscious. Whereas there are thousands upon thousands of psychologists around the world studying other aspects of human nature (especially the baser aspects!), very few of them are concerned with the superconscious.

What are the reasons for this strange state of affairs? Firstly there is man's basic materialism, in particular the theoretical and practical materialism of Western man. It seems that he is mesmerized by the sensations produced by the outside world and by those of his own body. He is fundamentally extrovert: he has a tendency to act outwardly; all aspects of his inner world frighten him or, at least, make him feel uneasy. He therefore tends to avoid and run away from anything which focuses his mind inwards and causes him to face himself. Another reason is the fear of being abnormal or of being considered abnormal by others. If a person has certain superconscious experiences there is the fear that he might 'lose his head', particularly when there are sudden, unexpected flashes of awareness which are seen in stark contrast with the narrow, restricted normality of everyday life. People sometimes fear that these are morbid or abnormal, whereas they are in fact *supernormal*. And lastly, in the scientific field, the greatest obstacle is the obstinate refusal to accept that these experiences are open to scientific investigation. Psychology, as the youngest of the sciences, has relied on or remained tied to the methods employed in the natural sciences, though these are not at all suited to it and serve it little better than the legendary 'bed of Procrustes'. Rather it has the right, and indeed the duty, to use methods which, though *equally serious and scientific*, are more suited to its nature.

There has been a group of brave pioneers, however, who have dared to venture into the field of the superconscious and who have sought to study it in a scientific manner. The first of these was the great American psychologist William James who, in a series of lectures which were later published in a volume entitled *Varieties of Religious Experience*, carried out a careful examination of religious experiences, sympathetically and respectfully, but at the same time with impartiality and objectivity. This is all the more commendable in that James acknowledged that he had not had these experiences himself and thus had to make a great scientific effort to study them through the experiences of others.

James's lectures were given at the end of the last century. Shortly after, an American doctor by the name of Bucke, following a sudden and unexpected experience of spiritual enlightenment which had a profound effect on him, began to study testimonies to what—though we might question the term—he called 'cosmic consciousness'. He collected and commented on numerous accounts, from many different ages, and gave his interpretation of them in the book *Cosmic Consciousness*, published in 1901.

Another doctor, Winslow Hall, made a collection of firsthand accounts of enlightenment, a valuable collection because it deals with the 'man in the street', i.e. people with no other ostensible claim to superiority who nevertheless had had remarkable superconscious experiences.

Among the modern psychologists we have Jung, who teaches that there are, within what he calls the 'collective unconscious', elements of a higher, superpersonal nature. The sociologist Sorokin devoted a chapter of his book *The Powers and the Ways of Altruistic Love* to the superconscious. Frankl, the Viennese neurologist, openly acknowledges the existence of super-conscious experiences. The psychiatrist Urban of Innsbruck speaks of 'higher psychology'. And lastly a comprehensive study of the superconscious has been carried out by the American psychologist A. Maslow, professor at Brandeis University, who has written up his findings in a book entitled *Towards a Psychology of Being* (Van Nostrand Reinhold Co., New York, 1968). He uses the term 'being' for the overall range of experiences we call superconscious, because one of their characteristics is to give a sense of 'fullness of being', or a sense of intensity in existing and living. Maslow collected a great deal of important data from personal interviews and from use of a questionnaire.

This leads us on to talk about the methods for examining the superconscious. First of all we need to collect together all the documents already existing on the subject: biographies, autobiographies, correspondence, etc., from different ages; then we need to obtain other data from personal interviews and questionnaires.

The second stage of scientific inquiry is the examination, classification, interpretation and assessment of the data that has been gathered.

The third method, and the most interesting, is the *experimental* one, that is to say the use of psychological methods. This could either be methods for calling down elements of the superconscious into the realm of the conscious, or it could be methods for raising the centre of consciousness to the shining regions above.

Let us take a look at the data that has been collected so far in our investigation of the superconscious: in other words, what are the characteristics of those higher levels or of the states of consciousness that they produce when they are brought into the realm of the conscious mind? I have listed and described 13 of these. The first is a sense of *depth*—in various accounts people have spoken about reaching the source or origin of their being, they describe leaving the ordinary level of consciousness and reaching the very depths of what they are. Another is the sense of *internalization*—moving from the external to the internal, from the periphery to the centre of our being. The third characteristic is that of *being lifted up*, or *ascent*: rising up to a higher level. The symbolism of climbing a mountain or of reaching a peak often occurs in testimonies to such experiences and it is tied up with the fourth characteristic of the *path* or *way* along which one must travel. The fifth is that of *expansion* or of the sometimes bewildering *enlargement* of the consciousness: the restricting limitations of the separate 'I' are transcended and momentarily removed, and one has the sense that one is partaking of a far greater consciousness. The sixth characteristic is *development* and *activation*, a sense of being freed from the tangles and hindrances that ensnare us so that we are able to 'blossom' or emerge. The seventh is an *empowering*: we feel a greater energy coursing through us, making us stronger and more dynamic; we experience fullness, that intensity of existence and being we have already referred to. Another frequently reported aspect of such experiences is that of *awakening*. In many accounts there are descriptions such as 'I woke to a higher reality', 'My senses were released from darkness', 'I moved from the "dreamlike state" of ordinary life to a state of enhanced alertness.'

It can be noted that the actual name of Buddha was Gautama, and that 'Buddha' means 'the Woken One' or the 'One who is perfectly awake'. Very often there is a sense of enlightenment, a new, unearthly light which transfigures the external world, and a light which reveals a new beauty. It illuminates the inner world, 'throws light' on problems and doubts and dispels them; it is the intuitive light of a higher consciousness. This is often accompanied by a sense of *joy* or *happiness* which may result in a state of bliss. Along with these, or quite independent of them, there may be a sense of *renewal* or *regeneration*, the birth of a new being within us. Then there is the sense of *resurrection*, of rising up to a state which had been lost and forgotten. Finally there is the sense of *liberation*, an *inner* freedom.

This array of characteristics corresponds largely to those borne out by the firsthand accounts collected and studied by Maslow, who identified 14 characteristics which he called the 'values of the consciousness of being'. These are: the sense of fullness, integration, totality; the sense of perfection, completeness, vitality and intensity of life; the sense of richness and, at the same time, a sense of simplicity; the sense of beauty, consciousness of goodness, absence of effort, spontaneity, joy, cheerfulness, humour; the sense of truth or *reality* of the experience, that is to say the experience reveals something *real*, more real than one is able to know with the ordinary consciousness, and lastly, the sense of independence, an inner freedom which takes away the need to rely on anything else; self-sufficiency in the higher, spiritual sense of the word.

Maslow is right in saying that all these outward manifestations are interpenetrating and linked together: 'They are all aspects of being, rather than parts of it.'

All this serves to produce in us a desire to have such beautiful and enticing experiences. How can they be brought about or encouraged? Before we go any further I need to paint a darker picture; that is to say, these very experiences can manifest themselves in a disruptive and even dangerous way. This may be the case either as the result of an incorrect understanding and assessment of the experiences, or because of their intensity. A wrong assessment, as I have already intimated, means regarding them as something strange or abnormal which may be a sign of mental imbalance, but quite apart from this false interpretation, the bursting in of superconscious elements, particularly if they are sudden and very intense, can disturb the former balance (however real that might have been) of the ordinary personality, producing various reactions, over-excitement or a sense of disorientation. Even when one is developing in this area, ascending to higher levels, various incidents and problems may occur. I cannot deal with these here, but I have dealt with them at length in an essay on 'Spiritual Development and Neuro-Psychological Disturbances'.[1]

[1] This essay appears as Chapter 10 of this volume.

However, the advantages and value of these experiences are far greater than any initial adverse effects they may cause. In an effective way they are able to resolve, or contribute to the solution of, all human problems, individual or social. They do so by incorporating them into a greater reality, reducing them to their true proportions, and assessing them in a different, more accurate fashion. This means that the problems either cease to preoccupy us and dissolve, or they are illuminated by a higher light in such a way that the solution is made clear.

I will give one or two examples. One of the greatest causes of suffering and incorrect behaviour is fear. This can be individual anxiety, or the collective fears which carry a nation into war. Now the experience of the superconscious reality cancels out fear, for any sense of fear is incompatible with a realization of the fullness and permanence of life. Another cause of error and wrong conduct is the urge to fight. This is based on the idea of separateness, on aggression, and on feelings of hostility and hatred. In the serene atmosphere of the superconscious, however, those feelings cannot exist. Anyone whose consciousness has been enlarged, who feels a sense of participation, a sense of unity with all beings, cannot fight any longer. He sees it as an absurdity: it would be like fighting himself! Thus the most serious of problems, the ones which cause the greatest distress, are resolved or eliminated by the development, enlarging and ascent of the consciousness to the level of a higher Reality.

Before completing our examination, albeit brief, of the superconscious, we need to highlight the distinction between the superconscious and the spiritual Self as shown in our diagram of the psychological make-up of a human being. This distinction is often omitted because the contents of the superconscious, particularly at its higher levels, are very close to the Self and therefore share, to some extent, its characteristics. But there is a fundamental difference: in the superconscious there are elements and different types of active, dynamic, changing contents which are involved in the overall flow of psychological life. The Self, on the other hand, is stable, unmoving, unchanging, and for this reason it is *different*.

It is important to remember this distinction, not least because

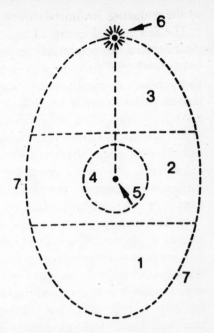

1. The Lower Unconscious.
2. The Middle Unconscious.
3. The Higher Unconscious or Superconscious.
4. The Area of Consciousness.
5. The Conscious 'I'.
6. The Higher 'I' or Self.
7. The Collective Unconscious.

this sense of permanence and stability, however mitigated and concealed it may be, is transmitted from the spiritual Self to its counterpart, the conscious, personal 'I'. It is this that gives us our sense of permanence and personal identity throughout changes and alternating states of mind, despite the changing contents of our awareness. However much we identify ourselves with various 'roles', with the various sub-personalities and emotions which successively occupy the realm of the conscious mind, through it all each person knows that he is still himself. Even if at times a person might say 'I no longer recognize myself' when some significant change occurs in his life, this actually means 'The thing I identified myself with before has gone and I now identify with something else.' But even to say 'I no longer recognize myself' implies, paradoxically, an obscure, hidden sense of an underlying continuity. If this were not so, there could not even be a sense of not recognizing oneself, in that this is based on a comparison, a clash between the previous state of consciousness and the present one. Thus the essential characteristic of self-awareness is continuity and permanence, but the self-awareness of the conscious 'I' is but a poor reflection of the enduring, immortal essence of the spiritual 'I', the Self.

The Self in the diagram is placed at the highest extreme of the periphery of the personality, partly inside it—in a continuous relationship with the superconscious—and partly outside of that personality. This helps to express its dual nature: individual and universal at one and the same time. This would seem to be a paradox, something the mind is unable to grasp, alien to personal consciousness, yet it is a state of consciousness which can be, and is being, experienced and *lived* at certain moments of heightened awareness when a person is lifted out of the limitations of ordinary existence. In such a state one experiences a sense of enlargement, limitless expansion and a sense of being pervaded by an intense joy and bliss. It is indeed a sublime experience which words cannot express.

It is here that one comes into contact with Mystery, with the supreme Reality. Of this I am unable to speak; it is outside the confines of science and psychology. However, psychosynthesis can help us to approach it and to reach the very threshold. And that is no small achievement.

3

PSYCHOLOGICAL MOUNTAINEERING

We have said that there are two different ways of exploring the superconscious and these are, in a sense, opposites. The most frequently encountered method may be called *descendant*: it takes the form of the flooding of higher elements into the realm of our consciousness. We might regard this as a form of vertical telepathy—telepathy because there is a marked distance between the conscious 'I' and the Self. These incursions take the form of intuition, inspiration, creative genius, and impulses leading to humanitarian or heroic action. There are also specifically parapsychological phenomena which would lead one to assume that the area of consciousness is penetrated through all three levels of the unconscious by influences and impulses which have their origin outside the individual.

The other type of relationship and contact we are able to establish with the superconscious is of the *ascendant* type. This takes the form of the conscious 'I', together with its realm of consciousness, being lifted up to higher levels, until it reaches an area we do not usually realize is there at all, because it is above our normal level of consciousness.

This is clearly shown in our diagram (see page 30). The area at the centre represents the level and normal area of awareness or consciousness, with the conscious 'I' at the centre. When an inner ascent takes place, this is completely shifted upwards to the level of the superconscious such that the area of consciousness now includes the content of the superconscious as it draws ever closer to the Spiritual Self.

Today I will be dwelling on this second method.

I have called this type of ascent 'psychological mountaineering', and this description is not merely a suggestive comparison, but points to an analogy which offers striking similarities, with readily transferable symbolism. In illustrating this point I will make use, among other things, of various remarks made by a skilled mathematician and an equally skilled mountaineer: Professor Ettore Carruccio.

The first analogy we can make has to do with the different motives which urge and persuade people to climb mountains, the physical motives and the inner ones. 'At times,' Carruccio rightly points out, 'the passion for mountaineering assumes proportions which link it up with the idea of the superman, as Nietzsche used the term, in the form of a blatant affirmation of individual power in overcoming extreme difficulties and the grave risk involved.' By analogy, the urge to leave behind the normal levels of mental life may actually represent a search for, and an affirmation of, superiority, or the desire to develop faculties in order to use them to dominate others: Nietzsche's 'desire for power', the yearning for the acquisition of superhuman or 'magical' powers. This is essentially a selfish motive, even if it is sometimes couched in pseudo-spiritual terms.

Another common motive in both types of mountaineering is the escape from everyday life, from everyday reality which is seen and felt to be narrow, boring or painful—in other words unsatisfying in various ways. This is a frequent reaction to the restrictions and the prosaic nature of modern life, particularly in cities.

A third motive is the fascination exerted by the unknown, the extraordinary and the mysterious. This fascination has always spurred men on to discovery, exploration, to search out the new and that which is beyond, in other words to experience the unusual. This motive, this compelling urge which at times is irresistible, was personalized by Homer in the figure of Ulysses, and this theme is developed throughout his *Odyssey*. Modern counterparts are the extraordinary experiences people now seek, and they use every means available, including various drugs. One must take this motive seriously if one is to understand many things that are going on at the present time.

A fourth motive is the enticing fascination with adventure,

difficulty and risk for its own sake, irrespective of the results and the rewards to be had from the exercise. A recent phenomenon has been that of the 'single-handed navigator' who has crossed oceans in a small craft—this is precisely what happens in the 'academic' type of mountaineering, that is to say when people look for and attempt new and more difficult ways to reach a summit despite the existence of less dangerous routes.

This motive is sometimes associated with the preceding one, and this explains why many young people are not put off by warnings and by demonstrations of the risks involved; indeed they expose themselves to such risks, paying no heed to bans or to external constraints. Recognition of this fact is important, for it shows that when one is seeking to prevent drug addiction or to help those already addicted, one must in some way appeal to other psychological incentives. Let us not deceive ourselves into thinking that merely to point out the risks and the dangers involved in some course of action will dissuade people from engaging in it. However, I must not dwell on this point.

A fifth motive, often very marked, and one which must not be confused with the motives described above, even if it is frequently encountered alongside them in various proportions, is that of attraction, or the fascination with something truly superior, something having a higher value and a genuinely spiritual quality. In this regard, as Professor Carruccio writes, mountaineering 'is seen as a branch of ascetics related to religious sentiments in their varied forms, all the way from ancient times to the present day'. Guido Rey, in a poetic frame of mind, imagined a monastery for mountaineers: 'The peaks all around,' he wrote, 'are the altars on which one is able to perform mystical rituals, far from the eyes of other men; rituals which can sometimes be frightening. There are even moments when they assume the most frightening and holy of aspects.'

This statement is a very significant one. It points to the reason for the intense attraction and fascination that mountains have always exerted and for the sacred nature people of all nations have attributed to them. It also highlights the enthusiasm and inner lift experienced by mountaineers.

Here is an enlightening quotation from an excellent study of this subject by Edoard Monot-Herzen entitled 'Ad summum per quadratum' (quadratum, or 'square', being understood as the base of a pyramid—an ascendant geometric symbol) published in the magazine *Action et Pensée* (Action and Thought) in December 1956:

> As we entered the shelter at the top of Cervino the guide, Joseph Pession, said: 'As we reach this point, all earthly burdens are left behind ... We will now find ourselves in an entirely new world.' Upon reaching the top, one of the porters said that he 'could hear the voices of angels and would now die a happy man'.

For some 70 years the painter Alberto Gross, his son Carlo tells us, had a passionate attachment to the Matterhorn and was enraptured by some mystical feeling about it. 'This,' Monot-Herzen tells us, 'also applied to Carlo Gross and Guido Rey. Both men wrote a book about the Matterhorn. It also applies to me, for over a period of 50 years I have made 19 ascents of it, each time coming away with a fresh revelation and a new sense of enchantment.'

It is well known that the Indians thought the peaks of the Himalayas were the abode of the gods, and that the Greeks believed their deities inhabited Mount Olympus. The great Japanese painter Hokusai painted more than a hundred times the sacred name Fuji, this mountain being considered as the temple of the deity known as the 'Princess of the Blossoming Flower', an allusion to the rose and the way in which it opens its petals. In one of these paintings by Hokusai we see the peak of Fuji glistening in the sun while half way up its slopes a storm is raging. Other testimonies to this are the temples which were located on mountains, the revelation to Moses on Mount Sinai, the transfiguration of Christ on Mount Tabor, and his sermon on the mount.

Let us take a closer look at the more detailed aspects of the analogies between the inner and outward stages of an ascent. Either type of ascent requires careful preparation. Preparation for the mountaineer means the training of his muscles down at ground level through gymnastics and other forms of muscle building. Before starting to climb he needs to be strong on level ground—it would be ridiculous to tackle a climb if he found even walking or gymnastics too tiring. This might seem self-evident, but it is not recognized and acted upon when it comes to psychospiritual ascents, for these are often attempted without the slightest preparation.

In psychosynthesis we always insist on there being an appropriate personal psychosynthesis, a control over and an ability to use the normal human energies and functions before trying to develop higher ones, that is to say before climbing to explore the superconscious. When this foundation has not been laid it can lead to mental disturbances, and these can be serious.

But physical or mental preparation alone are not enough. There must also be some knowledge, if only theoretical, of the region we are about to venture into. In the case of mountains, unless they have never been climbed before, there are maps, information and descriptions passed on by those who have been there previously. From a psychological point of view we see the parallel of knowledge of the superconscious that has already been acquired through the writings of those who have had experiences at those higher levels. Even more useful are the personal accounts of those who have explored these heights: the true spiritual instructors. I say 'true' because many who claim to be instructors are not.

Having undergone this twofold preparation we are ready to face the ascent. And it is an ascent, not a flight, and therefore has different stages and sections. There are two descriptions of this gradual climb, both of them instructive and enlightening. One is Dante's ascent of Mount Purgatory, the subject of the second book of his *Divine Comedy*. Read from an allegorical, psychosynthetic point of view it can give us many useful guidelines, still valid today, for the obstacles and difficulties to be overcome are to a considerable extent the same.

The other is the ascent of Mount Carmel, described in a large volume by St John of the Cross. Although this is specifically ascetic and mystical in nature, it also contains a number of treasures of psychological knowledge and instructions which, if translated into up-to-date language and removed from their historic setting, can be very instructive. I shall give but one example: St John of the Cross describes in painstaking detail the states of dryness and coldness and the darkness of the nights that follow one's first warm, joyful experiences, so abounding in feeling. These find their counterpart in the cold and the thick mist a mountaineer will encounter at a certain point in his climb before reaching the sun-drenched summit.

This symbolism of a mountain and an ascent has been used in various psychotherapeutic methods. Carl Happich, a professor of clinical medicine in Darmstadt and an active advocate of psychotherapy, made use of three symbolic situations which he called Meditation of the Meadow, of the Mountain and of the Peak.

This method of inner ascent, using the imagination to climb a mountain, was used by Desoille, among others, in his 'waking dream' technique, subsequently developed and modified under the names 'Mental Imagery' and 'Oneirotherapy' by Dr Virel.

With the spontaneous drawing method one also frequently comes across mountains to be climbed depicted as having been already conquered.

The importance of symbols as a mirror, or as a medium for spiritual reality, is shown in the following diagram:

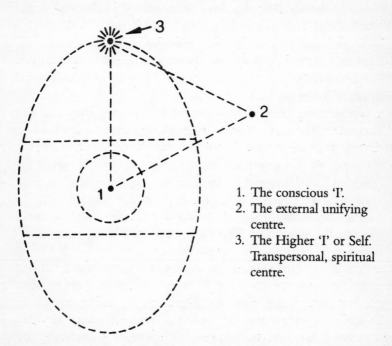

1. The conscious 'I'.
2. The external unifying centre.
3. The Higher 'I' or Self. Transpersonal, spiritual centre.

In this diagram we see an external centre which can act as a mirror for the Spiritual Self.

There are times when it is easier to see a reflection of the Spiritual Self by having it bounced off an external centre rather than by a direct ascent. This may be the therapy itself, in the form of an ideal model, but it may also be a symbol, such as that of the mountain. There are various types of symbols and various allegorical symbols of ascent may be used.

In psychosynthesis we make use of exercises of this type, firstly that of the mountain representing Purgatory which we have already referred to. The *Divine Comedy* may be considered as the poem of psychosynthesis in that it describes its three broad stages: first the descent into Hell, the psychoanalytical stage, the descent into the abyss of the lower unconscious; next the climb to Purgatory, which represents the inner ascent; and finally Paradise, which symbolizes ever higher levels of spiritual realization.

Another group of symbols is used in the exercise based on the legend of the Holy Grail. This is described in my book entitled *Principi e metodi della psicosintesi terapeutica* [The Principles and Methods of Therapeutic Psychosynthesis] (pp. 171–3).

These symbols are not only effective in therapeutic terms, they are just as, if not more, effective in conquering the glorious heights of the superconscious, in discovering all its wonders and in using its treasures.

Just as there are various ways up a mountain, there are also various 'inner ways' suited to differing temperaments or to differing psychological types by which one can reach the summits of the superconscious and make contact with the Spiritual Self. There is the way of mysticism, the way of love, the way of aesthetics described by Plato in his famous scale of beauty, the way of meditation, and so on. I will only comment here on the way of meditation because this has a more direct bearing on the area of psychosynthesis.

The first stage, which in one sense corresponds to the preparation we were talking about earlier, is that of attention or concentration, starting from the outside and working inwards, a conscious stepping back from one's outer identity, in other words freeing the conscious mind of its everyday contents. Our consciousness is generally dispersed across various areas of our conscious mind; in addition it is continually receiving messages or 'information', to use the current computer terminology, from various levels of the unconscious and from the outside world. First of all, therefore, one needs to 'get back into oneself'—in other words, withdraw one's consciousness into the conscious 'I', to the very centre of the area of consciousness, at its normal level.

In this there is a need for silence, not only outside but within. I will quote the apposite reply of one instructor. A disciple of his said, 'I shut my eyes and no longer see the outside world; I shut my ears to all speech and noise—yet I fail to reach the point of awareness.' The instructor answered, 'Try keeping your mouth shut as well so that you have silence not only outside but also within yourself.' Indeed, if we observe ourselves, we realize that we have a continuous inner voice—there are incessant voices from our sub-personalities or from our unconscious, a continuous inner din. External silence is not enough, therefore. Indeed one can be truly collected in one's mind in the midst of external noise.

The second stage is that of true meditation. Above all meditation on a theme, based on a phrase or suggested by a word. The first stage is *intellectual reflection*, but this is followed by something deeper and more vital. It is the act of truly perceiving and consciously confronting the nature, meaning, function and value of the object of one's meditation, almost as though we were able to feel it living and acting in us. Instead of words we may use images and symbols, observed externally and visualized inwardly.

An even higher stage is that of contemplation. It is extremely difficult, if not impossible, to convey in words what this consists of, we can only say that it is such an intimate state of identification with the object of contemplation that all sense of duality is transcended: it is the merging of the subject and the object into a living unity. When meditation is not based on a theme, the contemplation it gives rise to is a state of perfect repose, an inner silence, taking the form of pure consciousness of being.

One then arrives, fully conscious, in the region or sphere

which is normally that of the superconscious. At this stage one may have experiences of the various characteristics and of the various psychospiritual activities that take place in the superconscious. These are not abstract, vague or evanescent, as might be expected by those who have not had such experiences. They are *alive*, intense, varied, dynamic, and are perceived as being more real than ordinary, everyday experiences, be they inner or external. The main characteristics are as follows:

1. An awareness of light, enlightenment, either in a general sense or in the sense of light on specific problems and situations, the significance of which then becomes apparent.
2. A sense of peace, a complete peace which is independent of any external circumstance or inner state.
3. A sense of harmony and beauty.
4. A sense of joy and bliss—the bliss so clearly expressed by Dante.
5. A sense of power, power of the spirit.
6. A sense of greatness, vastness, universality, eternity.

These qualities are not separate from one another; they have an interpenetrating effect. This too was admirably expressed by Dante.

Such lofty experiences in contemplation cannot of course be permanent, but even when they are over they continue to produce effects and these can often take the form of profound changes in a person's everyday personality. Among other things, such an experience encourages a gradual stabilization of the centre of personal consciousness and of the area of ordinary consciousness at gradually higher levels. It may also happen that the area of ordinary consciousness is lifted to the line of demarcation (not division, but distinction) between the middle unconscious and the superconscious, with the result that then it remains continuously enlightened to a certain degree.

This may facilitate and make more frequent the coming down of intuition and inspiration. The greatest height attainable and the symbolic arrival at the summit is the union of the centre of personal consciousness with the Spiritual Self. I would point out that in the diagram above the 'star' representing the Spiritual Self is depicted partly inside and partly outside the oval. This shows that the Self partakes of both individuality and universality; it is in contact with the transcendent Reality.

Another effect of these experiences is the inspired *action*, the powerful spur to act. Above all it leads to the expression, pouring out or irradiation of the treasures that have been discovered and won, so that others can share in them. There is then a working together with other people of goodwill, and with all who have had similar experiences, to dispel the shadows of ignorance which grip humanity, to eliminate the conflicts that fragment people's lives, and to prepare for the coming of a new civilization in which people, now happy and having a common purpose, are able to realize the amazing, latent potential placed within them.

EXPANDING THE CONSCIOUSNESS: CONQUERING AND EXPLORING THE WORLDS WITHIN

Humanity today is in a state of serious collective and individual crisis: there is a general sense of dissatisfaction, a discontent with everyday life. People are looking for something different, something 'out of the ordinary'. There is no need to labour this point because it is a commonly accepted fact and is taking place continuously before our eyes. This search for something different and rebellion against ordinary, everyday life expresses itself in two ways, both of which favour an expansion of the consciousness.

The first of these leads to an increase in man's knowledge about the outside world, focusing on the exploration, conquest of and gaining dominion over space, through aviation and space flight. Alongside this are activities aimed at harnessing the forces of nature, all the way up to nuclear energy.

The second way of expanding the consciousness has to do with our knowledge of the world within, or the worlds within. Here we see the growing interest in psychology (in particular the exploration of the unconscious), and research into the nature of psychological powers and the laws that govern their use—and, all too frequently, abuse!

I therefore feel it appropriate to clarify certain important areas, to summarize the present situation, to point out the directions in which research is being channelled and the latest developments, and to indicate the ways that can be followed and the techniques that can be used. I will now give an overview and map out the form this will take. In the following chapters the various themes will be dealt with more specifically in greater depth.

Expansion of the consciousness can develop in three directions:

1. Downwards.
2. Horizontally.
3. Upwards.

1. As regards the *downward direction*, there are those who explore the lower unconscious or allow it to well up into the conscious mind. This is the area covered by depth psychology, and by psychoanalysis in particular. This is carried out for practical, therapeutic or educational reasons, and can be of some use. But there is also an unhealthy attraction to the lower regions. There is the fascination with horror, a fascination exerted by the primitive, instinctive aspects of human nature. This is clearly seen in the interest shown in the widely distributed books, films and shows which deal with violence and the darker side of the mind. Here, unfortunately, we have a vicious circle: the interest in the lower aspects of human nature is fed, and indeed intensified, by those who, for reasons of economic gain and the consuming urge to make money, cultivate these tastes and offer people increasingly worse books and films. The portrayal of horror is also seen in many paintings and drawings by modern artists. This attraction towards evil has been perceptively described by Erich Fromm in his book *The Heart of Man*. Rollo May also speaks of this fascination with the 'demonic' in his *L'amore e la volonta* [Love and Will] (Astrolabio, Rome 1971), but he does not make a clear distinction between different levels.

2. The second direction in which the consciousness can expand, what we might call the *horizontal* direction, is its participation and identification with others, with nature and with things. It is the impulse to flee consciousness of oneself and to immerse oneself in the collective consciousness. We should remember that the collective consciousness preceded individual self-awareness. We see this in primitive people, in children and, to a lesser extent, in various other groups: the social, military and

professional classes with which an individual readily identifies.

The best aspects of this horizontal broadening of consciousness are a sense of identification with nature in all its varied aspects and a sense of identification with cosmic life in general. It is the sense of participating in life, of becoming one with the universe.

3. The third direction is the *ascendant* direction, towards the levels of the superconscious, i.e. the transpersonal levels. This expansion of consciousness can come about in two different ways: the first consists of raising the centre of consciousness, the 'I', to those levels; the second has to do with opening oneself up to the influence of energies coming down from those higher levels.

There is thus an increasing interaction between the conscious 'I' and the superconscious levels. At its highest it takes the form of contact with the Transpersonal Self. We need to remember that the conscious 'I' is a 'reflection' of the Self and is thus essentially of the same nature, however much it is weakened and 'coloured' by the contents of the middle level of the personality. When one uses certain exercises (particularly that of dis-identification) it is possible to eliminate those contents; the conscious 'I' then tends to return upwards to its origin.

The various methods and effects of this type of transcendence, particularly in the upward direction, have been thoroughly expounded by Maslow who, in his article 'Various Meanings of Transcendence' published in the *Journal of Transpersonal Psychology* (Spring 1969), distinguishes different forms and aspects.

The differences between these three directions for expansion of the consciousness are often not recognized, and there is still much confusion about the subject. It is therefore important to point them out. But from now on I shall be speaking primarily of the upward direction, of the relationship with the transpersonal levels, with the superconscious, and above all of the means of receiving such influences from above, i.e. the descent— and at times the bursting in—of the contents of the superconscious at the ordinary, everyday level of the conscious 'I'.[1]

[1]The French writer, J. Wahl, in his study on existentialism makes use of a happy play on words in French in order to speak of two types of transcendence: trans-ascendance and trans-descendance.

This descent may occur in two ways: spontaneously or by deliberate action. The best known type of spontaneous descent is inspiration. The contents of the superconscious can come into the conscious mind with varying degrees of intensity: they may be almost formless, in a raw state, or they may be semi-processed, then again they may already be well structured, in more or less their final form. This often occurs in musical inspiration. A typical example is that of Mozart, whose compositions came into his conscious mind complete, without the need for further elaboration. When material presents itself in the raw state, on the other hand, it is often expressed verbally in a strange style, with no regard for the rules of syntax or grammar. A typical example is surrealist literature. But this literature comes from the various levels of the unconscious, including the lower level.

The simplest means by which the contents of the superconscious can come down to us is intuition. This may be compared to a flash of lightning which gives light, either for a moment or for a somewhat longer period of time, to the conscious mind in its waking state. Intuition can come in all areas of human activity, including philosophy and science. I will quote a worthy saying of Einstein on the subject of intuition. He said:

> Inductive physics poses questions to which deductive physics is unable to respond. Only intuition, similar to the relationship established between people in love, is able to take our knowledge beyond the confines of logical thought.

As a general rule, however, the great artists, writers and poets then had to work on the material that had sprung up before them or come down into their conscious minds and consciously develop this material. A typical example is that of Dante. Answering Bonagiunta, in the *Divine Comedy*, he says quite clearly that he had been inspired:

> And I to him: 'I am one who, when love
> Breathes on me, notices, and in the manner
> That he dictates within, I utter words.'
> *Translation: C.H. Sisson, Pan Classics*

His appeals to the Muses in the *Divine Comedy* are actually symbolic appeals to the superconscious and to the Spiritual Self. Afterwards, however, he consciously worked this inspired material into a rigid format, the *terza rima* of the *Divine Comedy*, and the fixed number of cantos in each of the three books. He makes this quite clear at the end of 'Purgatory':

If, reader, I had room to write more,
My poem could still not tell you everything
About the sweet drink of which I could never have had enough.
But since all the pages designed for this
Second part of the poem have been filled,
The rules of art stop me at this point.

Translation: C.H. Sisson, Pan Classics

There are various ways in which one can actively encourage the descent of transpersonal influences into the waking consciousness. One of the simplest, yet most effective, is free drawing. The unconscious expresses itself primarily in symbols, and drawing is a direct method for representing these symbols. We should remember that the first writing was ideographic: it used concrete images. (These can still be found today in the ideograms of the Chinese writing system.) The alphabet may be regarded as a type of shorthand or as a simplification of ideograms in letters.

Free drawing often produces surprising results in the form of real messages from the superconscious. One evidence of their origin is the fact that the conscious mind of the drawer is quite often unable to understand them unaided. It requires an expert in such mental processes to interpret them and reveal their meaning to the subject. The latter usually recognizes the interpretation as being correct and accepts it, but would not have been able to reach that understanding alone.

Another method is writing. This may seem a simple, obvious process, presenting few problems. It is actually a complex and varied psychological process. Very often we discover that if we start writing something we have thought of, new ideas start to flow through our minds. This thread or current of thoughts takes unexpected directions and what eventually comes out may surprise even the writer. We might say that in these cases the unconscious 'takes over' and begins to write itself. One very aware writer with an interest in psychology, Hermann Keyserling, describes this phenomenon in the following words: 'I do not usually write because I know, but in order to know, by raising the subconscious to the level of the conscious mind.'

We need to give a clarification and, indeed, a warning at this point, however. It is possible to move away from this partnership, in a sense, between the conscious mind and the unconscious and enter a state of 'automatic' writing in which the conscious 'I' plays little or no part—the subject is then in a trance-like state, similar to hypnosis, while the hand is busily writing. This causes problems and can even be dangerous: it is like opening the door without knowing what may come in. A great deal of material has been obtained by means of automatic writing and its value is very diverse. Some of these writings have literary merit and take the form of long novels. Sometimes they contain high-flown instructions of a spiritual nature or give helpful advice, but in the majority of cases automatic writing is of poor quality, clearly a case of the lower unconscious taking over.

Here we have a problem: is it possible that these manifestations have their origin outside of the subject, that is to say that they come from sources or centres other than the personality of the writer? This is a very confused and complex area. I will only say that we cannot exclude the existence of sources separate from the personal unconscious, if only because it is in a state of continuous interaction (what I would call 'psycho-osmosis') at all levels with the collective unconscious. For this reason it is difficult to say whether one is dealing with something strictly individual, or whether in fact certain influences come from the collective unconscious. I would repeat that this occurs at all levels, from the lowest level to the highest. We must therefore take great care. In any case the origin of the messages has no bearing on their intrinsic value.

The other type of higher transcendence is that of the active exploration of the levels of the superconscious, that is to say the deliberate raising of the conscious 'I' to ever higher levels. There are various methods of encouraging or producing this raising of the consciousness: prayer, meditation and various special exercises. I will limit myself to one observation at this point because I will be speaking later of other ways to the superconscious and the Spiritual Self. I will just say that in all the ways and stages of raising the consciousness it is necessary to use the will. The will is needed in order to overcome obstacles, to maintain a receptive state. It is needed as a propeller to attain ever greater heights and to stabilize the consciousness at those higher levels, and finally it is necessary for directing and making use of the energies released.

Among the special exercises are those of Raja Yoga, where ascent is encouraged by the use of allegorical symbols, the symbol of inner mountaineering we have already mentioned, for instance. One simple yet productive method is that of the 'guided imagination'. This often produces a steady flow of rich symbolic material which, when well interpreted by the person guiding the exercise, can result in a significant expansion of the consciousness.

Let us move on to the elimination of obstacles. These may be compared to 'weights', the ballast that hinders the ascent of the consciousness, or they may be compared to 'ropes', symbolizing our attachment to the ordinary contents of our personalities—these too can prevent upward progress. The obstacles may have to do with the body, the emotions, the imagination, the mind, the will or the environment.

Of particular significance are obstacles which have to do with the will. It is often the case that the conscious self does not wish to make the ascent—it offers resistance because it fears the unknown, the heights it has not yet seen. This resistance has been aptly named 'refusal of the sublime' by Dr Frank Haronian, who described this in an article of the same name. Quite often it is bound up with a presentiment that certain types of spiritual growth are demanding and impose responsibilities from which the selfish, self-centred 'I' wants to escape. There is then an intense battle between the personal 'I' and the Spiritual Self. A number of mystics have described this experience very clearly, and it has been portrayed in a particularly dramatic way by St Paul and St Augustine.

Very often the environment presents great obstacles, both the immediate environment of the family and the wider, social environment. We are engulfed by an oppressive, troubled, dense, heavy mental atmosphere which one might well call a psychological smog. But we should not use this as an excuse. Many people show a tendency to blame social structures and the modern materialistic lifestyle, claiming that this makes spiritual self-realization impossible. But this is not true. It is possible to rise above such obstacles. It is here that the indispensable purpose of the will comes to the fore. Instead of blaming outside influences, we need to resist them; not so much tackling them head-on, as protecting ourselves from them and continuing our ascent.

There are many different ways of expanding the consciousness as one moves upwards, and they are dependent on different psychological types and on different individual constitutions. We can identify seven main ways. I would point out at once that these ways are not separate and that in practice they tend to overlap, so it is possible for a person to proceed along more than one at the same time. The fact remains, however, that they are distinct and, to begin with at least—for the sake of clarity—we need to describe them and get to know them separately. We can then move on to possible ways in which they can be combined.

They are:

1. The Way of Science.
2. The Way of Enlightenment.
3. The Way of Regenerative Ethics.
4. The Way of Aesthetics.
5. The Way of Mysticism.
6. The Way of Heroism.
7. The Way of Ritual.

Let us now take a look at the way expansion of the consciousness affects the personality. We would do well to bear in mind that these effects can be harmful, and this is true even of upward expansion. Indeed, often when the contents of the unconscious burst in unexpectedly on the consciousness of an ill prepared, unstable subject, it can have an unsettling effect. Firstly it can result in self-exaltation: the personality feels full of new powers and becomes aware of the higher potential that resides in the superconscious and in the Self. Experiencing a Self which is essentially of the same nature as the Supreme Reality, something divine, can give the personality an inflated view of itself so that it deceives itself into believing that it is already at that higher level and that without undergoing the long process of transformation and regeneration it is already what it perceived or became aware of at the moment of enlightenment. An extreme expression of this self-deception is the statement 'I am God.' This illusion, this fundamental error may be seen as a confusion between what a person is potentially and what he is actually. It is as if an acorn, having been shown what it may one day become, i.e. a large oak, said, 'I am an oak.' Potentially it contains all that is necessary for becoming an oak, but it is not there yet, and it will need to undergo the long process of germination and development, as well as assimilating the beneficial effects of the earth, water, the air and the sun. The same applies to a human being who, having experienced a vivid insight into what he may become and having glimpsed what is latent within him, must then—upon his inescapable return to the level of everyday consciousness—come to terms with the long task before him: the complex and demanding task of moving on from his present potential so as to transform it into a reality.

Other effects may be an excessive nervous or mental tension produced by the energies that have burst in and by the conflicts arising between the conscious and unconscious, mediocre or inferior contents of the mind and those new energies.

But of even greater importance are the positive effects that an upward expansion of the consciousness can have. This may be divided up into temporary effects and into more lasting effects.

The first of these are the so-called 'ecstatic states'—vivid experiences of enlightenment, communion with that vaster Reality, contemplation of things that exist in higher worlds, and horizontal expansion in a cosmic sense. These are accompanied by joy, by a sense of empowering, love, inclusion and increased understanding. They arouse a surge of devotion and of consecration to the higher Reality or Being with whom one has come into contact. As far as the will in concerned, one experiences a merging or uniting of the personal will with the transpersonal will.

But these are passing experiences and they are quite frequently followed not only by a descent to the level of ordinary living, but also by states of negative consciousness. This is very painful and it produces an intense longing for those earlier states of consciousness which were so beautiful and joyful. This leads one to seek a repetition of those experiences which Maslow so appropriately termed 'peak experiences'. But they are like flying in an aeroplane to the top of a mountain—the aeroplane cannot stop there and has to return to the plains. But by repeating such flights, the gradual expansion of the waking consciousness and contact with higher values does result in the normal level of the personality being raised little by little. For ever longer periods the personality is able to remain on what an eminent Indian, Dr Asrani, who has had similar experiences and described them, calls the 'plateaux', a term picked up and developed by Maslow.

Then there are effects which we might call active, or effects of extroversion. These can be summed up in the word 'creativity'. This may be artistic, poetic, literary or even scientific and philosophical, in the context of the various forms of expression man has devised.

Let us now consider the tasks undertaken by psychosynthesis, i.e. what the personality, or the conscious 'I', after the consciousness has been enlarged and expanded, can and should do. These can be summed up as follows:

I.   An understanding and correct interpretation of what has happened, so as to avoid self-exaltation and inflation of the ego—in other words seeing what has been experienced in its true context. For this purpose there is great value in learning about the experiences other people have had and in studying the lives and writings of the 'host of witnesses' who have achieved this expansion of the consciousness.

II. Assimilation, that is to say allowing the new ideas which have come to enrich the conscious personality to become an integral part of it. This will of course entail its becoming more complex. This assimilation should lead to a proper balance between the various parts of one's being and at the different levels: in other words it should result in individual psychosynthesis.

To achieve this integration and synthesis, and to be able to make use of the energies that have flowed in, there is a need for:

1. The disintegration of our complexes, of the existing mental frameworks.
2. The transmutation and transformation of the lower energies. A regeneration of the whole personality.

III. In an overall sense we can speak of a process of 'death and resurrection' which is the specific task of one of the basic ways, the Way of Regenerative Ethics.

After all this—though in practice it takes place during the assimilation and regeneration process itself—comes the use of the new energies and capacities obtained through the expansion and lifting of the consciousness. This use can take one of two forms: it may be carried out in the form of inner action or external action.

Inner action consists primarily of irradiation. Energies radiate outwards from the personality as if from a great source of light, luminous rays shine out and pervade the atmosphere. This irradiation occurs spontaneously, I would almost say inevitably, and this explains the effect that the mere presence of a person who has had transpersonal experiences has on those with whom he comes into contact. This has been encountered and described on a number of occasions and may be referred to as a form of 'psychospiritual catalysis'.

However, there is also deliberate irradiation—the conscious action of sending out energies and beneficent waves. This is a form we might call psychospiritual telepathy, consisting not only of transmitting specific ideas, but primarily of a general channelling of goodwill or blessing. This was, and still is, used in the religious field, but it can be used anywhere, whatever one's philosophical or religious convictions. Recent studies in telepathy and telekinesis have given a scientific basis for this type of activity.

The other type of action is external. Anyone who has experienced an upward expansion of consciousness feels a natural, I would even say irresistible, desire to have others share in his own inner riches. We might call this activity a 'service'. It may be expressed in different ways, depending on the attitudes and interests of the individual. The most direct way consists of helping others achieve the expansion and raising of their own levels of consciousness. This may be done individually or in groups.

The other type of action is social in nature: it is directed at changing the existing conditions and structures insofar as they are inadequate and constricting, and in particular at establishing new forms of communal life, education, art and culture. It focuses on paving the way for a new and better civilization at an international level.

5

THE SUPERCONSCIOUS AND ARTISTIC CREATION

We have seen that there are various manifestations of the unconscious which have a higher qualitative value than that of ordinary consciousness, and that ordinary consciousness is unable to duplicate that higher qualitative value however hard it might try. These manifestations come from a higher psychological plane than the one we normally inhabit, and for this reason we call it the superconscious.

We find instances of astounding precocity among musicians: Mendelssohn began to compose at the age of five, Haydn at four and Mozart when he was only three years old. At that age the conscious personality is not even formed, so it cannot be that which produces the compositions. In adults the autonomous nature of the creative faculty is shown by the fact that it is normally expressed in a spontaneous, sudden and compelling fashion. This is what constitutes inspiration, which may be defined as the flow of psychological elements from the superconscious to the consciousness.

George Sand wrote that in the case of Chopin 'creation was spontaneous, miraculous; he found it without even seeking it, without anticipating it; it came complete, in a sublime flash.' The great naturalist Buffon says, 'It is like receiving a mild electric shock that strikes you on the head and in the stomach, as well as taking control of your heart. This is the moment of genius.' According to De Musset, 'One does not work; one listens. It is like some unknown person speaking in your ear.' Lamartine said, 'It is not I who do the thinking, but the ideas thinking within me.' The complex concept of quarternions suddenly came into William Hamilton's mind when he was walking with his wife. An inventor suddenly came up with the method of constructing a special prism (a problem he had been considering unsuccessfully for a long time) when reading a novel. The chemist Kekule tells how he saw atoms dancing before his eyes, enabling him to formulate his atomic group theory while travelling on the upper deck of a London bus.

Whether or not we are great artists or scientists, many of us have experienced the surge of new ideas when writing, with the result that what we are producing develops in a completely unexpected way. But there is more to it than this, for in some cases inspiration comes during sleep and wakes the sleeper.

Let us try to understand how this faculty operates and how it relates to the conscious 'I' and the rest of the psyche. First of all we must not confuse *inspiration* with *creation*. An analogy may help us here to make a distinction between the various stages of artistic or intellectual production and to gain an understanding of the mechanism of creation, or, to be more exact, the intimate, organic, creative process.

There is a close parallel between psychological creation and physical generation. To begin with, both types have a point of fertilization or conception. In the case of psychological creation, the fertilizing element sometimes takes the form of an external stimulus which suddenly strikes the imagination and evokes deep emotions, intense feelings, enabling the creative activity of the superconscious to be worked out.

A well-known example—all the more remarkable because it has to do with a writer who usually produced his works slowly and reflectively, with the greatest degree of conscious deliberation—is the 'Cinque Maggio' [Fifth of May] by Alessandro Manzoni. The unexpected announcement of the death of Napoleon had a profound effect on him and inspired him at once to write this ode. In it the poet gives a clear description of the reason or emotion that compelled his 'genius' (we would say his superconscious) to write:

> He in splendour on his throne
> Saw my genius and fell silent.
> As with unremitting alternation
> He fell, rose up again and lay down,

Not blending his own voice
With the throng of a thousand voices.
Untainted by servile praise
Or by cowardly outrage
He now rises, profoundly moved by the sudden
Disappearance of such a ray of light
And utters at the tomb an ode,
Which, perhaps, will not die.

Sometimes it is a case of less intense, multiple external stimuli which act directly on the superconscious in such a way that they are not noticed by the conscious mind of the artist. In many cases, on the other hand, the decisive stimulus is not external but from within, made up of inclinations, impulses, feelings and problems in a state of tumult in the artist's soul. Because they cannot find an outlet, a means of satisfaction or a solution in everyday life, they express themselves in a creation of the imagination, imbuing it with their compelling force. This is the transformation and the artistic sublimation of personal feelings. This has been simply and effectively expressed by Heine: 'I draw my modest songs from my great pain.'

A number of works on psychology contain analytical examples of this source of inspiration, but these are [to be] treated with some skepticism, given the tendency of many psychologists to exaggerate. The most rational analyses are contained in the book *Psychanalyse de l'Art* [The Psychoanalysis of Art] by Charles Baudoin.

The *Divine Comedy* itself may be seen, in part, as the sublimated expression of Dante's love for Beatrice, which knew no earthly consummation. Wagner himself described his *Tristan and Isolde* as 'a monument to my love which has failed to find satisfaction'.

The stimulus may also be of a higher quality, that is to say a vivid intuition of the Higher Reality, a flash of spiritual enlightenment. This was often the case in times of spiritual awareness when art was of a religious nature and the poet also a prophet and seer. Thus Dante, in his 'Paradise', uses his remarkable art to give expression to his mystical intuition and enlightenment.

When the initial stimulus for production by the superconscious is from within, we may speak of self-fertilization, that is
to say a creative relationship between the different parts and
aspects of a single mind.

But there is a third possibility, and that is the receiving of
stimuli from mental sources acting telepathically on sensitive,
receptive spirits. This possibility could be backed up by the not
infrequent instances of simultaneous invention or simultaneous
activity which take place despite the absence of any external
means of communication. One might label such manifestations
'products of the collective unconscious', but this expression does
not really say anything.

Next comes the period of 'gestation', a time for inner
development which, like its physical counterpart, may take place
simply, without causing any disruption. More often, however,
it is tiring, demanding and painful. Its duration can vary
greatly—sometimes it is a very rapid process, almost immediate,
at other times it is a long drawn-out process. At times the artist
will be overcome by a feeling of uneasiness or disquiet, perhaps
interspersed with fleeting glimpses of inspiration; in other cases
he will view this period negatively, with a sense of dryness and
lethargy, resulting in the inability to produce anything. The
artist often misinterprets this state as the paralysis of his
productive faculties, then torments himself and tries to force
inspiration using such stimulants as alcohol, but this is often to
no avail, as well as being harmful. When moments of insight
burst through they can give rise to the conscious, deliberate
collaboration of the artist with his unconscious. This
collaboration will be worked out differently depending on the
psychological type and on the make-up of a person's
personality.

Finally comes the moment of birth, the sudden entry of ideas
into the conscious mind, in other words true inspiration and the
external product. This too, like physical birth, can be easy and
spontaneous or it can be difficult and painful; it may require
artificial aids, and at times the product is not viable. In some
cases there is exultation and joy (we all remember Archimede's
shout 'Eureka!'); in contrast, others such as Alfred De Musset,
find it a painful experience and do all they can to avoid it by

excesses of various kinds.

The birth of an artistic product can occur at various stages: it may be like the offspring of certain animals which are ready for independent life, or it may be like the human baby which needs further care and feeding if it is to develop. Thus a work of art can come in an almost perfect form at the first attempt, requiring nothing more than some slight alteration or finishing touch, or it may come only in outline form, requiring that the bulk of the work be developed consciously.

The respective proportions and the mutual relationship between spontaneous creation and conscious activity can be varied and complex. There is sometimes a conscious, almost hallucinatory splitting of the mind. If one thinks of the references Dickens made in his letters to the independent personality, for want of a better term, of his characters and compare these references with other facts known to us, we must consider them authentic. Mrs Camp, his greatest creation, would 'speak' to him, as he affirmed, usually when he was in church, and in a voice which took the form of an inner prompting.

The French playwright De Curel carried out a careful analysis of his method, or more appropriately of his experiences when working. He begins by tackling the subject in the normal way, perhaps with greater difficulty and with less confidence than other writers. But then he notices certain characters coming to life in his mind and speaking to him, just as Mrs Camp spoke to Dickens. These characters are not exactly visible, but they move around him as though on a stage, be it a house or a garden, and he 'sees' this in a vague fashion, as though in a dream. From this point on he is no longer composing or creating: he is simply carrying out a literary review. The characters speak, act of their own will, and even when the writer is interrupted or when he is sleeping, the drama develops spontaneously in his mind. When he is distracted and not thinking of his work he often becomes aware of snatches of conversation or phrases which form part of scenes he has not yet reached. This means that the subliminal development, or the subconscious mind's processing of the drama has moved on from and anticipated what comes after the point at which the conscious mind stopped working.

In these small splits within one personality De Curel sees a type of bud, a source of growth within the primitive personality which the latter gradually reabsorbs, though not without a struggle, as soon as the play is finished.

This is a distinct manifestation of the sub-personalities which exist within each of us.

Luigi Pirandello, that gifted, restless analyst of dissociation and of psychological complexities, made similar statements and posed this very problem in his first play *Six Characters in Search of an Author.*

The source of artistic creation and invention which we have outlined, and the existence of various semi-independent psychological levels explain certain strange, paradoxical facts about the relationship between an author and his work. Sometimes his conscious state of mind is very different from the states of mind he is expressing in what he is creating—indeed, it may be the complete opposite.

By way of example, Rossini composed some of the most joyful sections of the *Barber of Seville* when he was angry. He was very lazy, which meant he was always late in producing his compositions. So for the *Barber of Seville* the date of its performance had already been announced, though as the day drew near Rossini had composed almost nothing. Then the producer, knowing Rossini was greedy as well as lazy, locked him up in his room and would not allow meals to be sent in unless the composer produced a given number of pages. As a result Rossini—in bed (where he usually composed)—wrote his music in a state of anger and then threw the sheets, one by one, from his window, whereupon scribes in the small square below would start to make copies.

It can also frequently happen that an author has a strange sense of disinterest, even of detachment from what he has produced, so when he rereads it after some time it seems new to him and he is surprised that it has come from his pen. But it can go further than this: it can even happen that an author finds it difficult to understand what he has written and does not appreciate its deep meaning, whereas another person, a sensitive critic, is able to see this and to bring it out.

I had experience of this phenomenon many years ago. An

intuitive and spiritually aware doctor gave a public reading, in the presence of the author, of some of the latter's poems and then gave a perceptive commentary on them, highlighting the spiritual and symbolic meanings they contained. After this address the poet said, 'I would never have believed that my poems could mean so much, but I cannot but recognize that this is the case!' It should be noted that this poet did not amount to much in his personal life, indeed he was something of a pleasure-seeker without any spiritual aspirations.

I will illustrate what I have said with some examples. These are very different from one another, but they help us to understand—to the extent this is possible—the amazing process of inspiration and creation. I will begin by quoting from the clear, I would even say frank, testimony of that great writer Hermann Keyserling.

> I became a writer—though originally I had had no leanings towards writing—only because, given the abilities, and more to the point the inabilities, I had, I saw no other way of making a living than expressing myself in writing. When I write I have always felt I am not unlike a medium: I never know in advance what I am going to say—it is only when I engage in this activity that I feel the urge to say something on a given subject. The first draft has always been produced as fast as is physically possible, and it always takes me by surprise—the surprise of joyfully recognizing what I had only had an inkling of before.
>
> When I had to get involved in an outside activity in Darmstadt (the founding and management of the 'School of Wisdom') to which I had never given any thought, and to which I was not at all suited, I was struck by the surprising fact that my production was guided by the combined effect of a lecture title and a particular deadline. I have no need to think about what I have to produce in the interim: when the agreed date draws near, my vague initial inklings take form of themselves.
>
> *My Relationship with the Superconscious*

The second example is that of a sculptor, Ernesto Masuelli. He was blinded in combat at the age of 19. He had never been particularly interested in art and had no involvement with it after losing his sight. But after some time, he happened to pick up a piece of plasticine and tried to make a model with it for fun. The results were so interesting that they led him to devote himself to modelling. In this way he developed a talent of the utmost spontaneity, which is all the more remarkable because of his blindness. When I asked Masuelli about the way he creates his works he replied, 'I do not guide my hand when I am working, I just feel what I am doing. At that moment I am the object I am representing, and I let my hands act of their own accord. I made the *Fante* (one of his most beautiful sculptures) in three quarters of an hour, in a dreamlike, almost unconscious state. I work with serenity and joy.'

This reference to the process of identification or impersonalization is very interesting.

The third example, and an even more significant one in certain respects, is that of the poetess and designer, Maria Gallotti. I will go into this case in more detail because I was able to collect the biographical data myself.

I will quote from part of my inaugural speech at the design exhibition for the Press Circle in Rome during April 1935.

From her earliest years Maria Gallotti was very unlike other girls and young women. She had a tendency to withdraw from her surroundings and to live in a world of her own, a world of beautiful visions, goodness and perfection. This intense introversion and the psychological dissociation it produced was heightened by a painful fact she referred to much herself.

I spent my childhood and youth in a nightmare I thought I could never wake from. To my great sadness—and I think this is a sadness that comes to and has such a pernicious effect on many young people—I had a teacher who, may God forgive him, rather than stimulate a love of learning in me and encourage me to find out more, took it upon himself to convince me with daily persistence that I was deficient as a person, incapable of wanting and even less of doing anything good, and that I was destined to become an academic drop-out. This labour of suggestion on his part must have met with a weakness in my will, because not only was I unable to rebel and react, I ended up thinking of myself as a wretched person who was incapable of seeing anything that other people seemed to understand, and marking out my own personal pathway through life.

This malevolent suggestion resulted in the best and truest part of Maria Gallotti's personality remaining in a state of paralysis, and she spent many years in a sleepwalking state. It then came out in weaker, less wholesome personality traits, indicating a stifling of the inner life; the depressing, destructive suggestions of other people put a brutal end to the sparks of spiritual life, producing psychological disturbances and even nervous and mental illnesses. What we are witnessing here is moral mutilation, which is in a sense more serious than physical mutilation. And those responsible for causing such states in others have much to answer for. The only excuse they can claim is that they are often unaware of the harm they are doing, but the time has come for such psychological crimes to cease. Everyone must come to realize that criticism, disparagement, pessimism and forecasts of failure are nothing less than poisons, whereas loving understanding, appreciation, encouragement and a healthy optimism are life-giving: they summon dormant energies and can lead to a wonderful inner blossoming and to precious works. There is so much ignorance here that mothers who love, and say they love their children, as they understand it, end up ruining them with these negative images and continuous criticisms.

Maria Gallotti lived for many years worthily performing her duties as a wife and mother, but she was never free from that subtle, unrelenting torment of a yearning for a spiritual life she felt was unattainable, and she was oppressed by the energies within her for which she was unable to find an outlet and to which she could not give creative expression. But then something surprising happened within her. One night she suddenly felt a strong urge from within to write some verses which came unbidden into her mind. She obeyed this urge, though in a state of bewilderment and hesitance, and the verses flowed out in a torrent, effortlessly. From then on this poetic vein did not cease to pour out its treasures, as living and fresh as a mountain spring. They were fluent, harmonious poems with the minimum of rhetoric, free from 'literary' contrivances, simply expressing the feelings, reactions and aspirations of a noble, sensitive soul, but a soul that is also full of life and intensity.

A few months later something even more surprising happened—Maria Gallotti began to draw spontaneously, without ever having done it before and never having had a drawing lesson. It was not a gradual apprenticeship or the steady unfolding of an artistic bent. She began at once by tackling one of the most demanding subjects in terms of technique and expression: a picture of Christ. The impulse which urged her on, with unselfconscious boldness, to dare such an undertaking was a fervent desire to have a picture of Him, one that matched her own inner vision, an image to which she could address her prayers—and she succeeded.

After this she produced many other pictures, with complete spontaneity, surprising ease and speed of execution. Worthy of particular note and of greatest merit is a series depicting Christ as he utters various words during his crucifixion.

In addition to this her favourite theme, Maria Gallotti drew other subjects, including St Francis, St Catherine and St Clare. She then produced a series of fine interpretations or 'transcriptions' representing the music of various great composers, including Bach, Beethoven, Haydn and Schubert, as well as symbolic representations of states of mind—regret, bitterness, attraction, reflection, meditation, happiness, serenity, etc. She also did many portraits.

Everything I have already discussed with regard to the process of inspiration and creation is clearly seen in the art of Maria Gallotti: external stimuli, and in particular inner spiritual stimuli, developed by a highly sensitive, lively superconscious; the easy, spontaneous birth of the artistic product, already complete in every detail, and thus requiring little or no participation of the conscious personality. It is all developed and prepared at a higher level of the mind and then passes to the conscious mind.

There remains the problem of her remarkable technical ability. But here I will do nothing more than formulate the hypothesis that the image, the inner vision of the drawing is so alive, so sharp and so exact in every aspect, that it automatically creates the necessary neuro-muscular coordination for producing the right pencil marks on the paper and for converting the image into a physical reality.

The strength of the superconscious in Maria Gallotti had also shown itself in other ways: on a number of occasions she had clear premonitions of things which later happened. She had compelling impulses to act in certain ways, and these later proved to be justified. Moreover she felt that she was guided and supported by a higher spiritual Force.

We are now at the threshold of mystery and I am not in a position to address this subject. I will conclude with a paraphrase of what Shakespeare said through one of his characters: 'There are more things between heaven and earth than the human mind will usually acknowledge.'

6

TRANSPERSONAL
INSPIRATION

If we examine the 'signs of the times', i.e. the present state of humanity, its interests and behaviour patterns, we will at once notice an increasing polarization between two opposing trends. On the one hand there is the frantic desire and restless seeking after material possessions, sensual pleasures, and domination over nature and over other human beings, with its consequent licence and self-affirmation in all areas, along with aggression and violence, both individual and collective; on the other hand, and visible to varying degrees, there is a sense of dissatisfaction with all this, even an open rebellion against it, especially on the part of the young, accompanied by the search, conscious or not, for different, higher values and means of fulfilment—a longing for what is generically termed 'spiritual' or 'religious'.

But in this area we are faced with countless uncertainties, misunderstandings and confusion. There is the strange paradox that despite the abundance of testimonies to the experiences men and women of all times and places have had in that higher realm, scientific studies and experimental inquiries into it have been sporadic and unsatisfactory. There are a number of reasons for this. To begin with there is a false understanding of the scientific method which restricts it to the quantitative and statistical techniques more suited to the natural sciences. Furthermore, the mind is reluctant to admit the existence of realities and values not consistent with the known rational world, confusing what is super-rational with what is irrational or anti-rational. Then there is the fact that the descriptions of these experiences have tended to be tied up with religious doctrines, images, symbols and forms which are no longer accepted or recognized by a growing number of people. As Keyserling put it, in his usual irreverent style, 'They have been exposed by their own prejudices.'

Another difficulty is the inadequacy of language and speech to communicate the true nature of transpersonal experiences. Everyone who has attempted to do so has said that such experiences are actually inexpressible.[1]

Finally there is the fear of entering a world different from the one we are used to—an unknown, disturbing world. This is accentuated by the fact that the attainment of such experiences has often been presented in the negative form of the renunciation of everything to which man is usually most attached, without placing sufficient emphasis on the positive, joyful compensations.

The result of all this is resistance and reluctance, or what has sometimes been referred to as 'rejection of the sublime'. Yet despite all this, the dissatisfaction we referred to earlier and the longing for 'something else', the fascination with exploration and conquest of the inner worlds, of which many people have had inklings, has produced flashes, and even vivid bursts of light, so that those who present themselves as messengers or guides in this area attract a large number of followers, building up an entourage of enthusiastic disciples and often fanatics.

But the value of the messages and the competence of these guides or 'masters' differs considerably. Alongside the noble, genuine teaching there is also the spurious, in which truth and illusion are mixed to varying degrees; alongside the truly wise guides there are also 'false prophets' who use and teach invalid and even dangerous methods. This highlights the urgent need for scientific study and experimentation in this area, independent of any doctrine, system or personal authority.

This study and inquiry are already under way and are developing rapidly. They represent a new branch of psychology referred to by the term *transpersonal* and which we might call 'higher psychology'. But this is only a start: there is a long way to go.

[1]This is one of the characteristics attributed to mystical experiences by W. James in his *Varieties of Religious Experience*.

For my own part, I have been engaged in this subject for most of my life and now intend to continue in the same vein, but in a more coordinated, systematic fashion (in the best sense of those words), by writing a book with the title *Higher Psychology or Psychology of the Self*.

One of the main themes of this 'higher psychology' is the relationship between transpersonal, superconscious activity and the conscious life or, to be more exact, the various means and stages of the transfer of superconscious ideas and energies into the realm of ordinary consciousness. These means are varied and may be listed as follows:

1. Intuition.
2. Imagination.
3. Illumination.
4. Revelation.
5. Inspiration.
6. Creation.
7. Understanding and Interpretation.

These do not develop separately; indeed they often occur more or less at the same time and, to varying degrees, in a united fashion. It is for this reason that they are often confused. But in order to study them scientifically we need to highlight the distinctions and differences between them. Only when we have done this will we be in a position to recognize and truly understand how they relate and interact.

This study in turn has various aspects or stages which also need to be kept separate:

1. First of all there is phenomenology, that is to say collecting data on experiences that people have had spontaneously, the observed facts as they have been described by many people from different times and places.
2. The means and processes whereby ideas and energies are transferred from the superconscious level to the level of everyday consciousness.
3. The techniques that have been and are still used to produce or encourage this transfer. These include the various

practices, external and internal, from different religions in addition to the various exercises called by different names which can be placed together under the general term of *yoga*.

4. The immediate results and the subsequent effects arising out of them.
5. The methods of forestalling the dangers and repairing the damage which can be caused by the descent or bursting in of transpersonal energies.
6. The ways of making best use of those insights and energies.

Let us first take a look at the means whereby superconscious elements and activities are passed down into the realm of the ordinary consciousness.

Intuition

We need to make a distinction here between intuition as a function of the mind and the results of its activity, i.e. types of intuition which are different in nature. The commonly accepted definition is the one indicated by the etymology of the word itself: *in-tueri*, or 'to see within'. It is the immediate sight or perception of a given object when considered in terms of its individual reality. Intuition as a particular, independent, cognitive function of the mind is generally recognized and has been spoken of in the past both in the East and in the West.

Self-defined scientific psychology, however, has not recognized it as a valid means of knowledge because of its own limited and one-sided view of this area and of the scientific method, or else it has simply identified it with the direct sensory perception of external stimuli. But there has been a reaction against this unwarranted exclusiveness. The two main proponents of the validity and value of intuition have been Bergson and Keyserling. They have been regarded and classified as philosophers, but both had a well-developed feeling for psychology, based on the very intuition we are discussing and, in Keyserling's case, on a marked ability to show empathy and identification. They have therefore made invaluable contributions to our knowledge about the human mind, contributions to which modern scientific psychology is indebted.

In the more strictly psychological field, Jung was sufficiently aware to reaffirm the existence and validity of intuition as a special independent psychological function. He spoke of it in these words:

> As I see it, intuition is one of the basic psychological functions; it is neither sensation, feeling nor intellectual deduction ... Through intuition each individual idea is presented as a whole, complete in itself, leaving us unable to explain or discover how it came about ... for this reason intuitive knowledge is intrinsically characterised by certainty and conviction, so much so that Spinoza felt it necessary to say that 'intuitive knowledge is the highest form of knowledge'.

Jung called it 'irrational', but this term is open to misunderstanding because this might be understood to mean contrary to reason, whereas it is only in fact different, not contradictory. We might perhaps call it 'para-rational' or 'transrational'.

There are various types of intuition. First there is sensory intuition—the conscious perception of visual, aural, tactile impressions, etc., produced by stimuli from our surroundings. I will not dwell on these because they take place at ordinary psychological levels and have nothing to do with the superconscious.

Then there is the intuition of ideas, in the Platonic sense, and these come from a higher region than the one in which the mind normally functions. We can therefore call them transpersonal. The same can be said about the other types of higher intuition, namely those types of intuition which have to do with aesthetics, religion, mysticism and even science (the use of intuition in higher mathematics, for instance). Indeed there are many people—people we must consider as being normal—who are not susceptible to intuition. This shows the distinction between the ordinary psychological life and the transpersonal one.

Intuition comes into the area of consciousness, or is perceived, in two ways. The first, more in keeping with the etymological meaning of the word, can be described as the opening of an 'inner eye' which enables us to perceive realities which our normal mental sight does not see. The second way can be compared to a flash, such as a flash of lightning, or as a sudden blaze of light pouring down into the area of consciousness and being perceived by the self, by the centre of consciousness at its ordinary level and in its ordinary sense. One special quality instances of intuition have in common is their authenticity. They give a perception of the object in its entirety, an overall view of that object as an organic whole. For this reason intuition is different from mental knowledge, which is analytical.

Keyserling demonstrated this very clearly:

> . . . After all man, like all the other animals, is intimately related to the whole order of beings and things, and if his instinct is defective or severely atrophied he will be unable to trust his basic impulses; man therefore needs the human equivalent of instinct if he is to find his way freely in this universe. In this sense only intuitive people are free; and it is for this reason that only they can give us our great discoverers, pioneers and innovators...

This is another special characteristic of intuition: it is directed towards continued development, towards the future.

Keyserling continues:

> ... Intuition penetrates the veil that hides the future, and thus penetrates the veil of the possible. Reality is in a state of continuous transformation, so it can only be clearly seen by someone who, when the opportunities present themselves, is able to take direct hold of what is possible. This applies in two senses: firstly, because above and beyond the facts certain 'possibilities' exist; and secondly, because from time to time and when the conditions are right, he is able at once to discern which of those possibilities can be made a reality. Both of these can only come about as a result of that primordial, inner experience of things in their entirety . . .
>
> Indeed, intuition is closely related to love.

For all these reasons intuition goes far beyond an appreciation of the qualities of an object—it assimilates its very essence, what it truly is. It is therefore one of the fields of inquiry covered by the new psychology of being pioneered by Maslow.

Imagination

This is closely linked with intuition because when intuition comes into the conscious mind it is often not in an abstract, simple, 'pure' form, but assumes the shape of images. The first task to be tackled, therefore, is to identify its contents—the essence or idea behind the intuition—and to separate it from its outward form or the clothing it is presented in. This is symbolic in nature and raises the significant, complex area of symbolism. We will deal with this later.[1] For the time being I will only highlight the dual, and at times contrasting, nature and function of symbolism. It can either conceal or reveal. When it is exchanged for the reality it is meant to express, it conceals and becomes a source of illusion. When it is recognized as a means of expression, on the other hand, it is a useful tool; indeed it is sometimes a necessary tool for perceiving and communicating a transcendent reality.

Apart from its cognitive function, as a means and vehicle for intuition, imagination has other varying aspects.

First of all there is straightforward reproductive imagination, the recorded image of sensations or impressions one has had in the past (mnemonic images). The most common type is the visual image, but there are other image traces left by different senses—most importantly aural images. These are latent and are kept in what we might call the 'archives of the unconscious'. They can rise spontaneously into the conscious mind or they can be recalled deliberately. The ability to keep and access such images is immense—one might almost call it unlimited. Under certain special conditions (hypnosis or feverish states) people are able to relive incidents from their early childhood in minute detail. Then there are the prodigious memory feats of great conductors, such as Toscanini, who are able to memorize whole symphonies and other musical works so that they can conduct them without a score in front of them. Indeed, so unbelievable is the ability of some chess players to visualize the pieces and their possible moves on more than one chess board that they are able to play 15 or more games simultaneously.

Then there is creative imagination, which is of great

[1] See Symbols of Transpersonal Experience, Chapter 8 in this volume.

importance, though it has not yet been properly recognized or used in areas such as education. Its activity usually comes to the fore in dreams, which are the mixed product of two types of imagination: reproductive and creative. But I will discuss this creative aspect later.

Enlightenment

One of the most frequent manifestations of the superconscious in the conscious mind is that of enlightenment, which follows on from the opening of the 'inner eye'. There are many similarities between intuition and enlightenment, but there are also significant differences.

In general terms we can say that intuition is a flash of illumination on a particular aspect or manifestation of Reality. Enlightenment, on the other hand, is broader and longer lasting. It is a vision that shows the essential nature and synthetic unity of all Reality, or of significant aspects of that Reality. It is the perception of light which differs from its physical counterpart, a light coming straight from Reality itself.

This type of enlightenment may be regarded as a revelation of the divine immanence, and as a revelation of the unity of Universal Life expressed in myriad forms. The most effective description is that contained in the *Bhagavad Gita* where it is referred to as the 'revelation of the Universal Form'.

Many poets have experienced this enlightenment and have attempted to express it. The greatest among them is Dante. His 'Paradise' is full of expressions of light. At the beginning of the book he states quite clearly that he had had the unspeakable experience of the supreme light, the light that shines in the highest heaven, closest to the Supreme Reality, God.

> The glory of him who moves everything
> Penetrates the universe and shines
> In one part more and, in another, less.

> I have been in the heaven which takes most of his light,
> And I have seen things which cannot be told,
> Possibly, by anyone who comes down from up there;

Because, approaching the object of its desires,
Our intellect is so deeply absorbed
That memory cannot follow it all the way.

Translation: C.H. Sisson, Pan Classics

This manifestation of light takes on different aspects in the conscious mind of the person to whom it is revealed, or rather different aspects prevail over the others depending on the individual differences of the beholders, since these aspects are not separate but interpenetrate and merge with one another to varying degrees. Sometimes the dominant factor is beauty, as in Tagore's case, in other cases it is the cognitive aspect which occupies the conscious mind, e.g. Plotinus and Eckhart.

For Christian mystics, as well as for Eastern mystics, this phenomenon is united with feelings of love and adoration. For others the main feeling aroused by enlightenment is one of joy which may reach the point of ecstatic bliss. I would nevertheless repeat that we are dealing with a situation in which one aspect is being stressed above others: in general they are all present in some measure. Dante gave fine expression to the way in which they blend together.

Revelation

There is one type of enlightenment which is different from the types of experience we have mentioned so far and that is the realization, and at times the sudden awareness, of what a human being is—the revelation an individual has about himself.

This revelation can have different aspects and effects, even opposing ones. The first type is extremely positive in nature: it is a vision of the amazing potential, latent or active, at the superconscious levels. This can come in a blinding flash, a light that reveals the Spiritual Self.

To this is added a new understanding: the true understanding of oneself and others. The field of consciousness is enlarged and expanded; it is pervaded by feelings of joy, goodness, love and gratitude.

But even this revelation, if it is unexpected, sudden or too intense, can result in undesirable, even morbid, reactions. It can give a sense of over-excitement and self-exaltation. If the distinction between the Spiritual Self and the personal 'I' is lost to the conscious mind, the qualities and powers of the Spiritual Self may be wrongly attributed to the normal personality, even to the point of megalomania.

The other aspect of inner revelation, in contrast with the above, is revelation of the lower, darker parts of the personality, which may before have been unknown, unrecognized or denied and repressed to a certain extent in the unconscious. These are what Jung called the 'Shadow'. This revelation, when it is sudden, can have a disturbing effect and produce states of depression, fear and even despair. In order to reduce such effects, a prior psychological knowledge—an awareness of 'depth psychology'—can be very helpful. This preparation can remove the shock of surprise and help a person to accept the revelation by showing him that this dark side is part of the common human condition.

There may also be other less extreme, albeit harmful, reactions, even at the physical level, if the nervous system is unable to take the intensity or voltage generated by the psychospiritual energies bursting in on the field of consciousness. Here too prior knowledge of the various levels of human nature, such as that provided by 'three-dimensional psychology', can ease the situation, enabling a person to accept the reactions and suggesting ways of eliminating them.

Inspiration and Creation

Other types of relationship and interaction between the superconscious and the conscious levels are inspiration and psychospiritual creation. It will be useful to have a clear idea of the differences between enlightenment, inspiration and creation, and to keep them in the forefront of the mind because they are often confused. Enlightenment can produce inspiration, and this is often the case, but not always. For some mystics, enlightenment remains a subjective thing: it can produce a state of contemplation, and it often produces intense feelings of love and the earnest desire to become united with God, to merge into the supreme Reality. But it does not inspire external expression and it does not call for action.

Moreover, there can be inspiration without enlightenment, without a raising or expansion of the consciousness. An example of this is the musical inspiration received by young children such as Mozart.

There is also a marked difference between inspiration and creation. Inspiration, in the true sense of the word, is the process whereby ideas, developed to varying degrees, are transferred or make their way down from the transpersonal levels into the field of consciousness. Creation, on the other hand, is the process, or rather a series of processes relating to the development of those ideas, before they descend or make their appearance in the conscious mind. Creation is like the conception and gestation period in the mother's womb; inspiration is like the birth, the emergence of the creature.

I developed these analogies in the last chapter, pointing out the various ways in which these processes operate. I said that 'birth' can take place at various stages of the development process. Sometimes the product presents itself to the consciousness well-formed and complete, ready for independent existence, as happens biologically in the case of many animals; other times, on the other hand, it presents itself in a raw, incomplete form, and then requires the conscious mind to spend time working on it before it has a proper shape. I also said that as with physical birth the emergence can sometimes be spontaneous, quick, easy, accompanied by a sense of joy; at other times it can be difficult, long and painful.

Understanding and Interpretation

In one sense this is the most important stage. Intuition, illumination, and the revelations they produce must be properly understood if one is to avoid wrong interpretations, applications and inappropriate, even dangerous, action. Such errors occur frequently and many examples could be quoted. I will give two which illustrate two different types: one has to do with wrong interpretations which lead to urges or inner 'commands' to act in certain ways; the other has to do with mental misunderstandings of truths when they appear in the field of consciousness.

The first example is a well-known episode in the life of St

Francis. Shortly after his conversion, when he was praying, he heard a voice within him saying, 'Go and repair my Church.' Because there was a small dilapidated church nearby, he interpreted the message as a divine command to repair it, and set about the task, Only later did he come to understand that the message had a different, far greater significance: it was the revelation of his mission to 'restore' the Catholic Church, which, at that time, was in a state of disarray. It is common knowledge how remarkably he fulfilled his mission.

The other example is completely different in nature and has to do with a very different man. It is the dazzling revelation Nietzsche had of the great cycles which run their course in the eternity of the development of the cosmos. He interpreted it, and expressed it in his theory of the 'eternal return'. As he saw it, given that time has no limit, whereas the number of the atoms of existing matter, however great, is finite, their possible combinations must necessarily be finite and must inevitably result in their being reproduced, always returning to the same point, and so on for eternity. This doctrine of despair was, of course, based on a wrong premise, namely that the number of atoms is finite and constant, whereas—apart from the intrinsic absurdity of this hypothesis—modern physics has shown that the atoms of matter are continually disintegrating and forming new atoms with different properties. What Nietzsche had felt intuitively was the cyclical nature of the cosmic manifestation or of its process of evolution. This is the oriental concept of the great cycles of appearance, disappearance of worlds, of the periodic emanation of matter and its evolution in countless forms, followed by its subsequent reabsorption into the formless spirit. Recent discoveries in astronomy concerning the formation and disintegration of the stars and galaxies fully support this idea. According to Eastern philosophy this also applies at a human level in terms of a cyclical manifestation of souls in a series of bodies (reincarnation). But this does not mean an identical return, rather a reappearance in ever higher forms, evolution in the form of an ascending spiral. Nietzsche's ideas are a clear example of the wrong interpretation of a valid intuition.

In the field of psychology there is the perennial problem of the interpretation of symbols. Even here one may note frequent, I would even say continuous, errors and confused thinking, for instance in the interpretation of the symbols found in dreams, and even in the interpretation of myths and of the symbolism found in artistic or literary works. The errors are often based on preconceived ideas and on the pet theories of those interpreting the symbols, but the difficulty is also due to the fact that symbols can have different meanings and different levels of reality, without being contradictory or mutually exclusive.

I will now illustrate this with a case of spontaneous inspiration which has much in common with that of Maria Gallotti, to whom we referred in the last chapter, but which is also different in a number of points, and highlights certain special character-istics of the activities which take place at the superconscious levels and their relationship with everyday consciousness.

It is the case of a young woman I have been treating for many years at irregular intervals because of my long absences from the town where she lives. The relationship has been continued by correspondence, however, except during the war years 1941 to 1945. I will call her Lucia (though this is not her real name). From the clinical point of view there was nothing unusual about her. Her symptoms came under the heading of neuro-psychological asthenia: physical debility, emotional depression, difficulty in applying her mind to a given subject as well as a number of phobias, in particular the fear of going out of the house alone. Her family environment was oppressive: an authoritarian father, a kind mother but narrow in her views. She was prevented from continuing her studies as she would have liked to, and suffered isolation and no emotional satisfaction. Following treatment, during which a number of the techniques of psychosynthesis were used, she gradually improved to the point of overcoming her agoraphobia and being able to make long train journeys by herself.

As I said before, there is nothing of particular significance here. But when she was introduced to free drawing she very soon started to produce some unusual specimens of particular interest from various points of view. To begin with the drawings consisted of lines, geometric shapes, diagrammatic representations of different aspects of nature (the sun, the sea, mountains) and of simple objects. After a short time, however, words and phrases were added to the pictures, referring to them and commenting on them. This development took place spontaneously, without any instruction or encouragement on my part. The phrases expressed various states of mind, but increasingly they referred to aspirations, yearnings for freedom and the desire to be lifted up, flashes of intuition which were universal or cosmic in nature. Here are a few from the many dating from the years 1932 and 1935:

> The face of the deity is hidden. Mysterious waves pass through the atmosphere. In the high spheres there blows the universal wind. The conscious mind is unwilling to recognize these things.
>
> The eye sees into the heights of space. Across all life is the cycle of history. The great all remains immobile.

The occurrence of such phrases became less frequent after this and almost stopped completely in 1940, but it then became active again and the drawings were gradually replaced by written words which were poetic in their style of expression. More and more they took on the form of messages from the levels of the superconscious levels. The clear distinction, and at times the opposition, between the everyday consciousness and this source of inspiration was recognized and verbalized by Lucia.

The style of the messages varies. It is often original, making use of strange, often bizarre expressions which are nevertheless vivid and effective. In certain respects the style is like that of the surrealist poets. These poets were sometimes suspected of expressing themselves in that way deliberately, artificially and even in bad faith. Often, at least, this suspicion is not justified, and it can be completely discounted in Lucia's case, for she was the first person to be surprised by what her hand wrote.

What is actually taking place in cases like this is a breaking through of ideas and activities from the unconscious in their raw form, without having undergone the usual processing and structuring to make them coordinated verbal expressions that can be readily understood. But what matters most is the nature and content of the messages. They can come from any level of the unconscious, from the lowest level to the highest. In Lucia's case the messages usually have a lofty tone and content, reminiscent of the transpersonal realm.

The most insistent themes are the vision of a bright future, the urgent need for the renewal of mankind, signs and indications of a New Era, and the appearance of Superior Beings who will be its pioneers and creators.

The attitude Lucia has adopted to the source of her inspiration is sensible and properly agnostic. She does not consider this source a living being, an external personality, but gives to expressions indicating this (God, the Singer, etc.) a symbolic nature of 'psychological personification'.

It should be noted that whenever Lucia wrote she did not lose consciousness of herself. This makes her different from all those people who have written things as long as novels in a state of hypnosis or trance, without knowing what they were doing. This type of automatic writing is not recommended because it tends to produce or increase psychological dissociation and can open the floodgates to undesirable influences. Furthermore, Lucia's case and the cases of other people like her show that keeping in a state of conscious vigilance does not hinder inspiration from the transpersonal levels.

What conclusion can we draw from the spontaneous production of drawings and writings done by Maria Gallotti and Lucia, to whom I have referred above, and from the countless other cases of the same origin, reported by Myers in his book *Human Personality*, as well as by many other academics? They act as clear confirmation of what humanist psychology and transpersonal psychology (the Third and Fourth Forces in psychology) have demonstrated: namely that there is a host of latent powers and energies, usually unrecognized, in the human mind, and a host of wonderful possibilities, both creative and expressive, just waiting to surface when they are given the right conditions.

The clearest evidence is given on the one hand by the spontaneous incidents I have already mentioned, and on the other hand by the many incredibly gifted children and young people, as well as other superior beings who exist: religious, artistic, scientific geniuses, great educators and the benefactors of humanity.

Highly gifted people who show special abilities, sometimes from their earliest years, are now beginning to be recognized and appreciated, but still to a limited, unsatisfactory extent. There is still misunderstanding, as well as reluctance and even hostility towards their being fully appreciated. There are various reasons for this, but I cannot go into them now. Yet there are two important reasons which should compel us to take note of the highly gifted. The first is that they represent the most precious human element, which we might compare to uranium among metals, in that both are able to release powerful irradiations.

The other reason is that the highly gifted often have an exuberance of energies at all levels of their being. When they are prevented from expressing their abilities, these energies can produce destructive effects, antisocial behaviour and even crime.

It has been noted that among the boys and youths held in what ironically are called 'Correction Homes' there is a significant percentage of highly gifted individuals, and at times some of them have had spontaneous spiritual awakenings. If this is not recognized and they are still kept under an oppressive regime, they become even more antisocial with the result that when they regain their freedom they can become violent and dangerous criminals. Society should therefore make it a matter of urgent concern to do all it can to prevent this danger materializing and to redirect those exuberant energies towards constructive, creative activities.

There is much that can be done towards this, but the necessary methods already exist. They are numerous and varied in nature, from the highest, such as understanding, compassion and love, to the various techniques of psychotherapy and education which are continually developing and amongst which are numbered such straightforward methods as drawing and writing.

We should all regard it as our duty to spread this knowledge, to encourage doctors and educators, and to help parents to make the maximum use of it. In this way, more than by any other expedient, it will be possible to anticipate the evils that threaten the very existence of civilized life, and to prepare for the coming of a New Age when psychosynthesis will be implemented at a worldwide level, and when, free from wars and violent social struggles, the highest human potential is able to find its widest and freest expression.

VERTICAL TELEPATHY

We will now turn to the relationship between the conscious 'I' and what it can receive or pick up from the superconscious. This ability to receive 'from above' may be called *vertical telepathy* in order to distinguish it from *horizontal telepathy*, which refers to signals from outside the subject, emanating from the currents of individual and collective thought, reaching that person horizontally through the atmosphere. We might also call it *internal telepathy* because it goes on within a single individual. We need to give a warning here, however: it is very difficult to distinguish what comes from the individual superconscious and what comes from even higher spheres or from the levels of the superconscious outside the individual. The higher one ascends, the more the limits of individuality tend to disappear; the higher one ascends, the more the individual becomes united with the whole. Thus any description or terminology can only be relative or indicative. Language is always symbolic and allusive in nature, and this is even more the case in the psychospiritual realm.

The word 'telepathy' means influence at a distance, referring here to a psychological distance, a distance in level between the conscious 'I' and the superconscious. Here again, as with horizontal telepathy, this type of telepathy can be either spontaneous or experimental, that is to say deliberate.

Spontaneous telepathy consists of receiving impressions from afar, without willing them, and then discovering that they tie in with reality, while in experimental telepathy one person projects a thought or image and another person tries to pick up what is being transmitted. The same distinction can be made in vertical telepathy. The type of vertical telepathy which might be called spontaneous covers all inspiration related phenomena: artistic, literary or musical inspiration; intuition; the higher forms of premonition; the urge to perform heroic deeds; and mystical enlightenment. Ideas and energies from the superconscious burst through or come down into the conscious mind and are perceived by the conscious 'I'. But here too the process can be encouraged or even deliberately caused by means of psychospiritual exercises which attract or facilitate the transfer of superconscious messages and influences to the level of everyday consciousness.

Vertical telepathy is of great scientific and human significance. It is important from the scientific point of view because it confirms the existence of this higher aspect to our being; and it is important in human terms in that it is the best part of ourselves which is being encouraged, made conscious and therefore used creatively and to good purpose. Its significance is not recognized, however, or we would live very differently!

An analogy may help us to understand this. If it were known that there was a great sage endowed with great spiritual powers, a loving, unselfish sage, we would certainly feel an eager desire to speak to him and to ask his help and advice. And if he lived as a hermit up in the mountains, surely we would be prepared to make the climb to find him. Would we not be willing to submit to the discipline of special psychospiritual preparation in order to win his precious teachings and to be made alive by the energy and love he radiated? We would realize that the help he offered could save us from making mistakes and from suffering and pain, as well as having the power to truly change our lives.

Such a sage or Master does actually exist. He is close at hand, indeed he is present in each of us. He is the Higher 'I', the Spiritual Self. To reach him does require a journey, but it is a journey through the world within. To reach the place where this Self resides means a climb, an ascent to the heights of the superconscious. It also requires proper psychospiritual preparation so that we will be able to withstand the impact of the force of the Spiritual Self and to pick up its subtle messages, distinguishing them from all the other voices within, so that we can understand and interpret its symbolism correctly. And lastly we need to be prepared to put into effect, with an unswerving, resolute will, what we have been shown.

This preparation is not easy, of course. The Self considers things, events, beings, etc., in a very different way to the personal 'I'. Its value system and its perspective are very different to the way the ordinary conscious mind looks at things, with its 'short-sighted views', as Dante put it. What the Self reveals is consistent with what is truly good, but it can be contrary to our wishes and personal preferences. The Self does not call for sacrifices in the usual erroneous sense of forced, demanding renunciations; it calls for them in the sense of a consecration which results in the gradual elimination of a number of habits and activities that are harmful and of no use, or of less importance, so as to create a space for us to devote our time to things of greater value.

Furthermore, the Self—in its wisdom and understanding love—does not require that we do this at a stroke and in a perfect fashion. It is patient, prepared to wait, knowing full well that, however slowly, we will reach the high goal for which we are destined, a goal on which the Self has kept its sights since the start of our evolutionary pilgrimage. In other words, the Self has a sense of what is eternal—or, to be more accurate, it lives in eternity. But it is the eternal 'now' that it inhabits, not merely a transcendent eternity, cut off from the evolutionary process of development.

'Eternal now' is a paradoxical expression which must be appreciated intuitively; but it provides us with a key to a fundamental truth, and that has to do with the relation between the transcendent and the immanent, between being and becoming. Both of these should be present, conscious and at work in us.

We need to live our lives with a keen awareness of each moment, but against the backdrop of eternity. Now the synthesis of the moment and of eternity is the cycle. Life proceeds in cycles, and these cycles are moments linked organically by something which transcends them: eternity. A synthetic expression of this is the phrase 'the glorious, eternal now'.

To enter into a conscious relationship with the Self requires that one become attuned to it. The analogy of a radio set may help us to understand this better. Initially an attempt was made to build the most powerful receivers possible by increasing the number of valves, but it was soon realized that power was often to the detriment of selectivity and purity of sound. Gradually the emphasis was placed on selectivity and clarity of reception, along with enough power to pick up the transmission.

The same thing applies to us. The problem is not so much 'receiving' (there is a sense in which we receive too much and from all directions), it is a case of developing an ever more refined and sophisticated selectivity. This necessary preparation requires overcoming the unwilling rebelliousness of our selfish attitudes and of our moral lethargy. (We are all morally lethargic, even if we camouflage it with outward activity which, more often than not, is a form of evasion—a passivity masked by activity.) But success is possible if we continually remember that *it is worth it*. The inner Master, the Spiritual 'I' is omniscient, it sees into the future and has remarkable powers on which we cannot set a limit. Its guidance, inspiration and multifaceted help can give us light, peace and security, producing joy and love in us, and making us effective instruments of good for others.

There are various symbols of the Self, and each of them portrays or suggests one aspect of it. Among the most commonly used symbols are a star, a sphere of radiant fire, an angelic figure which the orientals refer to as the 'Solar Angel', the inner Master, the Wise Old Man, the Hero, and the inner Warrior.

But it is we who must invoke the Self, we who must take the first step, open the door or create the channel. Only then can the Self intervene, for it will not force us or impose itself on us. We have the gift of free will, and though we make so little use of it, it is the most precious gift we have, because through our experiences, mistakes and suffering, it brings us to *reawakening*. The Self will not in any way force our hand, but if we address it, it will respond.

Time and time again one is brought up against the paradoxical duality and unity of the Deity. The personal 'I' comes down from the star, or from the spiritual 'I', in the form of a reflection. This fits one of the interpretations of the parable of the prodigal son. The personal 'I' is the prodigal son who has descended to the level of the material world and forgotten his origin, to the point where of his own free will he resorts to all the foolishness he is capable of, all the errors ('errors' both in the sense of making mistakes and of going astray), and only then feels a longing for his father's house, sets out in search of it and eventually finds it.

It is not enough, however, merely to admit or give intellectual assent to this duality in unity: this needs to happen, but it is only one step. One must then make it a reality by living it out. And before attaining reunification there is a time of dramatic 'inner dialogue'—appeals, questions and answers—followed by a gradual coming together and by ever more frequent and vivid sparks between the two poles as they approach one another until the point where they meet. They then separate again until that moment of great peace when the two become One.

SYMBOLS OF TRANSPERSONAL EXPERIENCE

Before speaking about the superconscious it would be useful to define what we mean by 'normal'. The term 'normal' is generally attributed to an average, law-abiding man who complies with the social norms of the society he lives in, in other words a 'conformist'. But looked at in this way normality is an unsatisfactory concept: it is static and exclusive. This normality is a form of 'mediocrity' which rejects or condemns anything not in accordance with the norm and calls it 'abnormal', without taking account of the fact that many of these so-called 'abnormalities' are actually the first steps in an attempt to overcome mediocrity.

Now at last people have started to react against this narrow-minded cultivation of 'normality'. The thinkers and scientists of our age have come out decidedly against it. Among the most authoritative, we might mention Jung, who had no qualms about saying:

> To be a normal man is the goal or ideal of this life's failures, of all those who fall beneath the general level of adaptation; but for those with far greater possibilities than the average man, the thought or moral straitjacket of merely being normal represents the torture of a bed of Procrustes, an unbearable boredom, or a hell of despair.
> *Modern Man in Search of a Soul* (Harcourt Brace, New York, 1933).

Another scholar, Professor Gattegno of the University of London, goes further, adding that in his view the average, ordinary man is a pre-human being, and he reserves the word 'Man' with a capital 'M' for those who have transcended the ordinary level or stage, and who are therefore supernormal.

In the past it has been a generally accepted practice for higher beings to be held in awe: geniuses, sages, saints, heroes and initiates were recognized as the vanguard of humanity, a great promise of what each man could become. This is apparent in the great statements of Christ: 'Be perfect as your father in heaven is perfect' and 'You will do greater things than I have done.' These higher beings, rather than looking down on common humanity, have sought to arouse in it a stimulus or a yearning to transcend the 'normality' and the mediocrity in which people's lives are lived, so that people might develop the latent potential which is within each human being.

In speaking of the superconscious we are up against a serious difficulty, and that is the inadequacy of human language. It is a concrete medium, especially modern language which is rational and objective. All the words used to refer to psychological or spiritual conditions and realities were originally metaphors or symbols based on concrete things. 'Soul', for instance is derived from *anemos*, meaning 'wind'; 'spirit' comes from *breath*; 'think' comes from *pesare*, meaning 'to weigh', and so forth. But this difficulty is not insurmountable if we are prepared to recognize and bear in mind the symbolic nature of each expression, be it verbal or of some other type. When the symbols are properly recognized and understood they have great value, for they are evocative and lead to direct intuitive understanding. Indeed, the fact that words representing higher realities have their roots in the experiences of the senses serves to highlight the essential similarities between the external world and the internal world, between the macrocosm and the microcosm.

These symbols can also be dangerous, however. Indeed, a person who takes them literally—going no further than the symbol towards the reality it represents—will not reach truth. Moreover, symbols are limited because of their one-sided nature: each symbol can only express one aspect, one mode and a partial concept of a given reality. We can get round this, of course, by using various symbols to describe the same truth. Then the sum, the convergence and the synthesis of all the different ways of looking at something can give us a greater, overall understanding of the reality they stand for.

For this reason, in our attempt to describe the higher experiences and conquests open to man we will use 15 classes or groups of symbols:

1. Introversion.
2. Going deeper, descent.
3. Elevation, ascent.
4. Broadening, expansion.
5. Reawakening, revival.
6. Light, enlightenment.
7. Fire.
8. Development.
9. Empowering.
10. Love.
11. A way, path, pilgrimage.
12. Transmutation, sublimation.
13. New birth, regeneration.
14. Liberation.
15. Resurrection, return.

These symbols are not only suggestive and enlightening, they can be used as themes for meditation, for real psychospiritual exercises. This has already been done for anagogic and psychotherapeutic purposes, and the use of such meditation and exercises has proved extremely effective, sometimes leading to surprising transformations. (One example of their use is the Exercise of the Rose, which is described at the end of this chapter.)

1. In the first group we find the symbols of introversion or internalization. Introversion is an urgent need of modern man. Our present civilization is so inordinately extroverted that man is caught up in a frantic round of activities which become ends in themselves. We could say that 'normal' man now lives 'outside himself' from the psychological or spiritual point of view—this expression which was once used to refer to people who were mentally ill is now quite an apt description of modern man! He lives his life here, there and everywhere, quite apart from within himself; he is 'eccentric' in the true sense of the

word, living outside of his true inner centre. (In French there is another appropriate expression, *désaxé*, meaning out of true or unbalanced.) There is then a need to balance the outward life with a proper inner life. We must 'come back into ourselves'. A person needs to turn away from the many continuous forms of evading this issue and turn towards the discovery of what has recently been referred to as the 'inner space'. We must recognize that there are, in addition to the external world, a number of inner worlds, and that it is possible, indeed incumbent on us, to get to know them, explore them and conquer them. This is a prerequisite for balance and wholeness.

Modern man, having dominated nature and exploited its energies, fails to realize that what he does in the external world actually has its origin within him, in his soul, and that it is affected by his desires, instincts, impulses, schedules and plans. These are mental activities, in other words internal ones. Each external action is the result of an inner prompting. It is therefore essential that we first get to know, examine and control these promptings. One gifted man, Goethe, who was very good at playing the part of the 'normal' man when he wanted to, said, 'When we have done what we need to on the inside, the outworking will come about automatically.'

In addition, this internalization can give us far greater balance as well as mental and emotional well-being. It can have effects we might well call 'supernormal'. When we come back into ourselves we discover our Centre, our true being, the most intimate part of us. It is both a revelation and an empowering. This is what Christ referred to as 'the pearl of great price'— anyone who finds it and recognizes its value will sell all else to acquire it.

2. The second group of symbols has to do with the idea of going deeper, descending to the 'bottom/depths' of our being.

Exploration of the unconscious is regarded symbolically as a descent into the depths of a human being, an exploration of the lowest regions of the mind. This symbol came into its own when psychoanalysis was developed, but was not invented then, for it has its origin in the remote past; indeed in antiquity it had a deeper meaning. We need only think of Aeneas' descent into hell in the *Aeneid* by Virgil, or of Dante's description of Hell. In addition to this, a number of mystics speak about the 'abysses of the soul'. Apart from psychoanalysis in the strict sense of the word, there is a branch of psychology known as 'depth psychology', represented by Jung and others. His basic principle is that man must have the courage to face up to all the lower, darker aspects of his own being, the things referred to as 'the Shadow', and then include them in his conscious personality. This recognition and inclusion are acts of humility and power at one and the same time: a person who is able to give conscious recognition to the baser characteristics of his personality, without being overwhelmed by them, is achieving a true spiritual conquest. But there can be dangers in this. The fable of the sorcerer's apprentice should put us on our guard: it is comparatively easy to let the 'waters' burst forth, but much more difficult to stop them and command them to withdraw!

It might be useful in this connection to remember what one gifted psychotherapist, Robert Desoille, does. This creator of the 'waking dream' method also uses 'descent' in his work, though he places greater emphasis on ascent. As far as descent is concerned, he says that it should be used wisely, a little at a time; i.e. start by seeking an experience of the higher realities and then, as you become gradually stronger, cautiously explore the region of the unconscious. The aim is to eliminate the dissociation between the conscious mind and the lower unconscious, which has been produced by repression, by the condemnation of the conscious mind and by not wanting to admit, out of presumption or fear, that this aspect of our personality exists. To repress it serves no useful purpose: far from ridding us of it, it aggravates the situation. Our task is to redeem this lower part of our being. 'Recognizing' this aspect of our personality does not mean allowing ourselves to be ruled by it. It means getting ready for it to be transformed. Christ's descent into Hell to redeem those imprisoned there has this profound meaning.

3. The third group of symbols, a frequently occurring one, is that of elevation, ascent or conquest of the 'inner space' in an ascending sense. There is a series of inner worlds, each with its own special characteristics, and within each of them there are

higher levels and lower levels. Thus in the first of these, the world of passions and feelings, there is a great distance, a marked disparity of level, between blind passion and the highest feelings. Then there is the world of intelligence, or the mind. Here too there are different levels: the level of the concrete, analytical mind, and the level of higher, philosophical reason (*nous*). There is also the world of the imagination, a lower variety and a higher variety, the world of intuition, the world of the will, and then, higher still, those indescribable worlds which can only be referred to by the term 'worlds of transcendence'.

The symbolism of elevation has been used throughout the ages. In all religions temples have been built on high places such as mountain tops, and indeed, many of the mountains of antiquity were considered to be sacred places. Then there are legends such as that of Titurel who climbs a mountain and builds the Castle of the Holy Grail. The symbol of the heavens as the higher region where the gods dwell and as the goal of man's aspirations is universal.

It would be useful at this point to make a semantic observation, namely the difference between 'ascent' and 'ascesis', the practice of self-discipline. These two words are phonetically similar, but they have different roots. 'Ascesis' comes from the Greek and means 'exercise' or 'discipline'; 'ascent' is from the Latin *ad scandere*, to go up step by step. But these two words, in addition to being similar phonetically, are also similar in the spiritual sense, because an ascent is the prize or reward for ascesis, not in the sense of 'asceticism', but in the Greek, psychagogic sense of 'psychospiritual discipline'.

4. The fourth group of symbols includes those of expansion, or broadening, of the consciousness. It is helpful to remember that though different symbols may appear contradictory, actually they complement one another in a consistent whole. Just as with descent to the lower regions it is useful first to ascend in order then to be able to descend without danger, so when one is seeking to enlarge the consciousness without becoming lost in its vastness, it is necessary first of all to take up a firm position at the centre of one's being. We might even say that a person's capacity for expanding the consciousness is in direct

proportion to the strength and stability of his centre. So rather than being mutually exclusive, those two groups complement one another.

The psychiatrist Urban talks about the 'spectrum of consciousness' and says that we are only aware of a limited range, similar to that of the spectrum of light from red to violet; but, he goes on, there are also psychospiritual regions corresponding to infra-red and ultraviolet. It is possible for our area of consciousness to expand or broaden so as to include ever larger regions of psychospiritual impressions and ideas. This expansion may be understood in 'spherical' terms, implying expansion in all directions, both vertically and horizontally from the individual to the group, to society and to the whole of humanity. But one needs to recognize oneself and not become lost in the whole. Leopardi and Carducci both spoke symbolically of these two possibilities: in his *Infinito*, Leopardi talks about 'losing oneself in the whole', while Carducci, in his *Canto dell'amore* [Song of Love], says, 'Is it I who embrace the heavens, or is the universe reabsorbing me from within?'

Another series of symbols of greatness or enlargement is based on the Sanskrit word *mah*, meaning 'great'. It is from this that we get *magister* (master), magician and *mahatma*. We speak loosely of 'great' men, in contrast with the small 'normal' men.

Expansion and the inclusion of others within oneself is also linked with the symbolism of love (see Group 10).

Another direction for expansion is the one which takes place over time. The normal man usually lives in the present, engaged in, if not enslaved by, the interests of the moment. But he can enlarge his consciousness to include ever wider cycles in a multidimensional time continuum. In this way he may come to understand that the significance and value of a human life does not reside in any specific, isolated moment, but in an ongoing process stretching at least from birth to physical death. This expansion in time and the inclusion of even greater cycles prepare one for the passage, we might even say the jump, from time to eternity, understood not as an unlimited period but as a dimension outside of time, a transcendent dimension in which our spiritual Centre exists and remains, independent of the flow of the river of time.

5. We now come to the fifth group of symbols. These are among the most significant and effective. They are the symbols of reawakening or revival. We might describe normal man's state of consciousness as a 'dreamlike' state in a world of illusion: the illusion of reality in the external world as our senses perceive it, and illusions produced by the imagination, the emotions and the usual thought patterns. As far as the external world is concerned, modern chemistry and physics have shown us that what to our eyes seems concrete, stable and inert is actually a seething mass of infinitesimal elements and energy charges fed by a mighty dynamism. Thus matter, as it appears to our senses and as it was understood by materialist philosophy, does not actually exist. The science of today has therefore aligned itself with that basic Indian concept, that ancient spiritual vision according to which everything we see is *maya*, or illusion.

There are then emotional and mental illusions which affect us at closer quarters and condition our lives, leading to continual errors of judgement, wrong behaviour and suffering of all kinds. Even in this field the science of modern psychology has come to the same conclusions as the ancient wisdom, namely that man is prey to inner 'phantoms', attachments and complexes. People live their lives seeing everything and everyone through a thick veil of coloured thought patterns and distorted views caused by their emotional reactions, by the effects of psychological traumas from the past, by external influences, and by strong psychological undercurrents, etc. As a result their minds become deformed. Thinking they are using their minds objectively, they are actually influenced by what Bacon called 'idols', by preconceived ideas and suggestion.

All this produces a true dreamlike state from which we can and must wake up. To achieve this we must first take the bold step of facing up to reality—we have to recognize the psychological complexity within us and the various subpersonalities in our being—we might almost say that each human being is a character out of Pirandello. The first step then is to become aware of everything within us that causes a sense of restlessness. The second step is to discover what we really are: the Self, the spiritual 'I', the Observer of the human tragi-comedy.

The doctrine and practice of 'awakening' dates from antiquity. Buddha placed particular emphasis on it in his teachings, to the extent of being called the 'Perfectly Awakened [One]'. To promote this 'awakening' there is an effective spiritual exercise one can use: having woken from sleep in the morning and entered the so-called 'waking state', move on to an equally real second awakening to the world of spiritual reality. We might express this in the form of an equation: sleep gives way to the ordinary waking state as the latter gives way to spiritual awakening.

6. The sixth group of symbols is that of light or enlightenment. As with the ordinary waking process, in a spiritual awakening one comes out of the darkness of night into the sunlight—that is why the awakening of the spiritual consciousness has been called 'enlightenment', i.e. the passage from the shadows of illusion to the light of Reality. The first step, corresponding to the first step in the awakening process, is a straightforward (though not necessarily easy) view of ourselves as we really are. The second step, or another effect of enlightenment, is that it becomes possible to solve problems which seemed insoluble by means of the special instrument of spiritual vision known as intuition. (The etymological definition of intuition, as we said earlier, is 'to see into', in depth, or to see the reality of things.) Thus intuitive knowledge replaces the knowledge of the senses, intellect, logic and reason; or, to put it another way, intuition complements and transcends the knowledge of the senses. It actually brings about complete identification with what one is seeing or contemplating, and enables one to perceive the intrinsic unity between subject and object.

But spiritual enlightenment is more than this. It is like a 'flash of lightning', the perception of immanent Light in the human soul and in the whole of creation. There are many testimonies to this—that of St Paul on the road to Damascus, for instance— while in Buddhism, particularly Zen Buddhism, one aims, through special disciplines, at producing this sudden enlightenment or revelation of the transcendent reality.

Dante's 'Paradise' might be called the poem of Light. The famous verse:

> Intellectual light, full of love;
> Love of the true good, full of happiness;
> Happiness which transcends any sweetness.
> *Translation: C.H. Sisson, Pan Classics*[1]

is a wonderful expression of the intimate relationship between light, love and intelligence (from *intelligere* meaning 'to understand spiritually').

7. The seventh group, symbols of fire, is one of the most widely used, as well as being one of the most essential. Adoration and veneration of fire are found in all religions and esoteric traditions. Everywhere—on the altars, in the torches and in the lamps—sacred fires burn with their glowing flames. Even the flame of the Olympic torch is a symbol of the competitions in which athletes push themselves to prove their exceptional physical abilities.

The inner experience of fire has been felt and described by many mystics—as examples, we need only mention St Catherine of Siena and Blaise Pascal. Indeed, fire is more than a mere symbol, it is a reality which exists and has its influence in the invisible worlds. Its function is above all else one of purification and it is used to this end in 'spiritual alchemy'.

8. The eighth group of symbols, which has much in common with human experience, is indicated by the words 'evolution' and 'development'. In a sense we might say that these words are synonymous. To develop, which literally means 'to become disentangled', refers to progress from the potential to the actual.

The two main symbols of development are the seed and the flower: a seed has all the potential it needs to become a tree, and a flower, from its closed bud, opens up and enables the fruit to form. We have grown so used to this that it no longer surprises us when an acorn by some miraculous process becomes an oak, or when a child becomes an adult. But where actually is the tree in the seed? Where is the oak in the acorn? Aristotle spoke about 'entelechy', and others have spoken about 'models' or

[1]Translator's note: the last line actually seems to have been mistranslated. The original is 'Happiness which transcends any pain.'

'archetypes'. One has to admit some pre-existent reality, an immanent Intelligence which guides the various stages of development from the seed to the tree, from the germinal cell or cells to the complete organism.

The other symbol, one that has been used extensively from the earliest times, is that of the flower, particularly the lotus (our waterlily) (India) and the rose (Persia and Europe). The symbolism of the lotus comes closest to what takes place in man himself. The lotus has its roots in the earth, its stem grows in water, and its flower opens in the air from the effect of the sun's rays. Oriental thinkers have seen this as a symbol of man, with his physical body, or earthly base, which then develops psychologically in the sphere of the emotions (the water) and the mind (the air). Reawakening of the spiritual consciousness corresponds to the opening up of a flower produced by the life-giving powers of the sun, a symbol of the Spirit. Eastern philosophers also maintain that man's soul is like the lotus flower, and that it has nine main petals, divided up into three groups. The first group stands for spiritual knwoledge, the second stands for spiritual love, and the third for spiritual strength. At the centre is the 'Jewel of the Lotus', the divine Essence, which is only revealed when a man's spirit has fully developed. Certain Eastern methods of development and meditation are based on this lotus symbolism.

The symbolism of the rose comes from Persia where the mystical poets speak of the rose in this symbolic sense. In Europe we find Le Roman de la Rose, the 'mystical rose' referred to by Dante, and certain secret movements, such as the Rosicrucians. The symbol of a rose has been used in a special exercise which is very effective in encouraging and bringing about an opening up and an unfolding of the spiritual consciousness (see pp 102—4).

The symbol of development can be applied in two stages: the first covers the transition from a child to an ordinary adult, and the second the transition from the 'normal' man to the spiritually awakened man.

Maria Montessori, who devoted so much of her life to the education of children and brought about a revolution in the education systems of her day, is right when she says:

The child is actively engaged in creating the fully grown person within him and gladly fulfils this task when the adult at his side does not hinder him by administering his own pearls of wisdom. The child is the human seed; just as the oak is contained within the acorn, so the child contains the adult in embryo form.

Although the method introduced by Maria Montessori was revolutionary, we should remember Plutarch's words, 'Man is not a vase to be filled up, but a fire that only needs to be kindled.' Education should be precisely what the etymology of the word implies: *e-ducere*, drawing out from within, or developing.

As regards the second stage of man's development, we can say that this truly represents the transition to what is practically a superhuman state—entry, symbolically speaking, into the Kingdom of God, the fifth realm of nature, as different from the fourth realm as the fourth is from the third, i.e. the animal kingdom. We should not look down on our bodies from the animal kingdom; despite having an animal's body, we are still self-aware beings. Thus the superhuman being (the genius, saint, sage or hero) has an animal body and a human personality, but at the same time something extra: he is a spiritual being.

9. The ninth group of symbols, and a very up-to-date one, is that of 'empowering' or 'intensification'. Spiritual conquest may be regarded as an empowering, an intensification of one's awareness of life. It is a force, a different psychospiritual 'voltage' which is superior to that of the average, normal man. Hermann Keyserling talks about a 'dimension of intensity', combining the symbolism of intensification with the symbolism of proceeding in a different dimension which he calls 'vertical' (in contrast with the others, which are horizontal). Speaking about this 'vertical dimension' he does not use the term in its ordinary sense; he uses it to refer to a type of verticality which rises from the world of becoming and flowing towards a world of being or transcendence. He also applies this symbol to time: a 'vertical transition' from time into an eternity which is outside time.

This empowering also has two stages or degrees. The first consists of the empowering of all those latent energies and functions which are underdeveloped or wrongly developed in man. An essay by William James entitled *The Energies of Men* clearly illustrates a number of possible energies in man if he is prepared to discover them, activate them and use them.

The second level of empowering is the one which makes possible the transition from the human realm to the superhuman realm we mentioned earlier. It is here that we see exhibited the various supernormal powers. In all ages these powers, alongside other superior spiritual-ethical gifts, have been ascribed to the enlightened, the awakened, the initiated and the 'wise men' from Moses to Pythagoras and from Buddha to Christ, as well as to various other saints. Some of these people used their powers deliberately and consciously, others spontaneously—even against their will—as in the case of the mystics or saints. One might say that these powers are a natural consequence or a by-product of spiritual realization.

10. The tenth group of symbols is that of love. This human love, looked at from one point of view, is a desire or attempt, conscious or otherwise, to move out from oneself, to transcend the limits of one's own separate existence, and then to enter into communion and merge with another being, a 'thou'. Devout people and mystics of all ages have told of their experiences of communion with God and with higher Beings using the symbolism of human love. We need only refer to the Song of Songs in the Bible and to the at times surprisingly bold phrases used by St Catherine of Siena and St John of the Cross.

11. The eleventh group of symbols covers that of the way, path or pilgrimage. This too has always been a universal metaphor. Esoteric tradition speaks about the 'path of the disciple' and about the way of initiation, with its various 'doors'. Religions refer to the 'mystical way'.

The symbol of 'pilgrimage' has been and is still often used in a physical, external sense, in the form of pilgrimages to various 'holy places'. Dante's journey through Hell, Purgatory and Paradise has been called a pilgrimage. One also remembers Bunyan's *Pilgrim's Progress*.

12. We now come to the twelfth group: symbols of trans-

mutation. The body can be transmuted by a process of regenerating psychospiritual transformation (during the course of which psycho-physical and parapsychological powers are also developed). The mind is brought into harmony with the spirit and includes the body, achieving an organic, harmonious unity of all aspects of a person's being, what we might call 'bio-psychosynthesis'. This is true spiritual alchemy.

When we speak of alchemy we usually think of attempts to 'make gold'—something which once seemed unbelievable, though it is not now so far-fetched since man has begun to manipulate atoms and transform one element into another. Often, however, the Arab and medieval books on alchemy used symbolic language to express a psycho-spiritual alchemy, i.e. the transmutation of man himself. This has been recognized by a number of modern scholars, especially Jung, who in the last years of his life devoted much time and much of his writing activity to the symbolism of alchemy. In his work *Psychology and Religion* he speaks about this at length, showing how he also found this symbolism in the dreams of his patients and in the drawings produced by both sick and well people.

13. The thirteenth group is that of regeneration or 'new birth'. This is linked to the the preceding group, because complete transmutation and transformation prepares a person and opens him up to regeneration. In its deepest and quintessential sense this represents a 'new birth': the birth of the new man, the spiritual man within the personality.

The Indians called Brahmins 'those who have been born twice'. This symbol has been used much in Christianity and many mystics have spoken about the 'birth of Christ in the heart'.

14. The fourteenth group of symbols is that of 'liberation'. This is related to symbols of development. The removing of the 'tangles' is a process of liberation from our complexes and illusions and from the way in which we identify with the roles we play in life, with the masks within us and with our idols, etc. It is a 'release', according to the etymology of the word, a liberation and awakening of hidden potential.

In this process of liberation there is an initial stage characterized by dualism: we must actually disassociate ourselves from the body, from the emotions and from that small personal 'I', and when this is accomplished, we will then be able to see ourselves as distinct from them and be able to transform them.

The symbolism of liberation has pervaded all the world's great religions. In India, the Buddha said, 'Just as water in the sea is saturated with salt, so all my teaching is saturated with freedom.' In Christianity St Paul affirmed the 'liberty of the Sons of God'. In their encounter with Cato ['Purgatory I'] Dante has Virgil say the following about him:

> He looks for liberty, which is so loved,
> As he knows who gives up his life for her.
> *Translation: C.H. Sisson, Pan Classics*

In our own era, during the Second World War, Franklin Roosevelt proclaimed the Four Great Freedoms to the world: the freedom of expression; religious freedom; freedom from want; and freedom from fear.

The last of these, freedom from fear, is fundamental, because only when a person is freed from fear is he truly free. A simple, unsophisticated expression, albeit a genuine one, of this longing for freedom is contained in Domenico Modugno's song 'Free', the lyrics of which communicate this longing very effectively.

But we are faced with a paradox here: in contrast with his spontaneous longing for freedom, man has a simultaneous fear of it! This is explained by the fact that freedom implies commitment, self-control, courage and other qualities of the spiritual life. It has been correctly stated: 'The price of freedom is continuous vigilance.' Freedom needs to be reconquered or safeguarded every day, we might even say every moment; it is not enough to 'become liberated' once and for all. Even those who do not fully understand this have an intuitive sense of it, and as a result they fear freedom and run away from it. In his novel *La Peur de Vivre* [Fear of Living], Henri Bordeaux highlights what psychoanalysis refers to as the desire to remain in the pre-adult stage, or even the desire to regress to the safety of infancy. This sort of desire is frequently encountered, and if we took a close look at ourselves who knows how many childish, regressive traits we might find. Throughout history there have been those who looked back wistfully to 'the golden age'. There are countless examples of this type of 'psychological torticollis'. But this attitude is unproductive and harmful. It is unproductive because any attempt to arrest the powerful, mighty flow of life within and around us is doomed to failure. And it is harmful because it can have no positive results—rather it can produce serious mental and nervous disorders.

15. We have now reached the fifteenth group of symbols, that of resurrection and return, what in the gospels is referred to as the return of the prodigal son to his father's house. This is a return to a previous state and points to a return to the original, primordial Being. It presupposes an emanatistic theory of the soul, descending, becoming one with matter, and then returning to its 'home', the heavenly homeland—not as it was before, but enriched by the experience of self-awareness which has come to maturity in toil and conflict.

There is another return, a higher form of returning, and this is the return to the world of those Beings who, in an act of love and compassion, have chosen to help those who are still blind, asleep or imprisoned. This is the return of those spiritual Beings who are free and unbounded, having nothing more to seek or desire in the world, but who nevertheless return to it in order to redeem others as God's fellow-workers, the 'liberated liberators'. In Buddhism this is referred to as the renunciation of Nirvana; in Christianity it is known as the work of co-redemption.

THE EXERCISE OF THE ROSE

Introduction

Flowers have been widely regarded and used as symbols of the soul, or the spiritual Self, both in the East and in the West.

In China an ancient Taoist text speaks about the deep meaning of the 'Flower of Gold',[1] and in India, as already mentioned, they have always used the symbol of the lotus, which has its roots in the mud and its stem in the water, but whose flower opens in the air in response to the sun's rays, but in Persia and Europe preference was shown for the rose. I will only mention the Troubadours' *Roman de la Rose*; the 'mystical rose' so remarkably described by Dante in his 'Paradise' (Canto XXIII), and a rose at the centre of a cross, the symbol of the Order of Rosicrucians.

The image of an open flower has been universally used as a symbol of the Spirit, and to visualize this is very inspiring and evocative. Of even greater effect, however, in awakening psycho-spiritual energies and processes is the 'dynamic' use of this symbol, that is, visualizing the transformation or development of the flower of the closed bud to the fully opened bloom. The symbol of development corresponds to a profound reality, a fundamental law of life, which manifests itself both in the processes of nature and in those of the human soul.

Our spiritual Being, the Self, which is the essential and most real part of us, is usually concealed, shut in or 'ensnared'. The main reason for this is the body with its many sensory perceptions. In addition to this there are the many emotions and impulses (fears, desires, attractions and repulsions, etc.), and the underlying restlessness of activity in the mind. We need to remove the tangles and iron out the folds so that the Spiritual Centre can be revealed.

Both in nature and in the human soul this comes about on the basis of the amazing, mysterious effect of a biological and psychological vitality which has an irresistible power to motivate from within. It is for this reason that the symbol, or indeed the principle, of growth, development and evolution has been and is still used in psychology and education; and it is on this that the concept and practice of psychosynthesis are based. One of the ways in which it is applied is the exercise which will now be described.

[1] This has been commented on at length by C.G. Jung in *The Secret of the Flower of Gold*.

The Technique of the Exercise

This exercise can be done individually or in groups. If it is to be done in private, it helps to familiarize oneself with the various stages so that they can be recalled without difficulty. If the exercise is to be done in a group, the person leading the session will announce the stages slowly, with appropriate pauses, as follows.

Let us imagine a closed rose-bud. Visualize the stem, the leaves and, at the top, the bud itself. It is green in appearance because the sepals are closed; then at the topmost point there is a pink tip. Try to visualize this as vividly as possible, keeping the image at the centre of your conscious mind. As you watch you gradually become aware that movement is taking place: the sepals begin to pull apart as their points turn outwards, enabling you to see the closed pink petals. The sepals move further apart … now see the bud-shaped petals of a beautiful, delicate rose. Then the petals also begin to unfold. The bud continues to expand slowly until the rose is revealed in all its beauty and you are able to admire it with delight.

At this point try to breathe in the scent of the rose and smell its characteristic perfume—delicate, sweet and pleasing to the senses. Take in its scent with pleasure. The symbol of perfume has also been used frequently in religious and mystical language ('the smell of holiness'), as indeed perfumes have been used in rituals (incense, etc.).

Next visualize the whole plant and imagine the force of life rising up from its roots to the flower, producing this development. Pause in awed contemplation of this miracle of nature.

Now identify yourself with the rose, or to be more precise, 'introject' the rose into yourself. Symbolically become a flower, a rose. The same Life that animates the Universe, that has produced the rose, is producing in you that same, if not a greater, miracle: the development, opening up and irradiation of your spiritual being. And we have the choice of taking an active part in our own inner flowering.

PART TWO

SPIRITUAL AWAKENING

9

THE STAGES AND CRISES OF SPIRITUAL DEVELOPMENT

Even if we take no more than a casual look at the people around us, we see at once that they are not equally developed from the psychological and spiritual point of view. Some of them are still in a primitive, even wild, state, others are a little more developed, yet others are more advanced, and finally there are those few who have transcended normal humanity and now stand at the threshold of the superhuman, spiritual stage.

We will not pause here to look into the possible reasons for these differences. It is an interesting question, but it will sidetrack us from our main theme. Whatever its causes, however, this difference in stages of inner development from one person to another is a useful, indeed a necessary, one. It makes possible the various relationships that come about between individuals: relationships of authority and obedience, teaching and learning, or oppression and revolt; and these can be very productive experiences. If humanity were all at the same level, these vital actions and reactions would not exist—life would, of course, be simple, but it would also be more monotonous, less interesting and less stimulating. It would be characterized by tedium and fall far short of its intended purpose.

In our study of the various stages of spiritual development we can be helped on our way by the principle of analogy, a method held in great honour by thinkers of old, but one which the modern world has neglected and overlooked. It is true of course that it can easily lead to far-fetched interpretations and arbitrary deductions, but when it is used discriminately and under the right circumstances it can provide the key to many secrets of the nature of the soul.

The use of this 'key' in our case is not difficult and can be very enlightening. The analogy between child psychology and the psychology of primitive individuals and peoples is an obvious one and has often been pointed out. Children, like primitive people, are simple, impulsive and easily distracted. They live only in the present, they are sensitive and emotional, but their feelings, though they may be intense at the time, are lacking in depth and short-lived. They are not moral beings because their sense of responsibility has not yet been developed, so they tend towards an unconscious cruelty—they tend to personify objects and the forces of nature. Their sense of responsibility is rudimentary and they are unable to distinguish it clearly from their surroundings.

At a certain stage, a little further on, we come across certain more highly developed children on the one hand, and souls with a corresponding inner age on the other, who we see most typically at the beginning of great civilizations. We may, for example, think of the men from the early Vedic age in India or those of the Homeric period in Greece, with their fresh sense of poetry and simplicity, their real sense of childlike communion with nature, and their somewhat childish gods who, as personifications of natural forces and human passions, were elevated only gradually to the position of symbols of high spiritual principles.

Before going any further in our analysis, we should remember that at every physical age or age of the soul, as with every psychological type and manifestation of the human personality, we need to distinguish the lower and higher aspects of the same principle and quality. Thus in primitive souls we find the lower qualities of roughness and violence, a certain barbarity, a typically primitive intelligence, a certain cunning and a tendency to deceive, in addition to an undisguised selfishness and little sensitivity to the sufferings of others. We can find many of these characteristics, to varying degrees, in the Homeric heroes described in the *Iliad*.

The higher qualities of this psychological age are described by the poets in what they refer to as the Golden Age, namely, purity, innocence, spontaneity, yielding, devotion and obedience to the gods, or a childlike faith in God. We do not find many people like this in our own civilization; they are only to be found among faithful servants and devoted followers, and mostly among country and mountain people. These men develop primarily through external activity which provides them with their experience of life. Their minds are developed and they acquire such moral qualities as wisdom, perseverance, courage and self-sacrifice. Their main ideal and the purpose of their conduct is devotion, faithfulness and obedience to God as well as to their superiors, to moral and religious precepts, and to the law as it stands.

But men cannot and should not stay at this childish level. Their development is marked, as during adolescence, by a series of contrasts and conflicts. As far as the mind is concerned we have the start of critical reflection which gives rise to problems and doubts. The inculcation of principles and dominant theories is no longer accepted without discussion; the mind demands some form of credentials—it has to know the origin and basis of those principles and theories, and to know that they fit the facts.

As regards the emotional aspect of the personality there is an intensification and complication of the feelings, the surfacing of new passions.

As far as action is concerned, we find an intense desire for independence, a proud turning away from 'gods' and from any form of authority. This is the Titanic or Promethean stage. We also find an accentuation of self-awareness and self-affirmation which often leads to subjective introspection and is the chief characteristic of the Romantic viewpoint.

This is a stage characterized by disharmony and chaos. It is painful and demanding for those going through it, as well as being difficult for other people to deal with.

The lower aspects of this age of the soul are an excessive self-affirmation, destructive impulses, anarchy, fanaticism, pride, intransigence, a tendency to take things to extremes, intolerance, and lack of respect for and understanding of others.

In contrast with this, the higher aspects are idealism, the willingness to make sacrifices for a cause, generosity, courage and boldness, an appreciation of beauty, a sense of honour, and all those qualities summed up in the attitudes and behaviour of the knights of old.

The 'dharma' of this age is the development of the mind and of the independent moral faculties, the affirmation of self-awareness and of spiritual independence, the study of life and the gaining of a broader experience. It is also the active devotion of oneself to a cause or ideal—no longer accepted from some external source, but felt within, so that one gives oneself to it by a free act of the will.

Many people today are at this stage and some of the characteristics listed may be attributed to the mental outlook of most of our contemporaries. We need only think of the way in which the old traditions and forms have so quickly vanished, and of the restlessness, critical individualism and rebellious attitudes which are now so prevalent.

Let us now take a look at the characteristics of the adult soul. If we compare the adult man or woman with young people we discover that what has taken place is a gradual reduction of their lively exuberance or emotional effervescence, alongside a parallel growth of their mental and rational faculties. The former state of chaos, the rapid changes, the swinging from one extreme to another, have given place to a certain arrangement or settling of the personality—the personality has now formed and become consolidated.

This stage also has its lower and higher characteristics. The former consist primarily of an excessive limitation, a hardening and dryness. Coming into contact with the harsh realities of life, its struggles, disappointments and failures, destroys the generous dreams of earlier years, dampens the enthusiasm, and severely tests the faith of a person. A reaction of skepticism and discontent can then set in, which may end in cynicism. Although it is essential, development of the mind has its attendant dangers, such as excessive criticism and a sort of intellectual crystallization which prevents and even destroys an awareness of what is Real.

Becoming engrossed in practical pursuits and personal duties can easily lead to isolation and to an unwarranted affirmation of the personal 'I' and of selfishness.

The higher aspects of this psychological age may be summed up in three words: harmony, balance and effectiveness. At this stage man is able to achieve a balance between spirit and form:

the personality is formed and perfected and becomes an instrument of expression for the 'I' which is well formed, structurally sound and resistant, but at the same time sufficiently mouldable. It is then equipped for acting out the will of the Spirit in the world.

This age, though it may seem more static and free from troubling crises, is actually the 'critical age' in spiritual terms. It marks the dividing of the ways, the point of decision which will determine the future of the soul. If the hardening and crystallizing process continues unchecked, and form or structure become more and more dominant over the living, spiritual part of the personality, old age will inevitably set in with its negative attributes of ossification, enfeeblement, self-centredness and a gradual withdrawing from life around. If this process is not interrupted by some balancing influence it can result in an extreme failure to respond to others and in an extreme self-centred isolation, culminating in spiritual death, just as senility results in physical death. Fortunately, other factors often intervene and intercept people on this downward slope, turn them around, gently or violently, point them in the direction of the upward path, and set them free from the attachments and illusions of 'normal' life, thereby bringing them into contact with the Spirit.

When this happens we come up against something rather strange (strange, that is, if looked at from the ordinary viewpoint). Those involved are suddenly imbued with power, enthusiasm and effectiveness. It is as if they had been rejuvenated: they have a new youthfulness within and the better characteristics of youth are added to those of maturity, without detracting from them. There is an interesting physical corollary to this. In some cases of robust men over 80 years of age the first signs of a third dentition have been observed, a very small, though significant, attempt by nature at physical rejuvenation. This is nothing more than a small start in such cases, because it is not matched by a corresponding psychological and spiritual rejuvenation to sustain it.

In other cases there is an attempt at a rejuvenation of the emotions. The best-known example is that of Goethe who, at the age of 74, fell in love with a young German woman. This happened when he was in full possession of his mental faculties and should not therefore be considered, as was first thought, as a sign of second childhood. It was a true feeling, idealistic and youthful in nature, which expressed itself in exquisite poetry. But even these flames, fanned into a conflagration by an old fire, quickly die out, because they are not fed by anything lasting.

When it comes to spiritual rejuvenation, on the other hand, we are dealing with something very profound and of fundamental importance, produced by what we might describe as the linking up of the personality with its intimate spirit, from which a powerful flow of spiritual energy, light and love is released, having a life-giving, transforming effect.

After this brief look at the stages of inner growth, we would do well here to make a somewhat closer examination of the two most important and decisive crises: the one we have already referred to, which precedes and determines inner rejuvenation, and another, dark and mysterious, which takes place at a later stage, corresponding to what mystics refer to as the 'dark night of the soul'.[1]

What is the meaning of these crises?

They are produced by the fact that the spiritual consciousness, i.e. that sense of what is eternal and transcendent, before revealing itself in its positive form of enlightenment and expansion, makes itself felt in a negative sense. In other words, it shows how every individual thing, even a good thing, when it is considered and loved in itself, divorced from everything else (as usually happens), is of transient value and useless; it shows us that nothing limited has value of its own, and that any isolationist, antagonistic statement made by the personal 'I' is false and doomed to failure, not because it violates some arbitrary, external code of rules, but because it is at variance with the very nature of spiritual Reality. But man—blind, ignorant—is afraid to let go, he does not want to give up the crutches he uses to support himself, or his attachment to people and things he is afraid of losing. So he resists with all his might the invitations and commands of the Spirit—until, when his resistance runs out, he has no choice but to give himself up.

[1] See Chapter 10, page 126.

Then, to his joy, he discovers that, instead of the feared annihilation, he has a new, greater and superior type of life. He is flooded by light and joy. The world itself is transformed in his eyes and, beyond changing appearances, he feels the powerful heartbeat of the supreme unity in all things and in all beings. This strange, intense battle between the personality and the Self has been admirably described by two modern poets: Francesco Chiesa in his poem 'The Voice', which appears in the collection entitled *I viali d'oro* [The Avenues of Gold], and Francis Thompson in his poem 'The Hound of Heaven'.

The awakening of the soul is usually followed by a period of joyful inner and external expansion, assuming different forms from one person to another. Sometimes it is the mystical aspect and enlightenment which are dominant; in other cases new energies are released in the form of selfless, heroic action, benevolent service or artistic creativity. This period may last for a long time, indeed it can last a lifetime.

In other cases things do not develop in such a straightforward, favourable way. Sometimes a person is ill-prepared or lacks the necessary psychological make-up, so he is unable to resist the spiritual force flowing into him and reacts in a discordant, morbid fashion. This can lead to the over-excitement, imbalance and fanaticism we observe in some spurious mystics and self-defined enlightened people who have discredited true mystics and truly enlightened people in the eyes of the public so that people are unable or unwilling to make a distinction between them, even though the former are nothing but a caricature and counterfeit of the latter.

In other cases the period of light, joy and productive activity is followed by a struggle. Here, the ordinary personality had only temporarily been under the control of the new spiritual consciousness—it had not undergone a permanent transformation. The 'old Adam' resurfaces with his habits, tendencies and passions, and the man now realizes he has a long, complex, demanding task of purification and transformation of various human building blocks ahead of him.

At times the Spirit itself imposes this work in a tough, inescapable fashion. Then the soul is obliged to enter that 'dark night', a phenomenon experienced and described by St Teresa,

St John of the Cross, Madame Guyon and many other mystics. This is an inner state of suffering and privation similar to that which precedes the awakening of the soul, but now it might be described as having been 'raised an octave': it is profounder, more complete and more radical.

The nature and meaning of this experience are well defined in the Christian tradition, and a similar stage and experience, at least in some descriptions—but considered more in a voluntary, active sense—are referred to in the hermetic, initiatory and alchemic traditions as a 'testing by fire', or as 'washing in the waters'.

Understanding the nature and purpose of this testing can make it less severe and not so long: instead of enduring it against one's will, one can yield to its working both the will and the mind, receiving rather than fighting the awesome and splendid gift it wants to bestow on us.

This conscious cooperation can be summed up in two words: acceptance and love. First we accept these sufferings and hardships, and this sense of annihilation, with an open heart and with full understanding. Then we go one step further and love them.

This is a less obvious form of heroism, though it is higher and more demanding than the heroism which is manifested in outward acts so readily understood and acclaimed by the crowd, and the conquests to which it leads are far more precious. In this way one arrives at what has been called the 'blessed liberty of the sons of God', or at the 'united life'. St John of the Cross asserted unequivocally that those who have attained this 'are like God himself and have the same characteristics as him'.

This is the state of victory and liberation which the eastern philosophers have called Nirvana. Here all desires, all personal yearnings are consumed, every attachment is severed and every fear dissolved. Thus released, the spirit acquires an acute, formidable power: it is capable of *wuwei*, action without action, which nothing can resist.

I have attempted, with this brief sketch, to give an overview (to use the current expression), or better still a perspective, of the stages and crises of spiritual development. On the face of it I have led you into a world that is very different from the world of restless clamour that surrounds us, far from the hum of traffic, the hooting of factory sirens, dances and theatrical spectacles, not to mention the ever present economic problems. But this distance is not as great as might be thought: it is only the facade of life in this modern world that we see, behind it is the life of souls in a state of turmoil, behind the external struggles are the harsh, unspoken conflicts of mental and spiritual forces. Behind the painted masks which writhe to the sound of modern music, behind the men in dinner-jackets gulping down their drinks, behind those gambling away their money in casinos, or those who are addicted to drugs, who can say how many tormented souls there are trying to escape pursuit by the 'hound of heaven'? Then there are the clinics and the mental hospitals: behind those despondent, static figures, speechless in their despair, or crying out wildly in their unbearable pain, who can say how many misunderstood, ignorant people are undergoing terrible trials of inner disintegration—a dark spiritual night?

I wonder how many fatal mistakes, how many painful and unnecessary conflicts and complications might be avoided if these souls could come to understand themselves and to be understood. To talk of spiritual crises in this present day, far from being out of date or an academic exercise to satisfy an empty curiosity, meets an urgent need and is an inescapable duty of anyone who has gained experience or knowledge of it, to however limited an extent.

Someone has to get it across to mankind, caught up as it is in a search for outward well-being and satisfaction, thirsty for pleasure and power, that all our achievements in taming the elements, our control over matter, and all the intensity and speed of technological advance, have at the most an instrumental value or a symbolic meaning. Only through an awakening of our deepest soul, only when the sovereignty of the Spirit is recognized and made a reality, will man be able to achieve that true power, that secure peace and that divine freedom—the unconscious goal to which he is aspiring.

10

SPIRITUAL DEVELOPMENT AND NEURO-PSYCHOLOGICAL DISTURBANCES

Spiritual development in a person is a long and arduous adventure, a journey through strange lands, full of wonders, but also beset with difficulties and dangers. It involves deep purification and transformation, the awakening of a number of formerly inactive powers, the raising of the consciousness to levels it has never reached before, and its expansion in a new internal dimension. We should not be surprised therefore that such a major change passes through various critical stages, and these are often accompanied by neuro-psychological and even physical (psychosomatic) disturbances. Though these disturbances might, to the ordinary clinical eye, appear no different from those produced by other causes, they actually have a completely different significance and value, and they are cured in a very different way.

Disturbances that are spiritual in origin are becoming more and more frequent today because the number of people troubled by spiritual needs, whether consciously or unconsciously, is increasing. Furthermore, because of the greater complexity of modern man and in particular the complexity of the obstacles put up by his critical mind, spiritual development has become a more difficult and complicated inner process.

It is therefore useful to take an overall look at the nervous and psychological disturbances that can occur at the various stages of spiritual development, throughout the transformation process, and to give some guidelines on the most appropriate and effective ways of curing them.

We can identify five critical stages in the process of spiritual realization:

1. The crises preceding spiritual awakening;
2. The crises produced by spiritual awakening;
3. The reactions which follow spiritual awakening;
4. The phases in the transformation process;
5. The 'dark night of the soul'.

Crises Preceding Spiritual Awakening

In order to fully understand the meaning of the unusual experiences that usually precede the awakening of the soul, we need to remind ourselves of certain psychological characteristics of ordinary man.

Instead of saying that he lives, we might say that an ordinary man lets life run its course in him. He takes life as it comes, he does not face up to the problem of his purpose, value and goals. If he is a common man he will only be interested in satisfying his personal desires: striving to gratify his senses, to become rich, or to achieve his ambition. If he is of a nobler spirit he may subordinate his own personal satisfaction in order to fulfil family and civil responsibilities that have been instilled in him, though he does not think to ask himself what those responsibilities are based on or how they relate in terms of priorities, etc. He may also claim to be 'religious' and believe in God, but his religion is an external, conventional thing, and he feels most at home when he has obeyed the formal prescriptions of his Church and taken part in its rituals.

In short, the common man believes implicitly in the absolute reality of ordinary life and is firmly attached to earthly goods, to which he attributes a positive value. In practice, therefore, he considers ordinary life an end in itself, and even if he believes in some future heaven his belief is completely theoretical and academic, as evidenced by the frequently encountered comic, yet genuine remark that he wants to go there ... but the later the better.

It can happen however—and in some cases this truly becomes a reality—that this 'ordinary man' is surprised and disturbed by an unexpected change in his inner life. This sometimes occurs following a series of disappointments, or often it comes after a great shock, such as the loss of a loved one, but at other times, however, it comes for no apparent reason. A person may be going through a time of prosperity with fortune smiling on him (as happened to Tolstoy), when he suddenly experiences a vague unrest, a sense of dissatisfaction or the feeling that something is missing. It is not so much the absence of something concrete, but of some vague, evasive thing he is unable to define.

Gradually this is supplemented by a sense of unreality, or the pointlessness of ordinary life. All those personal interests which used to occupy and pre-occupy his mind now fade, losing their importance and value. New problems are encountered. A person in this condition begins to ask himself *what is the meaning of life,* and he questions a great many things which he used to accept as a matter of course: the reason for his own and other people's suffering, how one is to come to terms with the great disparity between one person's fortune and another's, the origin of human existence, and his own destination.

This is where misunderstanding and error come in. Many people, not understanding the significance of these new states of mind, consider them unfounded or abnormal fantasies. As they suffer with these issues (and they do indeed cause pain) they try to fight against them in any way they can. Fearing that they are losing touch with reality, they make every effort to re-establish contact with the ordinary reality they feel is escaping them. Sometimes, as a reaction, they actually throw themselves back into this so-called reality with abandon, seeking new things to occupy their minds, new areas of stimulation and new sensations. In this and other ways they sometimes succeed in stifling their unrest, but they can never destroy it completely: it continues to ferment in the depth of their being, undermining the foundations of their ordinary existence, and can in some cases break out again with greater intensity, even after a number of years. The state of turmoil becomes more painful, and that inner void more intolerable. The person concerned feels that he is being destroyed: every aspect of his life seems but a dream, disappearing like a shadow, though the new light has not yet emerged. Indeed, in most cases the person will not even know of its existence, or he will feel it is unattainable.

Often this general sense of torment is supplemented by a more specific moral crisis: the ethical conscience has been awakened and the person is overcome by a profound sense of guilt or remorse for the wrong they have committed. He then passes a severe judgement on himself and is overcome by a deep sense of discouragement.

It is at this point that the idea and impulse to commit suicide may come upon a person. He sees physical destruction as the only logical response to the disintegration taking place within.

We should note that this is only a generalized description of such experiences and the way they develop. In practice there are a great many individual differences. Some do not come to the most acute stage, while others reach it almost at once, without the gradual process outlined above; some are gripped by the need to search and by philosophical doubts while with others it is the moral crisis which is in the foreground.

These outward manifestations of spiritual crisis are similar to some of the symptoms of such illnesses as neurasthenia and psychasthenia. One of the characteristics of this is precisely this 'loss of contact with reality', as Pierre Janet calls it, and another is 'depersonalization'. The similarity is heightened by the fact that the turmoil of the crisis often produces physical symptoms such as exhaustion, nervous tension, depression, insomnia and various digestive and circulatory disturbances, etc.

The Crises Produced by Spiritual Awakening

When the channels of communication are opened up between the personality and the soul, accompanied by floods of light, joy and energy, they often produce a wonderful sense of release. Inner conflicts, suffering and disturbances, both psychological and physical, disappear, often with surprising speed, showing that such disturbances were not attributable to physical causes, but were a direct consequence of psycho-spiritual turmoil. In these cases spiritual awakening is a real cure.

But spiritual awakening does not always come about so simply and harmoniously—indeed, it may even be the cause of complications, disturbances and imbalances. This happens in those who lack a sound mind, whose emotions are excessive and not under control, in people with too sensitive and delicate a nervous system, or when the flow of spiritual energy has an overwhelming effect due to its suddenness and violence.

When the mind is not strong enough and is not ready to take spiritual light, or when there is a tendency towards presumption and self-centredness, what is going on within may be misinterpreted. What we might call a 'confusion of levels' takes place: the distinction between what is absolute and what is relative, or between spirit and personality, is overlooked. The spiritual force can then produce over-excitement or a 'swelling' of the personal 'I'.

Some years ago, at the mental hospital of Ancona, I had an opportunity to observe a typical case of this. One of the inmates—a pleasant little old man—asserted calmly but firmly that he was God. He had built around this conviction a framework of the most fantastic, deluded ideas: he had heavenly hosts at his command, he had performed great things, etc. But apart from this he was the kindest, gentlest and most thoughtful person you could imagine, always ready to help the doctors and patients in whatever way he could. He had such a clear, attentive mind, and he worked so carefully, that he had been made assistant to the pharmacist, who entrusted him with the keys to the pharmacy and with the preparation of medicines. This never created any problems, apart from the disappearance of a small amount of sugar which he took to give pleasure to some of the other inmates.

From the ordinary medical point of view this patient would be regarded as a simple case of someone with delusions of grandeur, a form of paranoia. But these are nothing more than descriptive labels, a method of clinical classification, and ordinary psychiatry is unable to tell us anything about the true nature and the causes of such disturbances. It would seem legitimate therefore to find out whether there might be a deeper psychological interpretation of this patient's ideas. It is well known that when the reality of the Spirit is perceived within, and when a person becomes aware that it is intimately bound up with the human soul, it gives him a sense of greatness or inner expansion—in other words, the conviction that in some way he is participating in the divine nature.

Religious traditions and spiritual doctrine from all ages provide us with a great many testimonies to this, often expressed in very bold language. In the Bible we find the explicit, uncompromising statement: 'Do you not know that you are Gods?' while St Augustine said, 'When the soul loves something, it becomes like it; if it loves earthly things, it become earthly; but if it loves God (we might ask) does it become God?'

The most extreme expression of the identity in nature between the human spirit in its purest form and the Supreme Spirit is contained in the central teaching of the Vedantic philosophy: *Tat twam asi* (You are He) and *Aham evam param Brahman* (In truth I am the Supreme Brahman).

However one wants to think of this relationship between the individual spirit and the universal spirit—whether one thinks of it in terms of identity or similarity, participation or union—one most not lose sight, both in theory and in practice, of the great difference between the individual spirit in its essential nature— what has been called the 'depths', the 'centre' or the 'summit' of the soul, the higher 'I', the real Self—and the small ordinary personality, that small 'I' of which we are usually conscious. If this distinction is not recognized, it leads to absurd and dangerous consequences. This provides us with a key for understanding the mental imbalance of the patient I referred to above, as well as other less extreme forms of self-exaltation and self-promotion. The grave error committed by all who fall prey to such illusions is that of attributing the qualities and powers of the Spirit to the unregenerate, personal 'I'. In philosophical terms this is a confusion between relative reality and absolute Reality, between the personal plane and the metaphysical one. This interpretation of certain manifestations of delusions of grandeur also provides us with some useful means of curing this condition. It shows us that if we attempt to make the patient see he is wrong, that his ideas are utterly absurd, or if we ridicule him, it will serve no useful purpose. Rather it will encourage him in his views. Instead we should tell him that we recognize the element of truth contained in his claims and then patiently endeavour to make him understand the distinction referred to above.

In other cases sudden inner enlightenment produced by the awakening of the soul results in an excitement of the emotions which is then expressed in a noisy, muddled fashion, with cries, tears, singing and various forms of trembling or shaking.

Those who are active, dynamic or combative by nature may feel encouraged by the excitement of awakening to assume the role of prophet or reformer, and to form movements or sects characterized by excessive fanaticism and an eagerness to gain converts.

In some noble souls, who are nevertheless too rigid and extreme, the revelation of what is transcendent and divine in their own spirits arouses a strong desire for full and immediate achievement of that perfection. In practice this achievement can only come, if at all, at the end of a protracted and gradual work of transformation and regeneration of the personality, so this desire is bound to prove futile, resulting in depression and self-destructive despair.

In some predisposed persons, spiritual awakening is accompanied by various types of paranormal, psychic manifestations. They may have visions, usually of sublime beings or angels, or they may hear voices. They might also feel an urge to produce automatic writing. The value of messages received in this way differs greatly from one case to another; for this reason they must always be examined and assessed objectively, without prejudice, but also without allowing oneself to be swayed by the way they come or by the alleged authority of those to whom the products are attributed. One needs to be particularly careful with messages containing specific orders that require a blind obedience and messages that tend to exalt the person who received them. True spiritual instructors never resort to such methods.

Leaving aside for a moment the authenticity and intrinsic value of these messages, there is also the fact that they are dangerous because they can very easily have a serious disturbing effect on a person's emotional and mental equilibrium.

The Reactions which Follow Spiritual Awakening

These reactions normally occur after a certain period of time. As we have already said, a harmonious spiritual awakening causes a sense of joy and brings enlightenment to the mind, enabling it to grasp the meaning and purpose of life. It does away with a number of doubts, provides solutions to many problems and gives a sense of inner security. Alongside these benefits we might add a clear sense of unity, beauty and the sanctity of life, and there flows from the awakened soul a wave of love for other souls and for all creatures.

Indeed there is nothing more refreshing and encouraging than contact with a person who has been awakened in this way and is in this 'state of grace'. The former personality, with its sharp corners and disagreeable traits, has been replaced with a new person who is full of kindness and sympathy, a person who smiles at us and at the whole world, wanting only to give others pleasure, to be useful, and to share his new spiritual riches which seem to be overflowing from within.

This joyful state can last for varying lengths of time, but it has to come to an end. The ordinary personality, with its lower aspects, has only been subdued and put to sleep for a while; it has not been put to death or transformed. Moreover the flow of light and spiritual love is rhythmic and cyclic in nature, as is everything in the universe. Sooner or later, therefore, it fades or ceases altogether: the initial inflow gives way to an ebb-tide.

This inner experience is extremely painful and in some cases produces violent reactions and serious disturbances. The lower urges are reawakened with renewed energy; all the sharp rocks, the rubble and waste that had been covered over by the high tide now reappear. A person who, following such a reawakening, finds his moral conscience more finely honed and demanding, and in whom the thirst for perfection has been heightened, will now judge himself with greater severity, condemn himself more damningly, and may even wrongly think that he has fallen lower than before. This may be inferred from the fact that on occasions certain lower tendencies and impulses, which had lain dormant in the unconscious, are reawakened and aroused into violent opposition against the new lofty spiritual aspirations, thus constituting a challenge and a threat.

Sometimes the reaction is so extreme that the person comes to the point of denying the value and reality of that recent inner experience. Doubts and criticisms are roused in his mind and it is tempted to regard everything that happened as an illusion, a fantasy, or a 'sentimental exaggeration'. The person concerned becomes bitter and sarcastic, ridicules himself and others, and would even like to deny his own ideals and spiritual aspirations. Yet however hard he tries, he just cannot return to his former state. He has had a vision, and its alluring beauty remains in him; it simply cannot be forgotten. No longer can he be happy living the same ordinary little life he knew before. He is gripped by a divine longing and it gives him no peace. Sometimes this reaction has morbid consequences: he falls prey to despair and attempts suicide.

The cure for these extreme reactions requires, above all, that the person concerned be made to understand his true nature and be shown the only way in which his reactions can be overcome. He needs to realize that the 'state of grace' he experienced could not last forever, that his reaction was *natural* and *inevitable*. It is as if he had made a splendid flight to the sun-drenched mountain tops and had been given an opportunity to wonder at the vast landscape below him, stretching to the distant horizon. Sooner or later, however, every flight must come to an end: he comes back down to the plain and then, step by step, has to make the slow climb up the steep slope that leads to a lasting conquest of those peaks. Recognition that this descent or 'fall' is a natural event that everyone has to go through gives comfort and strength to the pilgrim, and encourages him to brace himself for the climb ahead.

The Phases in the Transformation Process

The ascent we have referred to actually consists of the transformation and regeneration of the personality. It is a long, complicated procedure, made up of phases of active purification during which obstacles to the flow and effect of spiritual forces are removed, phases when inner faculties that had been dormant or too weak are developed, and phases in which the personality must remain calm and still, allowing the Spirit to 'work' on him, and accepting the inevitable sufferings with courage and patience. It is a period full of change, a period that alternates between light and darkness, joy and pain.

The energies and attention of someone going through this experience can often be so absorbed in the struggle that he finds it difficult to cope with the various demands of his personal life. For this reason the casual observer who judges him from the point of view of normality and practical efficiency may find that he has grown worse and become less of a person. His inner turmoil is therefore compounded by unsympathetic and undeserved judgement from his family, friends and even from his doctors, and he will not be spared cutting remarks about the 'great results' of his aspirations and spiritual ideals that have made him so ineffective and weak in everyday life. Such judgements often cause great pain to those on the receiving end, with the result that they may be psychologically disturbed by them and fall prey to doubts and discouragement.

Yet this is one of the trials that has to be overcome, for it teaches us to triumph over our own sensitivity, and to acquire independence of judgement and a resoluteness in our conduct. This trial must therefore be faced without rebellion, but rather with serenity. If those close to a person in this condition understand what he is going through, on the other hand, they can be a great help in saving him from many unnecessary conflicts and sufferings.

What we are considering is actually a transition stage: having left the old stage, but not yet having arrived at the new one. It is like the state a larva is in when it undergoes the transformation process that will cause it to become a winged butterfly: it has to go through the chrysalis stage, a condition of disintegration and loss of power. However, the average man is not granted the privilege enjoyed by the larva when it undergoes this transformation, protected inside its cocoon. Today especially he has to stick to the place life has assigned to him and do his best to meet his family, professional and social obligations as though nothing were going on inside him. The demanding task he faces is like that given to the English engineers who had to convert and extend a large London railway station without disrupting the normal timetable in any way.

It should not surprise us if such a complex, demanding operation often causes nervous and psychological disturbances such as exhaustion, insomnia, depression, irritability and restlessness. These disturbances, given the fact that the mind has such a powerful effect on the body, can also easily lead to a variety of physical symptoms.

In order to cure such states it is necessary to understand their true cause and to help the patient with the appropriate, carefully selected psychotherapy, for physical cures and treatment involving drugs may help to alleviate the symptoms and physical disturbances, but they cannot of course do anything about the psychospiritual causes of the illness.

Sometimes disturbances are produced or made worse by excessive personal effort on the part of those aspiring to the spiritual life with a view to forcing their own inner development. Such efforts bring about the repression rather than the transformation of the lower aspects of the personality, and they greatly intensify the struggle, resulting in excessive nervous and psychological tension. What these over-zealous students need to realize is that the essential part of the work of regeneration is produced by the spirit and by its energies, and that once they have done what they can to draw those energies to themselves—through their fervent activity, meditation and a correct inner attitude—and sought to get rid of anything which might hinder the spirit in its work, they must then wait patiently and confidently for that work to unfold spontaneously in their souls.

In contrast with the above, another difficulty has to be overcome at times when the flow of spiritual power is full and free. This precious force can easily be dissipated in an emotional effervescence and in excessive, feverish activity. In other cases, however, too tight a rein is kept on this force: it is not translated into everyday life and used as it should be, with the result that it builds up within and, because of the great tension this causes, can then produce inner disturbances and stress, just as too strong an electric current can blow a fuse and even cause short circuits.

There is a need then for learning how to correctly and wisely regulate the flow of these spiritual energies, avoiding waste, and to use them actively in noble, productive works, both works within and works directed to the world around us.

The 'Dark Night of the Soul'

When the process of psychospiritual transformation reaches its final and decisive stage, it sometimes produces intense suffering and an inner darkness which has been referred to by Christian mystics as the 'dark night of the soul'. The characteristics of this condition closely resemble those of the illness known as 'psychotic depression' or melancholy. These characteristics are: an emotional state of deep depression which may even verge on despair, an acute sense of unworthiness which in some cases leads to a person's feeling himself to be lost or damned, a painful sense of mental impotence, a weakening of the will and of self-control, lack of desire and a great reluctance to act.

Some of these symptoms may present themselves less intensely at earlier stages, but that does not indicate the true 'dark night of the soul'.

Despite appearances, however, this strange, frightening experience is *not* a pathological state; it has spiritual causes and great spiritual value.[1] The experience, which has been called the 'mystical crucifixion' or the 'mystical death', is followed by the glorious spiritual resurrection which puts an end to every suffering and every disorder, is more than adequate compensation for what has been endured, and represents the fullness of spiritual health.

The theme we have chosen has made it necessary for us to dwell almost exclusively on the more painful and abnormal sides of inner development, but we would not want to give the impression that those who follow the way of spiritual ascent are more easily affected by nervous disorders than ordinary men. It will be useful therefore if we clarify the following points:

1. In many cases spiritual development takes place in a more gradual and harmonious fashion than we have described, so that difficulties are overcome and the various stages are passed without nervous or physical reactions.
2. The nervous and mental disorders suffered by so-called ordinary men and women are often more serious, more difficult to cope with and cure than those having spiritual causes. The disorders of ordinary men are often produced

[1] See St John of the Cross, *The Dark Night of the Soul* and E. Underhill, *Mysticism* (New York, 1961).

by violent conflicts between the passions, or between the unconscious impulses and the conscious personality. They may also come about as a result of rebellion against conditions or people who oppose their wishes and their selfish requirements. It is often more difficult to cure them because the higher faculties of their being are too weak and there is little to which one can appeal to get them to make the necessary sacrifices and to submit to the discipline required for creating the right harmonious framework in which they can be restored to health.

3. The sufferings and disorders experienced by those taking the spiritual path, however serious they may be at times, are actually nothing more than temporary reactions. We might think of them as the dross from the organic process of growth and inner regeneration. For this reason they often vanish spontaneously when the crisis which brought them into being is resolved, or they might respond more readily to an appropriate cure.

4. The sufferings produced by the low or ebb-tides of the spiritual waves are more than compensated for by the periods of free-flowing energy and by the experience of being lifted up, as well as by the great purpose and grand design of the inner adventure.

This vision of glory acts as a powerful stimulus, an unfailing comfort and an inexhaustible source of power and courage. We must therefore rekindle it as vividly and as often as possible, and one of the greatest benefits we can bestow on those who are tormented by crises and spiritual conflicts is to help them do the same.

Let us try in our imagination to form a vivid picture of the glory and bliss of the victorious, liberated soul as it consciously participates in the wisdom, power and love of the Divine Life. Now let us imagine an even greater vision of the Kingdom of God when it has become a reality on earth, the vision of a redeemed humanity, with the whole of creation regenerated and displaying with joy the perfection of God.

It is visions like this that have enabled the great mystics and saints to smile as they endured their inner torments and their physical martyrdom—the attitude which enabled St Francis to say, 'So great is the good I look forward to that I take joy in every pain!'

But for now we must come down from these heights and return for a moment to the valley where souls are in travail.

Considering the matter purely from the medical and psychological point of view, we need to realize, as we have already suggested, that whereas the disorders that accompany the various crises of spiritual development seem at first sight very similar, and sometimes identical, to those of ordinary illnesses, their causes and significance are very different in practice; indeed, in one sense they are opposites. This means that the cure must also be different.

The neuro-psychological symptoms of ordinary patients are usually *regressive* in nature. These patients have been unable to form the necessary internal and external frameworks which contribute to the normal development of the personality. For instance they may not have succeeded in freeing themselves from an emotional attachment to their parents, and thus remain in a state of childish dependence on them, or on someone else who has symbolically taken the place of their parents.

In other cases their inability or disinclination to face up to the requirements and difficulties of normal family or social life, cause them, without their being aware of it, to seek refuge in some illness which will free them from such obligations. In yet other cases we see an emotional trauma. An example of this would be a disappointment or loss that they are unable to accept and to which they react in the form of illness.

In all these cases we are dealing with a conflict between the conscious personality and the lower aspects of the personality which often operate at the level of the unconscious, and we see the latter gaining a partial victory.

In contrast with this, the ills produced by the travail of spiritual development are clearly *progressive* in nature. They are the result of an attempt to grow, and are of the upward quest; they are a by-product of temporary conflicts and imbalances between the conscious personality and the spiritual energies bursting through from above.

All this makes it quite clear that the cures for the two types of illness must be very different. For the first group the task of the person administering treatment is to help the patient get back to the level of 'normal' man, helping him to get rid of his repressions and inhibitions, his fears and attachments, and helping him to escape from his excessive self-centredness, false values and distorted perception of reality, so that he can gain an objective, rational view of life, accept his duties and responsibilities, and begin to appreciate the rights of other people. Those aspects of his personality which clash, which are not properly developed or coordinated, must be harmonized and integrated in the form of *personal psychosynthesis*.

For patients in the second category, on the other hand, the task is one of creating a harmonious framework which will favour assimilation and integration of the new spiritual energies with the existing, so-called 'normal' aspects of the personality—in other words, bringing about a *transpersonal psychosynthesis* around a higher inner centre.

Quite clearly then a cure that is appropriate for a patient in the first group is inadequate, and may even be harmful, to a patient in the second. His difficulties are added to rather than alleviated if he is in the hands of a doctor who fails to understand the turmoil he is experiencing and who is ignorant of, or even denies, the possibility of spiritual development. A doctor like this may undervalue or even ridicule his patient's spiritual aspirations, regarding them as nothing more than futile fantasies, or interpreting them in a materialistic fashion. The patient may then be made to believe he is doing the right thing in hardening the shell of his own personality and in refusing to pay attention to the insistent cries of his soul. But this may only result in his condition being worsened, making the battle even fiercer and delaying the solution.

If, on the other hand, the doctor is also travelling along a spiritual pathway, or if he at least has a clear understanding and a true appreciation of the reality of spiritual conquests, he may give such a patient invaluable help.

If, as is often the case, the patient is still at the stage of dissatisfaction, restlessness and unconscious aspirations, if he has lost all interest in everyday life but has not yet glimpsed the Higher Reality, if he is looking for relief in the wrong directions and is wandering up blind alleys, the revelation of the true cause of his condition and effective help in finding the right solution can greatly help in accelerating the awakening of the soul, which is in itself the most important part of the cure.

When a person is at the second stage, the stage where he is rejoicing in the light of the spirit and making joyful flights towards the heights of the superconscious, it can be very beneficial for him to have an explanation of the true nature and function of those experiences, and to be alerted to the fact that they cannot help but be temporary, as well as being given an idea of what he is likely to encounter as he continues on his pilgrimage. He will then be prepared when the inevitable reaction sets in, and this will save him a great deal of suffering caused by the surprise of 'falling' or by the doubts and discouragements that ensue.

Where such a warning has not been given, and the cure is started during the period of reaction and depression, the patient may be greatly relieved and helped by the assurance, backed up by examples, that this is only a temporary phase from which he will certainly escape.

At the fourth stage, where instances of 'ascent' are occurring—the longest and most varied of the stages—the work of the carer is equally more complex. The main components of this help are:

1. Explaining to the person suffering the meaning of what is happening in him and showing him the right attitude to adopt.
2. Giving him instruction in how to overcome his lower inclinations, without repressing them in his unconscious.
3. Teaching and helping him to transform and sublimate his own psychological energies.
4. Helping him to maintain and make good use of the spiritual energies flowing into his consciousness.
5. Guiding and working with him in the task of reconstructing his personality—or psychosynthesis.

At the stage of the 'dark night of the soul' it is extremely difficult to give help, because a person in this condition is enveloped in so dense a cloud, and so immersed in his sufferings, that the light of the spirit cannot reach his consciousness. The only way to offer strength and support is to tirelessly repeat the assurance that it is a temporary experience and not a permanent condition—as he is inclined to feel and which is the greatest cause of his despair. It is also a good idea to assure him, with the greatest insistence, that the torment he is going through, however terrible it may seem, has great spiritual value and will one day bring him so much good that he will turn round and bless it. This will enable him to bear it and accept it with a sense of peace, resignation and strong patience.

We feel it right to mention that these psychological and spiritual cures do not exclude the subsidiary use of physical expedients which may help to alleviate symptoms and contribute to a successful cure. These subsidiary expedients will be the sorts of things that assist the healing work of nature—such as a healthy diet, relaxation exercises, contact with natural elements, and a rhythm that is appropriate for different physical and psychological activities.

In some cases a cure is made more complex by the fact that the patient presents a mixture of progressive and regressive symptoms. This describes cases where the inner development is irregular and discordant. Such people may reach high spiritual levels with one part of their personality, but in other areas they are enslaved by childish attachments or are under the control of unconscious 'complexes'. We might even say that, on careful analysis, the majority of those travelling along the spiritual path show traces of such limitations, to a greater or lesser extent—as, we should note, is also the case for so-called 'normal' people.

The fact remains, however, that in the great majority of cases there is a marked prevalence either of regressive symptoms or of progressive ones. But we should always bear in mind that symptoms from both groups may be found together in the same patient, and it is necessary that each disorder be accurately studied and interpreted, so that the true cause may be determined and the correct cure found.

From all that we have said it is quite clear that in order to provide an effective, satisfactory cure for the nervous and psychological disorders that accompany spiritual development there needs to be a two-fold system in terms of know-how and practice: that of the doctor who is an expert in nervous illnesses and in psychotherapy, and that of the serious student or pilgrim travelling along the ways of the Spirit. It is rare at the present time to find these two areas of expertise working together, but given the growing number of people in need of such cures, all those able to provide such a service ought to apply themselves to the task of performing this good work.

Such cures might also be made easier if it were possible to establish a back-up of appropriately trained nurses and clinical assistants who would be able to work intelligently with all those involved, and finally it would help if the public at large were given some basic facts about the connections between neuro-psychological disorders and inner crises, so that other family members could assist the patient and the doctor in their task, instead of complicating it and hindering it through ignorance, prejudice and even active opposition, which unfortunately is often the case.

Once the initial groundwork has been carried out in the above three areas—doctors, nurses and the public—a great deal of unnecessary suffering will be able to be prevented and many pilgrims will then face a shorter, less arduous task in reaching the high goal they are pursuing: union with the Divine Reality.

MYSTICISM AND MEDICINE

Both in the last and the present century many positivist scientists (I will only mention Murisier, Janet, Ribot, Binet-Sangle, Portigliotti and some representatives of the psycho-analytical school) have claimed to explain away mystical phenomena by treating them as morbid manifestations. Because many mystics quite clearly suffered from nervous disorders, these scientists have deduced that all their mystical activity was the result of illness.

There is no need for me to bother to counter this crude idea, an idea which reveals a complete misunderstanding of what mystical experience is all about. But since this way of thinking is still prevalent among people in general and among doctors and psychoanalysts in particular, I do not think it superfluous, as a doctor, to restate that the discovery of symptoms of illness in a human being does not in any way justify discounting that person's spiritual experiences.

As I wrote some years ago:

... the intellectual and moral value of a personality is completely independent of any morbid symptoms he may be suffering from—symptoms he may have in common with baser or even truly degenerate people.

Even if it is true that Saint Teresa, Saint Catherine of Genoa and many other noble figures from religious history were affected by hysteria, this should in no way diminish our high regard of their spiritual gifts. Rather we need to alter our attitude to hysterics. If, as it is claimed, Saint Francis had degenerative stigmata in his body, this certainly does not diminish our veneration of the Poor Man of Assisi; it simply shows that these stigmata do not always have the 'degenerative' significance attributed to them, and this may cause us to reevaluate our concept of 'degeneration'. Even if it were true, as a certain French doctor has claimed to show, that Jesus—the highest goal of mankind—was mad, this would only mean that madness is sometimes infinitely superior to the wisdom of 'normal' people, including psychiatrists.

'Psychology and Psychotherapy', *Psiche*, 3, 1913, No.3, p.195.

Furthermore, even one of the most popular positivists of the last century, Max Nordau, realized what a gross error it was to consider the higher manifestations of the spirit as morbid phenomena. Repudiating the theory of his mentor, Lombroso, Nordau stated quite aptly that to say 'cleverness is a neurosis' is just as invalid as saying that 'athletics is a disorder of the heart' simply because many gymnasts have bad hearts.

This comparison shows us the true relationship between illness and mysticism. The nervous and psychological disorders of mystics, when they are not merely coincidental, are actually the effect or a direct consequence of their intense spiritual life, just as heart disorders in athletes are simply a result of their intense muscular effort.

The mystical life, with its various phases and 'critical points', and its exacting requirements and the extraordinary experiences they give rise to, actually serves to highlight the nervous and psychological resistance of an individual. Even at what we might call the pre-mystical stage, the period preceding the awakening of the soul, there are often disorders which can be attributed to the great inner tension caused by the promptings of the spirit and the tenacious resistance of the personality. At this stage one often has a negative first spiritual experience—an experience of insubstantiality, irreality, a feeling that the world of phenomena and one's own empiric personality have no value. On the surface this experience may seem the same as a state of depersonalization or the state in which one loses all sense of reality, the condition in which psychasthenics find themselves. But the significance and value of these are very different: in the first case we are dealing with a transient stage on the way to a fuller, richer life; in the second we are faced with a loss of normal faculties with no corresponding gain to offset them.

Awakening and enlightenment of the soul, which from the psychological point of view may be regarded as the bursting in and flow of a mighty flood of spiritual life into one's being, can easily cause temporary nervous disorders. The body may be powerless to resist the flow of such a force, and the psychological make-up unprepared to assimilate the new consciousness in a harmonious fashion. Quite often there needs to be a complex period of readjustment. However, this only points to the weakness of the 'old Adam', rather than laying any blame at the feet of the 'new Christ'.

It is also possible for morbid symptoms to surface at the active purification stage, the ascetic period of the mystic life, especially if this purification is carried out too violently and if, instead of endeavouring to transform and sublimate his instinctive, emotional energies, the mystic uses the wrong method of repressing them in his unconscious.

There is then the mysterious stage of the 'dark night of the soul', that 'passive purification' in which the mystic's consciousness undergoes a new, more radical, negative experience and in which the death of his old personality, or 'Adam', actually takes place—a necessary condition for his resurrection in Christ. It is in this mystical death, I believe, that human suffering reaches its highest level: it is an inexpressible torment, a real conscious agony. It is little wonder that in such a terrible experience, which can last for a considerable time, the health suffers and we encounter symptoms similar to those associated with the illness known by psychiatrists as 'melancholy'.

But here too the pathological similarities in no way detract from the reality and value of the spiritual experience. Indeed, I would go so far as to maintain the opposite: I have observed in a number of cases of so-called 'melancholy', when the patients themselves thought they were suffering from an illness alone, that a profound spiritual upheaval was taking place within them.

Recognition of the various connections between mysticism and illness enables us to avoid many of the misunderstandings, misinterpretations and even serious practical mistakes that either the doctors or the mystics themselves are likely to make. Doctors can learn to understand and respect the spiritual life of their patients and to encourage a harmonious development, rather than discredit and hinder it, as has happened too often in the past. And the mystics themselves, being made aware in advance of the nature and meaning of the disturbances that might come upon them, will not be overtroubled by them, nor—as sometimes happens—will they mistakenly regard them as signs of superiority or as a form of divine favour. Rather, they will recognize them as weaknesses and imperfections of their human nature, which has not yet become a compliant, suitable instrument for the Spirit, and then they will be in a position to endeavour to eliminate them and to aspire to perfect health.

This attitude towards illness is one of the main areas of difference between the mysticism of old (at least that of Western Christianity) and the new mysticism. The exaggerated spirit of asceticism, the thirst for suffering, sacrifice and abject misery, the hostile attitude to the body and the passive submission meant that many of the mystics of the past not only failed to seek release from physical ills that afflicted them, they actually accepted them with joy—indeed they almost cultivated them—because they saw in them a means of purification. Even though we might admire their strength of will and their generosity and love, through which they transformed weakness into strength and obstacles into stepping stones, we must nevertheless recognize that the attitude they adopted was based on false preconceptions and limited understanding.

As the new mysticism sees it, the body is not the enemy of the spirit: rather it is, or needs to become, its precious tool, faithful servant and temple. Asceticism, suffering and sacrifice are not ends in themselves, they have no absolute value. Rather, they are relative means and have a relative value. As for illness it has no merit of its own; it is merely an imperfection—if it is not a direct consequence of one's own or other people's actions, that is. Moreover, from this and other aspects, the new mysticism is less revolutionary than might first appear to be the case. As with all forms of renewal, it is in essence a return to the first, true sources: instead of calling it original in the sense of a new creation, we might call it original in the sense of something that has gone back to its origins. Indeed, in Jesus' attitude to health we see something far closer to what we are now claiming than to the attitude adopted by many mystics of the past. And Jesus (it should not be necessary to state this here, but since there are many who would deny it, we would do well to reaffirm it) was a true, great and perfect mystic. In him we see no sign of cultivating illness, no asceticism. Tradition does not hint at any physical imperfection or illness in him: the profound crises he underwent on various occasions—from his temptation in the wilderness to his suffering in the Garden of Gethsemane—though they caused him to sweat drops of blood, did not have the power to cause any lasting disorder in his body. Indeed it would be very difficult to imagine Jesus ill, passively accepting physical afflictions. Rather the Gospels describe him as strong, capable of exerting great effort, but also ready to rest, to gain new strength from solitude and prayer. Not only do they portray him as *healthy*, but also as a *healer*.

Throughout the ages men have sought the help of spiritual forces, powers and invisible beings to rid them of their physical ills. In the temples of Egypt and Greece, in the Serapeum of Memphis, the temple of Asclepius at Epidaurus and many others, the method of 'incubation' was used, that is to say the method of sleeping in the temple, during which the sick person would have benevolent visions and then wake up restored to health. In all civilizations and all religions those following the mystical way have acquired, at a certain stage in their development, the power to heal, which they have used for the benefit of suffering humanity. As the main proof of being the 'One who is to come' Jesus referred to this healing power when John sent a group of his disciples to ask him who he was. These are his own words:

Go and tell John what you have heard: the blind see, the lame walk, lepers are cleansed, the deaf hear, the dead are raised, and the Gospel is proclaimed to the poor.

He then gave this power to heal to the twelve disciples, commanding them to use it:

And having called to him the twelve disciples he gave them authority over unclean spirits so that they might cast them out, and the power to heal all sicknesses and illnesses.

He added:

> Restore the health of the sick, raise the dead, cleanse lepers, drive out demons; freely you have received, freely give.

The epistle of James confirms that in the early Christian Church use was made of prayer and anointing with oil for healing purposes. Thus the sacrament of extreme unction originated from this therapeutic use of oil:

> Is any among you sick? Let him call for the elders of the church to pray over him and anoint him with oil in the name of the Lord: and the prayer of faith shall save the sick man and the Lord will raise him up.

Thereafter the prevailing trend towards asceticism diluted this tradition and almost caused it to be lost altogether, with the result that until quite recently this important priestly, mystical role was almost completely neglected. Over the last few decades, however, we have seen a rapid burgeoning of spiritual and mystical healing practices, especially in America and England, through the activities of various movements, both unco-ordinated and organized. The most typical and widespread of these is the Christian Science movement, founded by Mary Baker Eddy. Also fairly widespread in America is the so-called Unity movement which has its centre in Kansas City. Meanwhile the Anglican Church has actively resumed the healing practices of old: the laying on of hands, anointing with oil, prayer, healing missions, etc.

Spiritual therapy raises many important questions, questions which are not easy to answer:

— What is the true nature of this healing power?
— How does one obtain it?
— What part does the patient's attitude of mind play?
— What actually is the substance of this necessary *faith* in the healer and in the one being healed?
— What are the differences and relationships between psychotherapy and spiritual therapy?
— What are the relationships between physical cure and inner regeneration?

I will not even begin to tackle these problems. It is only my wish to list them, to encourage those engaged in the area of mysticism not to overlook this very important aspect of their activities, and to encourage doctors—who only now are beginning to accept psychotherapy, albeit with diffidence and reservations—not to lag behind in this new spiritual awakening, and to recognize the value of this most noble and precious means of healing.

I confidently express the hope and wish that relations between mysticism and medicine would become closer, and that there would be greater understanding and harmony. This harmony would result in great benefits for mystics, for doctors and—most importantly—for poor suffering humanity.

THE AWAKENING
OF THE SOUL

The awakening of the soul, that first blinding flash of new spiritual consciousness which transforms and regenerates the whole being, is an event of fundamental importance and has an incomparable value in the inner life of man.

The great mass of humanity has not yet reached this stage in its evolution. For the most part people are unaware of it or deny its very existence. But throughout the ages, and in all parts of the world, there have been those souls that have received light and have left us a moving, joyful testimony to this experience. Let us listen to these testimonies with a reverent, attentive spirit, seeking to understand the profound meaning and true value of what they have to say, and let us, with those who have given us these messages, tread the strange, often difficult, winding and dark paths which led them to spiritual awakening. Such communion will make us wiser and better, encouraging us to work on our own spiritual development, and—who knows—it may create a spark of the great light in the depths of our hearts.

Anyone who reads and compares the testimonies of those who have been 'awakened' will first notice many differences in the language used, in the way the writers express themselves and in the way they regard and interpret the experiences they have had. But a closer and deeper study will reveal that these differences are to do with circumstances rather than with the substance of what they are describing; they are the result of the personality and temperament of the person concerned, the way in which that person has been brought up and educated, and the various slants and limitations of the race, civilization and time in which he or she lived. What we discover is that beneath these differences there is a basic unity and a remarkable agreement about the essential characteristics of spiritual awakening. We often find the same expressions, the same images, even the same words used in documents from very different times and places. This agreement is of great significance and it is firm evidence of the validity and universality of such inner experiences.

In the brief study of these experiences which I am now going to attempt it will be my aim to highlight these points of common agreement, ignoring any formal or outward differences, especially those attributable to the different religious creeds of the 'awakened' people I will be mentioning. In this study I will give priority to contemporary testimonies: these will be easier for us to understand in that they are expressed in terms that are more in tune with our own educational background. I also feel it appropriate to dwell on the preparatory stages of awakening because a knowledge and correct understanding of these could be of use to some soul that is seeking light.

It would be very interesting and instructive to make a study of the individual differences, but this is not the appropriate place for such an undertaking. It would be useful, however, in order to give a clearer and more vivid idea of such experiences, to give a fairly full treatment to one of the most notable and significant cases—this is the case of Tolstoy. This is how he describes it in his *Confessions*:

> ... Five years ago something strange began to happen in me: at first I experienced moments of stupor, a feeling that life had stopped and I knew neither how to live nor what to do; I would become restless and sad. Once these moments had passed I went on living as before. But then these moments of perplexity became more and more frequent, always taking the same form. These moments, when life seemed to be temporarily suspended, found their expression in the same questions: Why? Well? And then?
>
> At first I thought they were meaningless questions, questions that served no purpose; they seemed to be things I should know already, and I felt that were I one day to decide to sit down and answer them it would be very easy to do so; I imagined that though I did not have the time to consider them there and then I could have come up with an answer at once if I wanted to. But the questions came with increasing frequency; with increasing urgency they demanded

answers, and as happens when one is hit repeatedly on the same spot they ended up making a black mark [bruise]. I went through what happens to a person who contracts a mortal illness: first there are the minor symptoms of the illness, which the sick person hardly pays any attention to, then the symptoms become more frequent and become a single, continuous source of suffering. This then increases and before the sick person knows where he is, he realizes that what at first seemed a mild complaint has now gained a significance of the greatest proportions for him: death.

This is what happened. I realized it was not just a passing indisposition, but something far more serious, and that if the same question were asked over and over again, I would have to answer it. I attempted to do so, but the questions seemed so absurd, so simple, so childish! Once I attempted to study and resolve them, however, I was at once convinced that they were not at all childish or stupid, but the most serious and profound questions in life, and that they would require a great deal of thought: indeed I could not answer them! Before involving myself in the running of my estate at Samara, in my son's education, in the publication of a book, I needed to know why I was doing it. Until I knew, I could do nothing—I could not live. Right in the middle of my thinking about the organization of my affairs, which was a considerable preoccupation at that time, the question suddenly came into my mind: 'So I've got six thousand desyatinas of land in the Samara district, and three hundred horses. What of it?'

And I was completely at a loss, I did not know what to think. Then when I started to think about how to educate children the question would come into my mind: 'Why?' Or when I thought of the acclaim that would come my way as a result of the works I had written, I would find myself thinking: 'So you'll be more famous than Gogol, Pushkin, Shakespeare, Molière and all the other writers in the world. Then what?' And I had no answers to these questions.

Questions do not wait, they need to be answered at once. If one does not answer them, one is unable to live. But I had no answers. I felt as though the ground I was walking on was falling away beneath me, that there was no longer anything I could cling to, that whatever it was my life depended on was no longer there, and that there was nothing left.

My life came to a standstill. I could breathe, eat, drink and sleep, for I would have been unable not to do these things. But this was not life because there seemed no desire for which there was any reasonable satisfaction. Even if I desired something, I knew in advance that, whether it was satisfied or not, nothing would come of it. Were a fairy godmother to have come, offering to grant my every wish, I would have been unable to say what I wanted. If, in a moment of elation I rediscovered not so much desire as the habit of desire, as soon as I returned to my normal calm state I knew it was nothing more than self-deception—there was nothing for me to desire.

I came to a point where, although fit and happy, I felt I could not go on living. Some irresistible force was drawing me, intent on snatching life away from me in some way or other; I would not say that I wanted to kill myself, but the force which was drawing me from beyond life was more powerful, more complete, more universal—it was a force like my former eagerness to live, but in the opposite direction.

This happened at a time when, to all outward appearances, I had everything that is thought necessary for complete happiness. I was not yet fifty, I had a loving wife whom I loved, good children, a large estate which, through no effort of my own, was expanding and prospering; I was gaining even greater respect from my relations, friends and acquaintances; people who did not even know me were showering me with praise and, without any false modesty, I had good grounds for believing that my name had become famous. In addition to all this I was neither mad nor mentally ill, but enjoyed a moral and physical force I have rarely found in those around me. Physically I was strong enough to tend the land like a peasant, intellectually I could have worked eight to ten hours without a break and without feeling any adverse effects.

It was in this condition that I came to the point of no longer being able to face life, but fearing death I had to employ every trick I could think of to prevent myself from committing suicide.

What is the meaning of these strange inner states? Are they simply morbid feelings, fatigue, mental or physical imbalances? Can those people afflicted with them be released and get back to where they were before?

No. These are not simply nervous disorders, and the people involved cannot return to their former state. Sooner or later, however, something new and wonderful takes place within them, suddenly releasing them from their painful condition and completely transforming them.

For anyone who has not had direct experience of this it is

difficult, if not impossible, to fully appreciate what that great event within actually is and what it means. All who have attempted to describe it agree that language is inadequate and that ordinary words just cannot express such sublime facts, so far removed as they are from ordinary experience. Yet they have all felt a need or felt it their duty to tell other people about it. Such testimonies are better expressed in their lives than with mere words. The transformation of one's whole being displayed in its outward form in how one behaves towards and affects other people is far more eloquent and meaningful than any verbal expression. Thus no description can come anywhere near a deep knowledge of their lives and above all a personal relationship with them; but failing this, we can still catch a glimpse of what they have experienced from their writings, because they have often succeeded in transforming the common building blocks of our language into instruments of profound meaning and given them a new lease of life.

Let us endeavour then—through the veil of words, and despite differences due to the mental outlook, temperament and circumstances of various witnesses—to gain an insight into the essential characteristics of the event we have referred to above. The first and most frequently encountered manifestation of this is that of an extraordinary dazzling sense of light.

We all remember how the conversion of St Paul began, as recounted in the Acts of the Apostles, with 'a light from heaven which blazed all around him'.

A modern writer, the doctor R.M. Bucke, describing in the third person his own inner experience, says:

Suddenly, without the slightest warning, he found himself surrounded by a flame-coloured cloud. For a moment it seemed like a fire, an unexpected conflagration in the town, but after a moment he realized that the light was inside him.

James relates the testimony of an uneducated man:

It seemed as if the sky itself had opened and was showering down rays of light and glory. Not just for a moment, but throughout the day and the night it seemed that rays of light and glory were passing through my soul, and I was changed—everything was new.

President Finney described a similar experience in these words:

> All at once the glory of God shone down on me, all around me in a wonderful way ... An utterly indescribable light shone into my soul; so intense was it that I fell to the ground ... This light seemed like the splendour of the sun shining in all directions. It was more than my eyes could take.

The poet Walt Whitman points to this experience in the short but effective phrase: 'A rare inexpressible light that illuminates light itself.'

But the simplest, and at the same time the most powerful expression of this, in its stark brevity, is found in the famous amulet of Pascal—a piece of parchment on which, around a crude drawing of the blazing cross, is a brief reference to his experience of spiritual awakening:

> In the year of grace 1654, Monday 23rd November, St. Clement's day ... from ten thirty in the evening to half an hour after midnight, fire.

Pascal's inner fire is both light and heat. Other accounts of spiritual awakening emphasize the sensation of heat and burning. Richard Rolle, an English mystic of the fourteenth century, wrote with delightful simplicity:

> I was in such awe, indeed more than I can express, when I first felt this heat and burning in my heart, not something in the mind but a tangible fire ... that I, in my ignorance, repeatedly put my hands to my breast to feel whether this burning had some physical cause. But when I realized that the fire was within, and had a spiritual origin, I then knew that it was a gift from my Creator.

The significance of these sensations of light and fire will be readily understood if we combine them with the other characteristics of spiritual awakening that we will now turn to.

The effect of the new light is the transformation of the visible world: every being and every object assumes a new beauty—it seems suffused with an aura of glory.

Describing his own conversion, Jonathan Edwards said:

Everything was altered in appearance. It seemed that everything bore an imprint of serenity and gentleness as it displayed the glory of God. I could see God's excellence, wisdom and purity in everything: in the sun, the moon and the stars, in the clouds and the blue sky, in the grass, the flowers, the trees, in water and in the whole of nature.

Alongside this transformation of one's view of nature, there is often an even greater sense of inner enlightenment through which the soul discovers new and wonderful truths, and in a flash of intuition solves besetting problems that had troubled it so much. The soul now sees the universe as a living Whole and recognizes itself as an indestructible particle of it—tiny but necessary—as though it were one of the notes, inseparably linked to other notes, which go to make up the cosmic harmony.

The soul now appreciates that every contrast and every discordant feature are included in this supreme Unity, and it begins to understand the mysterious significance and true nature of evil. This is now seen as unreal, not in the sense that it does not exist, but in the sense that however serious and painful it might be for the limited creature experiencing it and being oppressed by it, it is nevertheless transitory and insubstantial; it is the absence of good, disharmony, a partial imbalance which is destined to disappear. The soul that has been thus enlightened sees every fact and every event as being connected with other facts and events, justified by a higher logic; it sees the universe upheld and permeated by a perfect justice and an infinite goodness.

In many cases this manifestation of the divine nature of all things is supplemented, or even replaced, by a more definite, more intimate manifestation. There is a real sense of the presence of some other being, a great Being—invisible but intensely real—a Being who is more certain and real than visible things.

This light of consciousness is accompanied by a powerful, indeed overwhelming flood of new feelings. The universe, transfigured by the new light of the spirit, appears wonderfully beautiful, and in contemplating it the soul is first gripped by a sense of wonder and admiration, immediately followed by a joyful exaltation together with an inexpressible peace.

A hymn of gratitude rises up to the Creator of such magnificence and the heart burns with an unspeakable love for Him and for all his creatures. Totally absorbed in this vision and in these feelings, the soul has forgotten itself; it has, without noticing it, transcended its limitations and hardships, and when it again looks at itself, it realizes, to its great joy, that all the pain, fear and despair that were there before have mysteriously vanished—that burden which so oppressed the heart, that sense of dissatisfaction with oneself, and those feelings of guilt and inferiority have gone. One feels a lightness and expansion of the spirit, pervaded by a new sense of security and power. In the context of this new awareness, this range of feelings, this vision and love, the will now joins in with complete commitment as an expression of the spontaneous desire of the whole being to undergo a transformation that will unite it with the new ideal that has been glimpsed, to purify itself from all blemishes, to undergo a complete regeneration, and from this point on—at all times and in all things—to do the will of the Spirit.

These, in brief outline, are the main characteristics of the awakening of the soul. In order that we might gain a better grasp of them, as well as seeing how they interrelate and different ways in which certain characteristics can dominate in individual cases, we will hear some more testimonies of those who have been 'enlightened'.

I well remember the night and almost the exact point up on the hill when my soul opened up, as it were, to the infinite and the two worlds, the inner world and the external one, merged into a single entity. It was like deep calling to deep; the depth of feeling opened up within me as a result of my struggle was answered by the unfathomable depths of the external universe which stretches beyond the stars. There I was alone with the One who had made me, the One who had also made love, pain and even temptation. I was not seeking Him, yet I felt a perfect unity of my spirit with His. My awareness of my surroundings faded. At that moment there was nothing in me but inexpressible joy and exaltation. It is impossible to give an adequate description of what I felt. It was like the effect of a large orchestra when all the individual notes merge into a growing harmony so that the person listening is only aware that his soul is being carried aloft and that he feels giddy with the excess of emotion. The perfect quietness of the night was imbued with an even more solemn silence. The darkness held a presence which was felt rather than seen. I was just as certain that He was there as I was of my own presence. Indeed I felt that if anything I was the less real of the two.

It was then that my faith in God and my deep awareness of Him were born. Since then I have been up the Mountain of Visions on other occasions, and have felt the Lord all around me, but never again have I felt the same deep emotion in my heart. If I have only once been in God's presence and been renewed by His Spirit, I believe it was on that occasion. There was no immediate change in my thoughts or beliefs, except that my former rudimentary understanding blossomed. There was no destruction of the old, but a rapid, wonderful development.

Tolstoy's spiritual awakening was more difficult, complex and gradual. On many occasions he had a real sense of the presence of God and the joy that accompanied it, but within a moment doubts and intellectual misgivings of all kinds would cloud his vision, throwing his soul into turmoil, and he would fall back into his former despair. But one day, at last, he had an experience which was to be a turning point. This is how he describes it:

I remember being alone in the forest one day in spring, listening to its thousand different sounds. My ears were free to listen and as always my thoughts returned to what had been preoccupying them for three years: the search for God ... The idea of God is not God, I told myself; the idea is something that happens in me. The idea of God is something I can work up within myself, but that is not what I am looking for. I am looking for something without which life could not exist. And seeing how everything around me was dying, I again felt that desire to put an end to my own life. But then I examined myself and remembered all those pangs of despair and hope that had assailed me one hundred times before. I remembered that I only truly lived when I believed in God. Whenever, as now, I believed I knew God, I lived; but as soon as I forgot and stopped believing in Him, I stopped living.

What then is the essence of this exaltation and this despair? I am not alive when I lose faith in the existence of God: I would have killed myself long ago if I had not had that vague hope of finding Him, whereas I live, I am truly alive when I feel Him and seek Him.

'What am I still looking for, then?' a voice inside me cried out. The One without whom it is impossible to live. Knowing God and living are the same thing. God is life. You live in search of God, so there is no life without Him. More than ever before I felt as if my whole being had been enlightened, as well as everything around me. From then on this light did not leave me again.

Of particular interest from a number of aspects is the account of the spiritual awakening of Rabindranath Tagore, the great Indian philosophical poet and mystic, whose wonderful writings, full of wisdom and beauty, have now become very well known even in Italy.

The most notable feature in Tagore's case was the independent, separate manifestation, at different times, and under the influence of various stimuli, of two of the above-mentioned aspects of 'awakening', namely the transfiguration of the external world, on the one hand, and the feeling of freedom and peace, on the other—a feeling that comes after the terrible experience of the impermanence and futility of personal life separated from the universal life. It is very instructive to read what Tagore had to say about the contrast between the deep 'I' and the superficial 'I', and about the spiritual clarity of vision we get when we succeed in putting aside our limited, ordinary personality, with its narrowness and pettiness, and in silencing its jarring notes and raucous cries.

Here is the description of the first external crisis and the first stage of 'awakening' that Tagore gives us in *My Reminiscences*.

When the outward life is not in harmony with the inner life we are wounded in the deepest part of our being and this suffering manifests itself in our external consciousness in a way that is difficult to describe and which has more in common with an inarticulate lament than with a discourse made up of words with a definite meaning.

The sadness and suffering I tried to express in the series of poems entitled 'Songs of the Evening' that had their origin in the depths of my being. Just as our conscious mind when under the spell of sleep fights against a nightmare in an attempt to wake up, so the deep 'I' within each of us struggles to be released from its difficult surroundings and to emerge into the open. Those songs of mine are the story of such a struggle.

Awakening and release were close at hand, however. As he tells us a little later on:

One late afternoon I was walking up and down on the terrace outside our house. The splendour of the sunset joined with the shade of the twilight in such a way that it seemed to me to lend a special charm to the approaching evening. Even the walls of the nearby house seemed to take on a new beauty. Does this disappearance of the apparent triviality of everyday things depend on some magic effect of the evening light, I asked myself? Of course not.

Suddenly I realized that as the evening set in within my own soul, its shadows had put aside my ordinary personality. As long as this ordinary 'I' was present in the full light of day, everything I perceived was confused and hidden by that personality. Now that the everyday 'I' had been put to one side I could see the world as it really was. And there was nothing trivial about its appearance; instead it was full of beauty and joy.

After this experience I would make deliberate attempts at obliterating this 'I' and to look at the world as a simple spectator. I was always rewarded with a sense of special pleasure.

Shortly after this I gained a heightened power of vision which has lasted all my life...

One morning I was on the verandah of our house ... the sun was just rising and could be seen through the foliage of the trees in front of me. Suddenly, as I watched, it felt as if a veil had fallen from my eyes and I could see the world pervaded with a wonderful splendour, with waves of beauty and joy rising on all sides. This splendour penetrated in a moment the accumulation of sadness and depression which had been oppressing my heart and bathed it in a universal light.

It was that day that the poem entitled 'The Awakening of the Waterfall' bubbled forth and cascaded down like a true waterfall. The poem came to an end, but never again did the veil block out the joyful aspect of the Universe. Consequently no person or thing in the world ever seemed trivial or displeasing to me again.

Now let us turn to Tagore's other experience which he had shortly after the first at the age of 24, on the occasion of the death of a loved one:

The fact that there could be any gaps or interruptions in the procession of life's joys and pains was something I still had no idea of. I could see nothing beyond this life, and I had accepted this life as though it represented the whole of reality. When death came suddenly, tearing a wide gap in the apparent reality of life, I was quite perturbed and confused. Everything around me—the trees, the ground, water, the sun, the moon and the stars—were unchangingly as real as before, whereas the person who before had been so present and who, because of a thousand points of contact with my own life, mind and heart, was even more real to me than nature, had disappeared in a moment, like a dream. How contradictory this all seemed to me as I looked around! How could I reconcile what remained with what had been lost?

The terrible darkness I saw through that gap continued to preoccupy me night and day...

I tried to penetrate the mystery and to understand what remained in place of what had disappeared. A void is something man cannot believe in; what is not there is false, and what is false does not exist. Thus our attempts to find something where there is nothing to see go on incessantly.

Just as a young plant, plunged into darkness, struggles upwards in search of light, so when death suddenly casts its shadow of negation around a soul, that soul endeavours in any way it can to seek out the light of affirmation. And what pain can compare with that state in which darkness prevents a person from finding a way out of that darkness?

Yet in the midst of this intolerable pain, rays of joy escaped from within me, in a way that surprised me very much. The fact that life was not a stable, permanent thing was a painful discovery which nevertheless gave me a sense of relief. Recognizing that we are not prisoners for ever within the solid walls of ordinary life was a thought which unconsciously impressed itself on my mind, causing waves of contentment. I had no choice but to let go of what I had possessed—that was the sense of loss that made me unhappy—but when, at the same time, I considered this from the point of view of the freedom that came with it, I was overcome by a great peace. As the attraction of the world palled on me, the beauty of nature acquired a deeper significance in my eyes. Death had given me the right viewpoint from which to contemplate the world in the fullness of its beauty, and when I saw the picture of the Universe against the backdrop of death, I found it a source of ecstasy.

Now that we have spent a few moments at the sublime heights

where the light of the spirit shines, let us return to the dark valley. We will now be in a better position to understand the meaning and function of the troubled, tormenting period preceding the awakening of the soul. We now realize that it is the very fact of approaching spiritual awakening which causes a crisis within.

In view of the intensity and duration of this suffering, one cannot help wondering whether it could be avoided, at least in part. Would it not be possible to shorten the pathway to light and to make it easier to travel along? Indeed this is a possibility: whereas certain fundamental experiences are necessary and no amount of teaching or help from other people could make up for them, many of the pains, many of the useless forms of rebellion, and many of the deviations and falls can be avoided through a knowledge of the mysterious ways of the soul, and in particular through the direct help of a wise guide who has already walked that way himself and lived through its experiences.

There is another natural question which deserves a brief answer at this point: what happens to a man once his eyes have been opened to such a spiritual vision? The adventures that ensue are varied, complex and a source of wonder. After the solemn, pivotal experience in which the soul is awakened, it truly begins a new life: it is now driven by an intense benevolence, feeling the need to come into complete harmony with the universal life and obeying in all things the divine will. To begin with, when it is still under the influence of its communion with the Spirit, it believes it can do this easily and directly, by a simple act of the will, but when it sets to work it is sadly disappointed. The lower human nature resurfaces with its habits, inclinations and passions, and the man realizes he must make a pilgrimage across the uncharted waters of his lower nature in order to understand it, bring it under control and transform it. The results of this long, hard work are of great value: a new and deeper enlightenment and greater revelations are the reward of the purified soul.

Before the full and final victory, however, the soul has to undergo another test: it must pass through the 'dark night' which is a new and deeper experience of annihilation, or a crucible in which all the human elements that still go to make it up are melted together. But the darkest nights are followed by the most radiant dawns and the soul, perfect at last, enters into complete, constant and inseparable communion with the Spirit, so that—to use the bold expression employed by St John of the Cross—'it seems to be God himself and has the same characteristics as him'.

These are the main stages in the pilgrimage of the soul. It is a long road and there are few who manage to reach the end of it in this life, but knowing of such wonderful possibilities of development and conquest, and knowing that some have succeeded in appropriating these and making them realities, is a great encouragement to us all, as well as being a sober warning and a compelling incentive for us to shake off our lethargy and awaken our own souls.

PURIFICATION
OF THE SOUL

We will now begin to examine the work of purification we must undertake in order to transform the lower characteristics of our personality and bring unity to our being. As we start our examination I will take a lead from Dante Alighieri.

Everyone knows the *Divine Comedy*, but few understand its most intimate, deep significance, so although everyone studies it and admires it as the highest work of literature in our [the Italian] language, few appreciate it as a true 'holy poem', that is to say as a wonderful description and guide for the inner life and for spiritual development.

As with all writings and words which are attempting to express the inexpressible, Dante's work is allegorical and symbolic. Furthermore each symbol is complex and multi-faceted—in other words it has different meanings at different levels, so in order to discover each of these meanings we need to be in possession of the appropriate 'key'. To begin with, as we all know, the *Divine Comedy* has an historic and political meaning, and in order to understand this aspect we need the 'key' of knowledge about the political conditions in Italy, and indeed in Europe, in Dante's time, as well as knowledge about his political opinions and ideals and the activities he engaged in during his life.

The same applies to the spiritual and esoteric meaning of the symbols used by Dante. Here too we need the 'key' so that we can get beyond the threshold of appearances and forms, and discover the great truths the symbols represent. Let us attempt this for the theme we are dealing with here. The part that interests us comes at the beginning of the divine poem.

'Half way along this life's pathway' Dante finds himself, without knowing how, in a 'great, rough, wild forest'—but even here he finds something of benefit. For it is as he wanders through this forest that he reaches the foot of a hill; he then looks up and sees that it is lit by the sun.

In the form of a brief synthesis this simple allegory symbolizes everything connected with the first stages of spiritual development. The wild forest represents not only (as commentators are wont to tell us) the harsh life of ordinary man, but also, and indeed more significantly, that special state of restlessness, that acute suffering and inner darkness which usually precede the awakening of the soul. What Dante says about the forest has far more to do with this state than it does with the life of ordinary man. Indeed, the mere memory of it filled him with fear: 'So bitter is it that death could hardly be any worse.' What comes next confirms this interpretation. Indeed, his discovery of the hill lit up by the sun and the raising of his eyes clearly point to that decisive moment when the soul is awakened. Fear is then quieted in the lake of the heart and, after a short rest, he begins to climb the slopes of the hill. This clearly refers to the stage we will now be examining, the stage following this spiritual awakening.

Anyone who has had a first glimpse of the blinding light of the spirit and who has experienced, if only for a moment, the great peace and perfect bliss of those who have been awakened, will naturally feel rising up within him an intense desire to receive more of this light and to live continually in those serene regions of bliss. He will then set out to reach the dazzling heights of that light. In the enthusiasm of that first revelation he thinks he can go straight ahead without any problem. It is not long, unfortunately, before he runs into difficulties and dangers. Thus 'almost at the first upward step', Dante tells us, he comes up against a wild beast which continually blocks his path:

> And somehow it managed to stay in front of me
> In such a manner that it blocked my way so much
> That I was often forced to turn back the road I had come.
> *Translation: C.H. Sisson, Pan Classics*

This first wild beast, a 'fast running, slender leopard' symbolizes above all the attractions and temptations of the senses.

When it comes to the moment of enlightenment and joyful exaltation, man is no longer drawn by such attractions: he feels that every illusion has vanished, that every earthly bond has been severed. But this is not the case. The soul suddenly realizes, with a painful surprise, that the lower nature has only fallen asleep or become paralysed for a moment; it has not been killed. Very soon it will reawaken and rebel violently: it will stand in front of him and block his way.

But the awakened soul does not allow itself to be won over by the attractions of the senses. Instead, buoyed up by its aspirations, and lifted and encouraged by various signs and indications, as well as by helpful influences within and without, it has hope that it will triumph.

This is expressed by Dante in the following verses:

> . . . .; and this,
> With the hour it was, and the delightful season,
> Gave me reason to entertain good hope
> Of that wild animal with the brilliant skin.
> *Translation: C.H. Sisson, Pan Classics*

But very soon new and more serious obstacles present themselves to the man, producing new and stronger apprehensions:

> But not so that I found myself without fear
> When a lion appeared before me, as it did.

The lion stands for one of our worst inner enemies: spiritual pride, which can so easily take over a man when he discovers new forces and new powers within himself and catches a glimpse of the wonderful possibilities for development that lie before him. But when this happens he is developing that sense of separation which is the very antithesis of spirituality and places a great barrier across his own path.

This is not all, however. Soon the lion is joined by a she-wolf, full of 'excessive appetites'. This beast represents the very essence of separateness, of selfishness, the true source of all appetites. This is what the Orientals call the 'tomb', the thirst for living, the root of desires in the individual soul.

We should not be surprised, therefore, that it is the she-wolf who not only blocks Dante's path, as the other beasts did, (that is the path up the hill) but who also forces him back down to the place where 'the sun is silent'. It is in this dangerous state that he encounters Virgil and calls out to him in humility, asking for help.

Having gone through the painful experiences and difficulties of life, and having suffered the first bitter defeats, man loses his self-confidence and presumption; he recognizes his weakness and powerlessness, thereby attaining true humility, and is then in a state where he can be helped. Indeed, as soon as reaches this position, help comes.

This is a great, comforting law of the life of the spirit, and one which we often forget at times of doubt or discouragement, though we ought always to keep it at the forefront of our minds. Help from above is always at hand; it is never denied. We ourselves are the only obstacles that make that help seem distant. We do not know how, or want, to ask for it in the right way.

But what does this help actually consist of? And where does it come from?

Let us consider who Virgil is. We are usually told that he is the personification of reason. This explanation is not wrong, but it is inadequate: it does not provide sufficient comment to throw light on the true nature and true functions of the principle Virgil symbolizes. This principle might accurately be defined as 'spiritual discrimination', what the Indians call *viveka*, that is to say the power that human reason has—when it is not obscured or sidetracked by passions and personal feelings—to recognize the right way to go and to guide the personality along that path, giving him encouragement and keeping him safe from all dangers.

But who is behind this power? What is its inspiration? Dante gives a very deep answer to this question, an answer that calls for a lengthy commentary. The first initiative relating to this help comes from the exalted spheres of Paradise, from a generous lady who has pity on Dante. She symbolizes the mystery of the divine principle of compassion which sets in motion divine grace, the light of the soul, personified—as Dante sees it—by Lucia; and grace in turn enlists the divine wisdom, represented by Beatrice:

She said: 'Beatrice, you who are a glory of God,
Why do you not help him who loved you so greatly
That for your sake he left the common crowd?'
                    Translation: C.H. Sisson, Pan Classics

From this we learn that Dante had endeavoured to attain divine
wisdom, that is to say his soul had seriously resolved to travel
along the way of the spirit; this is why it receives help from a
higher source. But still the divine wisdom is not revealed to him
direct: in his impure, unregenerate state, still surrounded by the
impenetrable veil of matter, man is unable to directly
contemplate the supreme truth. Thus Beatrice sends Virgil to
arouse and inspire the power of awareness already present in
ordinary man. It is this power of awareness or discrimination
that must guide Dante's soul in the first part of his pilgrimage,
that long difficult path of purification and expiation across the
kingdoms of his lower nature.

But before describing the various stages of this pilgrimage,
and before indicating the methods of moral purification, we
must pause to discuss and resolve an important question that is
central to our understanding.

There are various schools of thought which state, some
openly and explicitly, others more or less by way of inference
and more in practice than in theory, that moral purification is not
necessary, and that one can enjoy great revelations without the
need for this painful, unwelcome work. This type of teaching
fits in very well with our selfishness and laziness, of course, but
the temptation to adopt such a costless view is both wrong and
dangerous. We must therefore clarify the issues here, especially
since the arguments adopted by what I will call the immoralist
schools are specious and could easily deceive untrained or
incautious minds.

Good and evil are relative, say the immoralists, for the same
action can be good in one instance and bad in another. The Spirit
is above such human distinctions and is indifferent to them: the
Spirit justifies everything. Morals, they go on to say more
explicitly, are a product of society, made up of a series of
traditional standards which ordinary men accept uncritically;
but the initiated, the superman, can be free from such limiting

standards of behaviour, for he has such important tasks to accomplish that he is allowed to do what others cannot or dare not do, using means forbidden to ordinary mortals.

But anyone who does not allow himself to be readily taken in by these fine-sounding claims will quickly realize how fundamentally ungrounded they are. In the first place these lofty claims are based on a confusion between the great moral principles of a universal nature, and the particular, imperfect application of those principles that men have made at various times and in various places throughout human history. Actual moral standards and the various codes of moral law are, of course, relative and at times contradictory, but this does not in any way detract from the validity of the great moral principles which are as fixed and certain as the laws of physics. The reason for this is that in both cases what in essence is being demonstrated is the great Law of Causality, or Karma. Thanks to this every effect is not only a necessary outcome of its cause, it is also implicit in that cause.

So a man who commits some wrong action is not punished because he is breaking a human law, nor because he has offended a personal God: he is not punished *for* his wrong action, but directly *by* his wrong action. The first and most important effect of an action is the immediate effect it has on the soul that committed it: a good action lifts a person up and ennobles him, we might almost say automatically, whereas a bad action debases the person who commits it. This is a fixed law, and the justness and necessity of such a law is obvious. No fine sounding claims or juggling with words can do anything to change this fact.

As for the other argument put forward by the immoralists, this is based on confused ideas. It may be true that the pure Spirit, or to be more exact the Absolute Being who cannot be perceived by the senses, is essentially without attributes, which means that among other things he is above good and evil. But since the first moment of cosmic manifestation the Eternal One has been two—that is to say there appeared a polarity, an infinite series of opposites, one of which is good and evil. Now which of us can claim to be pure Spirit and therefore above good and evil? Anyone will recognize the enormity of such a presumptuous claim.

We see something quite different in the unanimous teachings of both Eastern and Western schools involved in developing true, pure spirituality. They tell us that every passion and every selfish desire are like a ball of lead tied to the feet of anyone eager to climb the spiritual heights; they represent a state of slavery to lower forces and elements. They teach us that every manifestation of selfishness, however well-hidden and subtle, is by nature divisive, whereas spiritual development consists of the gradual, successive overcoming of every division and the harmonization of various conflicting elements into a higher synthesis, as a necessary preparation for conscious union with the universal Principle, and this unity becomes a reality at all levels and from all aspects.

One comes to the same conclusion if one looks at the question from the point of view of the powers that emerge naturally at the various stages of spiritual progress. There are great difficulties, dangers and responsibilities that accompany the achievement and use of those powers. We need to learn how to control and use wisely the universal forces (macrocosm) of the universe and to use them for good. But how can we presume to do this if we are still slaves to the small forces of the 'microcosm', the narrow passions of our small individual personality?

In summary, then, obedience to these moral principles, far from restricting us and slowing down our progress unnecessarily, is the only way in which we can truly become free, and any form of immorality, amorality or supermorality— however liberating it may appear—actually makes us even more enslaved because we are deceived and ignorant of our chains.

We have a great many sober warnings in this area, handed down to us by those who truly know, in that they have reached the lofty summits, the summits we look up to, full of longing and eager expectation, from the depths of the valley. From Buddha to Jesus, from the unknown wise authors of the Upanishad to the great Christian mystics, every awakened soul impresses on us that it gained victory through a purification of the personality and through the elimination of selfish attitudes.

All this shows us that anyone advancing along the way of the spirit must not only observe the great ethical principles of humanity, but must actually have a purer, stricter and more conscious concept of morality than the ordinary man. As he increases in knowledge of the existence of the laws governing the higher levels, he assumes new responsibilities and new duties. For instance, when he learns that thoughts, feelings and the intents of the will are not abstractions, but living forces, powerful realities operating at subtle levels, and that they are real creations for which we are responsible, he becomes more conscious of the use of those forces than a person with no knowledge of them. For him wrong thoughts and unworthy intentions now become faults as serious as those committed in reality.

Great truth is contained in the apt statement by the author of *The Imitation of Christ*: '*Quanto plus et melius, tanto gravius judicaverit nisi sanctis vixeris*' ('The more you know and the better your understanding, the more strictly will you be judged if you fail to live a holy life.')

I think I have now made this point clearly enough. I will only add that the question of ethics is the safest yardstick for judging various movements, schools of thought and trends, and for assessing not only the theoretical claims made, which sometimes seem quite exemplary, but also and more significantly the practical applications and actual results, always bearing in mind that great truth: 'You will know the tree by its fruit.'

This indispensable requirement of moral purification is the key to understanding the true reason for the long pilgrimage through the inner worlds which is the fabric of Dante's famous epic.

Virgil, representing reason and the power of spiritual discrimination that resides in man, recognized that the soul, in its impure state, is unable to tackle and beat the wild beasts and to make an immediate ascent to the glorious peak. Thus, when Dante calls for help, Virgil says:

> You will have to go another way than this ...
> If you want to get away from this wild place.
> *Translation: C.H. Sisson, Pan Classics*

He then suggests that Dante set off with him to cross the abyss of darkness and expiation and then to ascend the mount of purification. He also promises him that once he has done this he will be permitted, with another to guide him, to ascend to the eagerly sought spheres of Light.

At this Dante sets off resolutely, without a moment's hesitation, in the wake of his wise guide.

> As little flowers, which in a frosty night
> Droop and shut tight, when the sun shines on them
> Stretch and look up, erect upon their stalks,
> So I recovered from my failing strength,
> My heart so filled with satisfying courage
> That I began, like a man just released:
> 'How generous she was to give her assistance!
> And how courteous you were, to obey her so quickly,
> When she proffered her help and spoke the truth!
> My heart is now so set in its desire
> To come with you—and it is your words that have done this—
> That I am back again with my first intention.
> Now go, for a single will informs us both;
> You are my guide, my master and my lord.'
> So I spoke to him and, when he stirred from where he was,
> I entered upon the deep and thorny way.

These first two cantos of Dante's *Divine Comedy* represent the human soul at the start of its spiritual journey—in other words it represents each one of us. Each of us has the opportunity, if we really want it, of travelling along the path he trod, and of following him through the various stages of his pilgrimage, climbing with him to the sublime spheres of Light and Love.

THE SCIENCE OF APPLIED PURIFICATION

Purification has rightly been referred to as a science. Indeed this is a very broad subject in that it has various aspects and different areas of application, and many techniques have been developed to meet different requirements. To do this subject justice would require a lengthy work. Even a brief examination, however, will be of value in laying the proper foundation for that inner attitude needed if one is to engage in dynamic meditation.

If we have focused our inner eyes on the light, we have already begun to travel along the path that leads from slavery to freedom; in other words we have to a certain degree, consciously or otherwise, applied the science of purification. Thus, although the overview which follows contains ideas many of you will already be familiar with, it may be useful to list the various tasks involved in purification, as well as being an incentive for us to use those means which will enable us to fall into step with the unfolding of that great evolutionary plan. Purification can and must be applied at all levels in that process.

Physical Purification

The first step is purification of the physical body.

The means for this are well known: the use of water, fresh air, exposure to sunlight, a simple, healthy diet that is suited to one's constitution, the avoidance of alcohol, tobacco, drugs, etc. Observance of these basic tenets is, however, only a preliminary, serving to make performance of subsequent tasks easier and more effective. If too much emphasis is placed on physical purification, it can be a hindrance to other, more important practices.

Purification of the Emotions

It is here that we have an urgent need for a thorough application of the purification process. It might be said that the suffering, illnesses and problems that beset humanity have their origin primarily in selfish desires, and in the search for personal satisfaction. This was clearly shown by Buddha in the Four Noble Truths he formulated to show the causes of suffering and the way to be free from them.

All people are moved—we might even say possessed—by a desire of some kind, or indeed by desires of many kinds, ranging from those which have to do with sensual pleasures to the more idealistic aspirations. Desire is the common root of three causes of attachment and slavery: the attraction of material things, the confusing effect of jumbled emotions, and mental illusions. All these culminate or combine in creating a basic attachment to one's personality, in the identification with the personality which is mistaken for one's true 'I'.

Purification of the Imagination

The power of the imagination to condition both the inner life and the outward behaviour of man has always been recognized, both in the East and the West. In recent times, however, it has been regarded as increasingly important: it has been widely studied and made use of—unfortunately some have even exploited it. The basis of this power is the motive force inherent in every idea and image. An image acts like a force which stimulates mental activity and draws out emotions and feelings. It is still used as an effective form of treatment in psychotherapy; it is also beginning to be used in education, though there is a lot more that could be done in this area.

Businessmen have become very aware of the importance of the imagination, and are using it on a large scale for their own benefit by appealing to basic instincts and needs—usually the less noble ones. Indeed the art and techniques employed in publicity are far more sophisticated than those used to achieve more worthy goals. This has brought about an artificial reinforcement of the urge to seek pleasure and to possess a large number of useless objects. It is to this we can attribute the problems of the consumer society and, by way of reaction, the rebellion against it, particularly on the part of the young.

In addition to this way of using images, however, there is another more pernicious way, expressed in literature, in theatre productions and in films, which exploit man's morbid fascination for violence, horror, cruelty, and what are often perverted sexual images.

Great, indeed enormous, is the unwholesome power of suggestion aroused by this type of imagination, yet not only the public in general, but even those occupying positions of authority show an amazing lack of awareness of the harmful effects of such influences. It would not be an exaggeration to call them a collective poison, a 'psychological smog', even more harmful than the chemical variety.

This general acquiescence and apathy make possible the systematic and cynical exploitation of people's imagination for financial gain by those involved in the production and dissemination of such poison. Editors, directors and film producers have the impudence to defend and justify this type of 'entertainment' on the pretext of its claimed 'artistic value', and in the name of freedom of expression. An extreme example of this deplorable state of affairs is the film *The Exorcist* which has caused a real collective psychosis. It seems incredible that, given the morbid effect this film has on people, it should still be possible to show it!

There are a great many methods and techniques for attaining purification. Some of these are generally applicable, others are specific and relate to particular types of impurity.

The elimination of mental illusions requires a clear understanding of the dual nature of the mind:

The Analytical Mind

It is the nature of activity in the analytical mind, all the more if it is stimulated by impressions, impulses, desires and emotions, that it produce a constant and often feverish jumble of thoughts and wrong ideas, often self-centred in nature.

The Higher Synthetic Mind

This gives a correct and clear view of whatever it focuses its attention on. In addition to its capacity for true perception, it has the function of recognizing and correctly interpreting intuitions when they present themselves to the conscious mind. This is the true meaning and function of discrimination. But before it can perform this task, the area of the consciousness needs to be purified, that is to say emptied of the contents with which it is normally occupied, preventing the free use of the higher mind and intuition. This highlights the need first of all for reflective meditation, which only allows mental activities aiming at the desired knowledge. After this must come the attainment and practice of 'mental silence' which removes all obstacles from the channel linking the mind with the higher cognitive functions or intuition and enlightenment. On a broader scale, this means eliminating all impurities from the channel linking the personal 'I' to the transpersonal Self. This actually means a purification of the whole personality and a conscious withdrawal from identification with that personality through the cultivation of a 'divine indifference' to its demands, so that one can then identify with the Self.

The achievement of a certain measure of individual purification enables us to participate in the great work of group and planetary purification. This needs to be carried out at all levels. At the physical level the first task is to purify matter from the contamination produced by man's use of it for selfish purposes. The emphasis now being placed on ecology shows the growing recognition of the importance of this task. It is, however, in its initial stages, and much more needs to be done before the laying waste of nature perpetrated by man can be put right.

Another work in this connection involves what we might call the redemption of matter, its refining and transmutation. This means man's redemption of the countless beings that make up the three lower kingdoms: animal, vegetable and mineral. At the emotional level purification requires dispersion of the miasma and poisons which are the main feature of the emotions today. This can be achieved in the first instance by the elimination of emotional fog in groups.

Purification of the mental world requires the melting and destruction of old concepts and dogma, and freedom from the false, one-sided fanatical ideologies that the minds of men have come up with in the past and actively continue to produce even today (the dispersion of illusions).

PROGRAMME FOR MEDITATION ON PURIFICATION

I. Preparation
    1. Physical release.
    2. Stilling of the emotions.
    3. Mental silence.
II. Consecration
    'May I become so pure that I can embrace the world without wanting to keep hold of it.'
III. Elevation
    'On the wings of aspiration, I project my personal centre of consciousness upwards towards the Self.'
IV. Affirmation
    Assertion of one's own essential identity with the Self, 'purer than snow'.
V. Proclamation
    Proclamation by the personality that has become pervaded by the Self of its own desire for purity.
VI. Meditation on means of purification

1. Purification with water:
    Seed-thought: reflect on water as a symbol of purity, healing and universality. Visualize a waterfall in which water is cascading down from far above you, washing away all kinds of impurities and obstacles (mud, rocks, etc.).
    Think of a powerful current of life and light coming down from the transpersonal kingdom and cleansing the whole personality from all impurities.
2. Purification with fire:
    Reflect on fire as the destroyer of impurities and obstacles. Visualize:
    a) A great fire burning up a heap of rubbish.
    b) A burning landscape in which the bushes are being consumed.
       Imagine a deluge of fire coming down from the Self and purifying all aspects of the personality.

OBSTACLES TO SPIRITUAL DEVELOPMENT: FEAR

Anyone who wishes to travel along, or who has already embarked upon, the way of spiritual development must overcome three different types of obstacles: these have to do with the mind, the emotions and the will. We will deal here with the emotional obstacles, partly because they are the most frequent, and partly because intellectual obstacles, such as doubts and skepticism, are often produced or accentuated by obstacles of the emotions and the will. They are smoke-screens or pretexts which we use to hide the fears and the reluctance we are not even aware of.

The first emotional obstacle we will concentrate on is that of fear. Indeed, fear is the most frequently encountered emotion. Everyone is victim to fear to a certain extent, and it often assumes a great intensity, with harmful effects.

I think we would be justified in saying that most of the ills and sufferings afflicting humanity are a result of fear. Fear has no boundaries or limits: it is possible to be afraid of anything! Fear is like Proteus—assuming a thousand different forms. There are many ills that cause mankind to suffer, but far more in number are the misfortunes, accidents and catastrophes that never actually materialize! They produce as much, if not more, fear in people than they would if they were real, because in the fear-gripped imagination they are lived through and suffered over and over again.

But fear not only produces internal suffering; it is also a very bad counsellor and often results in actions which harm both us and others. It causes people to commit cruel acts of violence. Who can say how many struggles and wars have been encouraged by fear? Montaigne's apt motto is more serious than we might think: 'We have nothing to fear but fear itself!' For there are indeed people who reach the point of being afraid of fear itself!

If fear is a poison, then, a poison that destroys human life, life that without it would be so beautiful, joyful and creative, it is well worth our mobilizing our forces so as to become gradually freer from what we could call, using the well-chosen expression of St Paul, this 'thorn in our flesh'.

We may say there are five main forms of fear, and these form the basis of five fundamental instincts:

—the first is the instinct of self-preservation, the root of which is the fear of death.
—the second is the sexual drive, underlying which is a sense of incompleteness and the fear of loneliness.
—the third is the herd instinct, again caused by the fear an individual feels when he is separated, weak, insecure. This fear causes him to seek support and security by associating with other people.
—the fourth is the tendency to affirm oneself. This might seem the opposite extreme of fear, but careful analysis shows that at least one of its roots is the fear of not being appreciated, recognized and respected as much as we deserve (or believe we deserve!) and therefore not having the power we would like to have over others.
—the fifth is curiosity, that thirst for knowledge based on fear of the unknown or of mystery.

It ought to be recognized that these instincts or tendencies have spurred man on to useful, indeed necessary, activities, so even fear has had and can have a useful function. In contrast with this, however, it does far more harm! We might say about it what Alessandro Manzoni said about love: 'There is six hundred times more of it than is needed!'

I will only mention here the morbid forms of fear (for it would otherwise require special treatment of its own). These are anxiety, anguish, phobias and collective fears.

How can we rid ourselves of fear? There are two types of

means we can employ: psychological means and spiritual means. They operate at different levels, and it is a good idea to use both. The most effective, of course, are the second; but the first group is also useful and can be applied more readily in certain cases when one is waiting to know how to use the others.

Psychological Methods

I. Use of the Mind—Reflection—Persuasion.
    The relationships between the mind and the emotions vary according to the different stages of psychological development:
    a) The mind is a slave to the emotions.
    b) The mind is not captive to the emotions, but it is unable to modify them at all effectively.
    c) The mind has control over the emotions and is able to transform them.
II. Psychoanalysis. Exploration of the unconscious. Finding the roots of fears and bringing them into the light of the conscious mind.
III. Diversion and substitution by means of:
    a) Physical activities and sport.
    b) Channelling the imagination in other directions.
    c) The use of humour. (This can be very effective—the novelist Talbot Mundy saved his life when he recalled a comic scene which had the effect of freeing him from the paralysis caused by fear in a dangerous situation.)
    d) Cultivating positive emotions and dynamic emotions, such as courage, happiness, etc.
IV. Psychagogic Exercises.
    a) Suggestion and affirmation.
    b) Training in the imagination: going through the feared event in one's mind before it happens (e.g. an examination, a public concert, etc.), and repeating this until the fear subsides.

Spiritual Methods

Every fear is based on ignorance or error and is overcome at its roots by the light of truth, or spiritual realization.

Let us take a look at the various tendencies or instincts.

1. The self-preservation instinct, or the fear of death.
   From the spiritual point of view death does not exist. When we leave the physical body we pass on to a more beautiful, freer life.
2. and 3. Fear of loneliness and isolation.
   This is overcome:
   a) By communion with God, with Life, with one's own immortal Self.
   b) By spiritual love, friendship and group-focused living. (Paradoxically, the less one fears isolation the less one requires love and the company of others, and the more one is loved and sought after).

   Let us endeavour to understand and recognize that isolation is an illusion. At all times we are participants in the universal Life, in the presence of and in union with the Supreme Being.
4. Fear of failure, an inferiority complex, expressing itself in self-affirmation in an excessively separatist fashion.

   One gets rid of this by becoming aware of one's latent powers, and of one's true spiritual nature.
5. Fear of the unknown and of the future.
   This is overcome:
   a) By reflecting on the fact that feared ills often fail to materialize (even if other ills do!)
   b) By believing that we will not have to endure hardships beyond our ability to cope. Difficulties produce the necessary energy for overcoming them.
   c) By developing our awareness and growing in wisdom. Science has removed many superstitious fears: the more one knows, the less one has to fear, but the true form of spiritual awareness is intimate, direct intuition, enlightenment, an identification of one's being with the truth and with life which are essentially one and the same reality. Through this identification one overcomes the limitations of separate consciousness. Each new understanding about the truth expands the consciousness, imparting joy and a sense of freedom.

THE FEAR OF SUFFERING: REFLECTIONS ON PAIN

One of the greatest obstacles to our spiritual development is the fear of suffering. It brings us to a standstill when we face the inevitable difficulties and struggles that clip our wings and paralyse our most generous urges. And this is not the worst of it: it often causes us to neglect our duties, to fail in our inner and external commitments, and to fall into those sins of omission that are often just as serious as sins of commission.

It is necessary then that any man who seriously intends to travel along the way of the spirit resolves to overcome this obstacle by conquering or at least minimizing this fear of suffering within himself.

But to succeed in overcoming this basic fear which is so deeply ingrained in our psyche, we need to know the true nature, meaning and function of suffering. We need to discover the best attitude to adopt towards it. Above all we need to learn how to transform it and make it into a source of spiritual blessing.

The first lesson we must learn about pain is a lesson of knowledge and wisdom. Indeed, as long as we regard suffering as an evil, as something unfair and cruel, or even just as something incomprehensible, we will not have the key to accepting it, transforming it, and using it for good.

Many people in the past have made do with dogmatic explanations, or they have simply stopped trying to understand suffering, leaving the matter with God. For some this is still a satisfactory solution. However, most people today find themselves unable and unwilling to remain within these limits. They want to know and to understand, at least to the extent this is possible for human reason and spiritual intuition.

The great spiritual concepts provide healthy, life-giving nourishment to meet this irrepressible need of modern man, this inner hunger. They are able to give full satisfaction, and those who have lived them out in their experience will testify to the light, power and peace they can give. These concepts are widely known, so I will only refer to them insofar as they throw light on the problem of pain.

Mankind now finds itself at the ascendant stage of its evolution. After descending into the depths of materialism, it is now rising up, slowly and painfully, to the spirit, towards its eternal homeland.

Having reached the greatest extremes of separateness, self-sufficiency and selfishness, man must now gradually extend the limits of his personal identity, and enter into a harmonious communion with his fellows, with the universe and with the Supreme Being.

When man begins to feel this deep need or duty, an intense, hard fought battle begins within him: the impulse and spur towards the widening or expansion of the mind comes up against the rigid, hard barriers of separateness and self-centredness. The soul then feels like a bird shut up in a cage, or like a prisoner locked up in a narrow cell, and it struggles and suffers. This is the critical, painful stage that has to come before there can be release, or to be more exact the first release of the soul.

In this present period of spiritual awakening it is precisely this stage that many people find themselves at today. In the light of this composite concept, which shows us that suffering is necessary and inevitable in the great process of evolution, we will be in a better position to understand in a deeper way and to accept more readily the various meanings and the various specific functions of pain.

In the first place we can see that suffering is a form of expiation, linked inevitably to the law of cause and effect. But this expiation is not the only function of suffering, nor even the most important or essential function. Suffering has a direct and powerful effect in helping the soul to ascend and to become free. It purifies—its beneficial fire burns away our worldly dross. It also sculpts the soul, releasing the god that has been locked up inside a shapeless block of matter. As the saying so aptly expresses it: 'The gods are formed by hammer blows.'

Suffering can toughen and strengthen us, developing in us that remarkable and difficult power of inner resistance which is a prerequisite for spiritual development. Many people fail to realize that the spirit is awesome in its power and that we do not yet have the strength to sustain or contain it. This strength and resistance is developed primarily through pain.

Suffering also develops and brings maturity to every aspect of our being, particularly the deeper, less obvious ones. Pain forces us to take our attention away from the phantasmagoria of the external world, freeing us from our attachment to that world, and causing us to come back into ourselves. It makes us more aware, causing us to look inwards, to the spirit that is within us, to find comfort, light and guidance. In other words, it awakens us and reveals to us what we are.

Finally pain enables us to better understand and feel for others in their pain. It makes us more sensitive and ready to help other people. To quote from the fine poetry of Virgil: *'Non ignara mali, miseris succurrere disco'*, or 'Not unacquainted with ills, I am learning to help the unfortunate.'

One might object here, however, asking why it is that pain often has the opposite effect. Why does it sometimes provoke people, hardening them and causing them to do wrong and to engage in hate and violence?

That this happens, and happens all too often, cannot be denied, but it should not be regarded as a necessary, fatal effect of pain. Closer psychological examination will show us quite clearly that these effects are dependent on how we react to a painful event.

An extremely important fact deserves our close attention: the quality and consequences of suffering depend above all on the attitude we adopt towards it, our inner acceptance and our outward reaction. It was St Paul who summed up this truth in the words: 'Pain that lifts up and pain that puts down.'

Let us take a look then at the attitudes we can adopt in the face of pain and at the consequences of each of them.

If we are powerless (as very often happens), we rebel, and the result is an intensification of the pain, pain on top of pain, the creation of a vicious circle of mistakes, guilt, blindness, despair and acts of violence.

If one endures pain, one suffers less and some of the worst external consequences are avoided. But the inner effects remain: feelings of dejection, depression and emptiness. No positive lessons are learned, apart from that of enduring and putting up with the pain itself.

Acceptance of pain, on the other hand, requires the awareness we have been talking about above or an act of faith: faith in God or in the goodness of life—but to be effective this must be a living, active faith.

By consciously accepting pain one learns the various lessons it can teach us, and as one cooperates with the process one receives comfort and the suffering is shortened considerably. Indeed, something surprising often happens: once the relevant lesson has been properly learned, the cause of suffering disappears.

In all cases, then, acceptance gives a wonderful serenity, a great moral strength and a deep sense of peace.

In some cases one can achieve so full an understanding of the function and value of suffering, such a willing acceptance, that one experiences a joy which transcends the suffering itself. St Teresa, who speaks of this from personal experience in her biography, calls this fact a 'mystery'.

With the benefit of the concepts now available to us we can shed light on this apparent mystery. We know that man is not simple, but that he has a multifaceted psychological make-up. There are various levels within us, so it is possible when we are suffering at the emotional level to rejoice at a higher level. Sometimes this joy we obtain through spiritual acceptance can become so dominant that it overcomes the pain, causing it to vanish from consciousness.

This brief outline, which has been too rapid and incomplete given the enormity of the subject and its complexity, may at least help us to understand and appreciate the profound reasons for pain in human life, the necessary function it performs in our development, and the precious, saintly goals to which it can be directed.

OBSTACLES TO SPIRITUAL DEVELOPMENT: ATTACHMENTS

In our examination of the difficulties and obstacles that make it an arduous task for man to ascend to the heights of spiritual consciousness we have already mentioned fear. This may be compared to a paralysis which stops the wayfarer in his tracks, sapping his strength and robbing him of the courage to proceed.

Today we will be talking about the many forms of attachment—attachment to people, things and ways of living— which may be compared to heavy balls of lead tied to the feet of one who would like to advance, or to snares along the path, things that can sometimes even cause him to go back.

A man who 'lets life take its natural course', who allows himself to be carried along with the current, and who fails to stop and examine himself, will not realize—unless something serious happens—how in bondage and enslaved he actually is. But anyone attempting to turn his back on the usual lifestyle of those around him, leave behind the well-worn paths across the plain and begin to climb to higher levels will soon realize how many and how tenacious are the attachments that hold him prisoner.

These attachments are of two types:

1. Active attachments: instincts, passions, desires and affections connected with people and possessions that absorb one's energies and require time, attention and looking after, sidetracking a person from the high goal to which he or she is aspiring.
2. Passive attachments: these are less obvious, but no less real obstacles. They are inertia, physical and moral lethargy, the

'heaviness' that immobilizes a person, all those forms of routine behaviour, traditionalism and habit which make up the ruts from which people are loath to escape.

From the spiritual point of view, that is to say from the point of view of true value, every strong, exclusive attachment and every instance of moral lethargy is based on false understanding and a distorted vision. They reveal a lack of perspective, an incomplete, distorted view of reality, and a violation of the law of harmony and of the great hierarchical principle which requires the Deity, the Reality, the Source of Good and the Being of Supreme Worth, to have the first place in our minds and hearts, to be the highest goal to which our will is addressed.

To look at it another way we might say that every attachment is an error, at variance with the law of life, because it is a vain, desperate attempt at laying hold of part of that life and making it fixed or rigid in isolation from the rest of life, whereas in fact life is a unified whole, an immense current in a continual state of flow, and a dynamic phenomenon which is being continually transformed. In light of this we can say that what at one moment was a help, a stimulus or a condition favouring expansion of the consciousness may later become an obstacle, a tie or a hindrance.

This, for instance, is at the heart of maternal love when a mother lacks the wisdom to allow a transformation of the quality and the expression of her love in step with the development of her children's personalities.

An important fact emerges from this: attachments are obstacles to spiritual realization not only when they are unworthy or 'bad' so to speak, but even when they are thought of as 'good'. Indeed the latter are often the most insidious and tenacious, precisely because they are apparently justified.

It can be a great help to see this clearly and to be released from illusions and blindness—in fact it is a necessary first step. In itself, however, it is insufficient, marking only the start of the battle and hard work that needs to be done to achieve inner release.

Even when this is clearly perceived and one wishes to be freed from an attachment, however, the attachment can put up an obstinate resistance in us. This has been very well expressed by

Rabindranath Tagore in one of the short poems in his *Gitanjali*:

The chains have a tenacious grip, but it produces pain in my heart when
    I try to break them.
I want only freedom, but hoping for it makes me feel ashamed.
I am sure that in You priceless riches are to be found,
that You are my best friend, but I lack the courage
to throw away the tinsel that decorates my room.
It is as though I were covered with a sheet of ashes and death,
I detest it, yet hold it tight to my breast.
Many are my debts, great are the things I lack, secret
and oppressive is my shame; but when I venture to ask
for what would be best for me, I tremble with fear that my prayer will
    be answered.

Let us now take a look at the methods for bringing about detachment.

The Method of Sudden Separation

Often life does this to us in various ways, against our will, removing people and things to which we are attached. This is the fastest and most radical method, but it is also extremely painful and can produce serious reactions. After a period of emotional upheaval, however, during which little helps to ease the pain, a person usually comes out of it with a greater maturity and strength.

The Method of Transmutation

This method transforms our attachments by sublimating the emotional energies that produce them, and by widening and replacing the objects to which they are directed. It is the most gradual and harmonious method, and in the end it achieves the same result. The ease with which it is accomplished depends on the individual make-up, which can differ greatly in this area. In some people emotional energies are plastic and readily mouldable, indeed they are sometimes too fluid. In other people they are, to use a physical metaphor, dense, viscous and tenacious, which makes it very hard work to mould and transform them.

Let us see how this method can be applied to the typical, central attachment—what we call love.

Many different things are meant by love: sexual or instinctive love, the various kinds of passionate, sentimental love, mystical love and spiritual love. This subject needs to be dealt with in depth, but I will restrict myself to a few remarks in this instance. Further comments are contained in my work 'Transmutation and Sublimation of the Emotional and Sexual Energies'.[1]

The most important and most frequently presented form of sublimation is when passionate love becomes spiritual love. Let us be clear about the differences between the two.

Passionate love is possessive, demanding, exclusive, selfish and jealous. Spiritual love is generous and open-handed. A person who loves spiritually remains free and gives freedom to others.

The characteristics of spiritual love are as follows:

a) To love the Deity, the Supreme Being, above any other thing or creature. Because He is the Ultimate Good He deserves, and rightly asks for, the first place. This is the true meaning of the symbolic expression which has been the object of wrong interpretations: 'God is a jealous God.'

Even love for the Deity, or whatever other term one might prefer to refer to the Universal Being or Essence (the Supreme Value, the Cosmic Mind, the Supreme Reality) can assume different levels of attainment or purity. Thus to begin with people tend to love God for the inner delights this gives them, for the grace they receive, and for the benefits they hope to receive from Him. Then, after successive, painful purification processes we succeed in loving Him in an increasingly disinterested way, a nobler, more generous way. These stages in the relationship of love for God have been very well described, with perceptive psychological analysis, by St Teresa and St John of the Cross in their famous works, and have also been expressed succinctly in another fine short poem by Rabindranath Tagore:

Many are my desires and pitiful my cry, but You have always saved me
with hard refusals; this great mercy has become the fabric of my life.

[1] Included as Chapter 20 of this book.

Day by day You make me worthy of those great, simple gifts which you bestow unbidden—this sky, the light, this body and the life of the mind—and you keep me distant from the danger of desiring too much.

Sometimes I am overcome with a lazy slowness; sometimes I awake and hasten in search of the goal; but You cruelly hide Yourself from my sight.

Day by day, with continual refusals, You make me worthy of being completely acceptable to You, and You save me from the dangers of too weak and uncertain a love.

b) To love everything and everyone in God. That is to say with reference to God, as a manifestation of God, as souls proceeding—as we ourselves are—along the path back to God.

c) Spiritual love differs depending on its object. Spiritual love is not a cold, abstract, indifferent thing; it is alive, full of warmth, and assumes different specific qualities depending on the varying nature of the beings to which it is directed, and on the relationships of affection that we have with them.

The enlargement of the sphere of our relationships of affection and, as a result, the reduction of a narrow, exclusive attachment to a single relationship or object, is greatly helped by the new characteristics life is taking on today. The broadening and strengthening of human relationships produced by rapid, easy means of communication and the new forms of communal life today encourage various forms of friendship and cooperation which are acting in a timely fashion to correct the tendency towards exclusivism and over-attachment.

The same can be said about the replacement of objects on which the force of people's emotional energies are concentrated, the sentimental treasures which are the painful 'embarrassment of riches' for many souls, particularly for women. The enormous, growing number of varied social activities provides ample opportunity for the healthy expression of feelings for which life has not been able to give direct, personal satisfaction.

Then there is the replacement of human objects with spiritual ones, referred to by R.W. Emerson in his brief but telling remark: 'When the demi-gods leave, the Gods arrive.'

The Method of Defusing the Intensity of Life and the Method of Humour

Many people become over-attached because they tend to take life, situations and other people too seriously. They see everything in tragic terms. To be free of this they should cultivate a more detached, calm and impersonal attitude.

This is a matter of learning to observe the human comedy from a distant vantage point, not becoming too emotionally involved, regarding life in the world as a sort of play in which each person is playing his own part. The part is to be played as best one can, but without identifying oneself completely with the character one is portraying.

One of the most profound and illuminating of the Indian concepts is that of the 'cosmic dance' of Siva, one of the aspects of the Supreme Being. It has been briefly described as follows:

> The essential meaning of the dance of Siva is threefold: first it is the image of his rhythmic game as part of the whole movement of the Cosmos; secondly the purpose of this dance is to free the countless human souls from the slavery of illusion; and thirdly the place where this dance is performed, the Centre of the Universe, is within our hearts.

The same idea has been beautifully expressed by Hermann Keyserling in a chapter actually entitled 'Divine Comedy' in his *Meditations Sud-Americaines*.

When we regard and live life in this more dignified, open fashion we realize that it has its serious, difficult, painful side, but that it also has light-hearted, bright and joyful as well as comical and amusing aspects. The latter are the proper and necessary counterbalance to the former.

The art of living consists of alternating between these different elements and attitudes at the right times, and to do so is far more under our control than we might imagine. Humour is a valuable weapon for this, and in its better, wide-ranging manifestations (very different from the superficially comic or vulgar forms), it is full of feeling. We may say that humour involves understanding, sympathy, compassion, and at the same time detachment.

The Method of Inner Independence or Spiritual Autonomy

Many attachments are based on a sense of dependence on others, that is to say on the need—or the claimed need—of support and help. Many people think or fear that they are incapable of managing themselves and that they would be lost if they did not look and cling to others for support.

In order to become free from such attachments, which are nothing more than forms of limitation and slavery, one needs to have confidence in the powerful latent energies of the human spirit. One must appeal to the true being within, the higher, spiritual 'I'. This part of us is in communion with the Supreme Spiritual Reality, and it is here that we are able to find all the light, strength and help we need.

In conclusion we should point out that becoming free from attachments does not mean some negative activity; it does not involve any form of mutilation or loss.

As one Oriental teacher put it, 'As you learn to become more and more detached, you discover that you are then able to love those who are dear to you in a deeper, more constructive way.'

Being detached means that one has achieved the highest form of freedom, indeed the only true freedom, 'the liberty of the sons of God'.

EMOTIONAL AND MENTAL OBSTACLES: AGGRESSION AND CRITICISM

We will now examine another of the greatest obstacles standing in the way of spiritual development: the tendency towards personal self-affirmation, and the aggressive ways in which this manifests itself. It can take various forms: some impulsive in nature, others of a more calculated type. We will take them together because it is often the case that emotional elements and mental elements coincide within us in a complex fashion.

Among the manifestations of aggression we might mention antagonism in its various forms: anger, rage, resentment, condemnation, reproach and criticism.

Anger or rage is the reaction brought about by any obstacle or threat to our existence or to our sense of self-affirmation in a given area. The fact that it is a 'natural' reaction does not of course mean that it is an appropriate one, nor even that it serves any useful purpose for those selfish goals of self-affirmation that it seeks to promote. Quite often in fact it only serves to cause damage: anger is the worst of counsellors and if it is not brought under control it will result in violence and all manner of excesses. Anger, like the Australian boomerang, returns to the one who launched it. This is so obvious it hardly needs stating, but unfortunately we often forget the most obvious, basic things in life!

Another harmful effect of anger is that it plays a decisive role in the production of poisons in our system. These poisons are also produced by resentment, which we might regard as a chronic irritation.

I think it appropriate, however, that I focus our attention on one aspect of the fighting instinct which, because it is so subtle and insidious, because it is so widespread, and because of its serious harmful effects, deserves special attention. That is the area of criticism—the tendency (indeed I might even call it a universal mania) to blame and belittle our fellow human beings at every opportunity.

Let us try to understand why this tendency is so widespread and so strong, why it is that people who in other respects have good moral qualities devote themselves with a passion, I would even say with enthusiasm, to criticizing others, and in doing so experience a real pleasure throughout their being—as shown by the inflection of their voice, the animation of their gestures and the twinkle in their eye.

A brief psychological analysis will readily give us the reason for this state of affairs. Indeed, we will see that many of man's basic tendencies find a considerable amount of satisfaction in the exercise of criticism. In the first place criticism satisfies our self-affirmation instinct: discovering and pointing out the shortcomings and weaknesses of others gives us a pleasurable sense of superiority, as well as pleasantly bolstering our pride and arrogance. In the second place it provides an immediate outlet for our aggressive energies, and while giving us all the satisfaction of an easily won victory free from any danger (because the enemy is not present), it seems no more than a harmless pursuit—often, in fact we feel it our duty to criticise— so it is not subject to any check or inner censure, and our moral conscience is taken in.

We might add that for many people who have to suffer domination by others without being expected to fight back, or who have to put up with situations and circumstances they find disagreeable but can do nothing to change, criticism is the only way in which they can give full vent to their hostility and to their repressed resentment. It is the only safety valve they have for reducing their inner tension. This fact also helps to explain why criticism has become more highly developed in women than in men. (This finding is not my own.) Men have other, worse, ways of expressing their fighting instincts and make frequent use of them.

Finally, and curious as it may seem, criticism serves to satisfy the desire for communion with others, though it is only partially successful and destructive in its effect.

This apparent paradox should not surprise us too much, indeed what can most readily unite and reconcile people and groups of human beings is having a real or assumed enemy in common. We should not be surprised therefore that men are all too eager for the pleasurable fellowship and agreement that comes from sharing their criticisms of others! This is not true fellowship or union, however; it is merely a temporary, superficial coming together, because it is based on separateness and not on unity. For this reason such negative bonds are usually severed without great difficulty. In the area of criticism, then, it is not unusual for Tom and Dick to speak ill of Harry, and then for Tom and Harry to speak critically about Dick—nor will this prevent Dick and Harry getting together to talk about Tom behind his back!

The mental attitude of the systematic critic, with all his ridiculous arrogance, is well portrayed in a story from England. Two elderly Scotsmen are having an enjoyable time running through the follies of their mutual acquaintances. When they have completed this demanding task, one of them makes the concluding remark, 'Well, my friend, you could say that all men are mad, apart from you and I ... but I'm not sure whether there might not even be a trace of madness in you!'

One particular form of criticism is ridicule or mockery. All innovators and pioneers have been laughed at and regarded as cranks.

It is important to note that there is a fundamental difference, often not appreciated, between ridicule and humour. The first is antagonistic, lacking in understanding and often cruel, whereas the second is characterized by indulgence, kindness and understanding. Humour consists of seeing human weaknesses from above, in their right perspective. Indeed the true humorist is smiling primarily at himself.

How can we escape the inclination to criticise? There are a number of effective methods.

Transformation and Sublimation

The critical urge can be transformed into wise, finely tuned discrimination. This is not only a legitimate process, it is also a necessary one. Some people think that not criticizing means not even noticing the shortcomings of others or choosing to shut one's eyes to them. But we must not do this, and we should certainly not give in passively to the unjust demands people make on us.

What distinguishes criticism from true discrimination is the attitude within us when we become aware of the failings of others. Whereas the critic—consciously or unconsciously—feels complacent, the person with discrimination will feel the pain of those failings. He will not seek to highlight or broadcast them, but instead will feel moved to sympathy and to helping the people concerned. Far from feeling smug about his own superiority, he would rather that the other person be the same or better than him, so he prays for the other person to be changed. If on occasions, out of love for the truth, in order to be true to his own principles, or for the good of others, a person with spiritual discrimination feels obliged to state his disagreement openly, warn people or alert them to the need for caution, or to defend a cause, institution or person that is being unjustly attacked, he will do so with courage and firmness, but his involvement will always be calm and impersonal.

Development of the Opposite Characteristics

These characteristics may be divided into two groups. The first consists of goodness, gentleness, generosity and love.

It should be noted that we are not speaking here of that passive, sentimental pseudo-goodness, but of a true spiritual goodness which is powerful, dynamic and radiant. It is the goodness of someone like St Francis of Assisi who was able to tame the wolf of Gubbio and many other 'human wolves', the goodness of his namesake St Francis of Sales whose imperturbable restraint and gentleness brought about many conversions. The power of gentleness is also contained in a perceptive Tuscan proverb: 'You can catch more flies with one drop of honey than with a hundred barrels of gall!' This is all so obvious, it seems unnecessary to state it. Here again it comes down to 'merely' putting it into practice!

The other group of characteristics is made up of appreciation, praise, gratitude and a constant emphasis on the good qualities of things, people and circumstances. This emphasis is usually referred to as optimism, but it is not a blind, superficial optimism. It is possible to see quite clearly all aspects of life, including the darker, negative ones, but then to consciously direct one's attention, interest and appreciation towards the positive aspects.

According to an aphorism of Alphonse Karr: 'The pessimist sees the thorn behind the rose; the optimist sees the rose on top of the thorn.' Or to use another image: 'One man sees a half-filled glass as half empty, another sees it as half full.'

This attitude has been expressed in poetry by Vittoria Aganoor Pompilj in the following dialogue between St Francis and one of the brothers:

'Saint Francis, I'm frightened that I can hear snakes hissing in the bushes.'
'I hear nothing but the rustling of the pine-trees and the song of the birds.'
'Saint Francis, a terrible stench is coming from this overgrown path and from the pond.'
'I smell thyme and broom, I have joy and health for my drink.'

'Saint Francis, we are sinking, the evening is coming on and we are far from our cells.'
'Lift up your eyes from the mud, man, and you will see the stars blossoming in the heavenly gardens.'

This benevolent appreciation of the goodness and light in every thing and every being makes life easier and more joyful. It gives us the light and strength to free ourselves from that attitude of discontent, ill humour and resentment, and from that rebellion against circumstances, life and God Himself which is the most bitter, tormenting, blind and we might even say petty aspect of all our pains and hardships.

We dare to criticize God and accuse Him—whether consciously or unconsciously—of insensitivity, hardness and cruelty towards us and towards others, without realizing how gross and ridiculous is the implicit arrogance of such reactions, and without remembering how often we ourselves, under more favourable circumstances, have recognized the spiritually beneficial function of pain.

We need to learn how to see God at work even when this means hardship and adversity. Victor Hugo wrote a fine apologue in this connection:

. . . the horse must be Manichaean.

Arimane does him ill, Ormuz does him good;
Every day he feels the crack of the whip on his back,
he hears the terrible, invisible master behind him,
that unknown demon who deals him blow upon blow.
In the evening he sees a kind being, good and gentle,
who gives him food and water,
and lays fresh straw in his dark stable;
who seeks to soothe away the pain with ointment
and to replace the labours of the day with rest.
Someone, alas, pursues him, but someone loves him.
And the horse says, 'There are two of them': but it is the same
    person.

Many people testify that appreciation, praise and gratitude have what might be regarded as a magical power over circumstances themselves: they open pathways, remove obstacles and attract good. One thing we can be certain of is the remarkable inner transformation they produce. They create in us a harmony, a serenity and a profound peace 'that nothing can disturb, in which the soul grows like the sacred flower on the tranquil waters'.

PART THREE

SPIRITUALITY IN
EVERYDAY LIFE

19

TWENTIETH-CENTURY SPIRITUALITY

The title of this study may seem something of a paradox. Indeed I can imagine the pessimists, those who denigrate modern life, and the prophets of decadence, such as Spengler, considering this title sadly ironic. We have to recognize, too, that the most blatantly obvious aspects of the first half of this century seem to justify them in their views.[1] The external landscape has characteristics that are clearly materialist and often anti-spiritual.

At the start of the century there was a rapid development of technology, a growing appreciation of and ever more determined quest for material well-being, the worship of money and its growing prestige and power, and the view that success in life was an indication of one's individual worth.

This thirst for gain and power, individual and collective ambition, dreams of material strength, rivalry, lack of understanding and mutual fear between nations culminated in the terrible world wars. After these came the turbulent post-war years: the spread of violence, unrestrained economic greed, sexual licence, the thirst for pleasure, the squandering of easily gained money, and harsh conflicts both within and between nations.

In the area of culture we see a lack of concern for the traditional values and ideals, a growing preoccupation with science, the focus of people's attention being directed almost exclusively at the external world, and philosophies character-ized—consciously or unconsciously—by materialistic, pos-

[1]The original text of this article was written in 1935; it was then republished in 1962. This chapter is based on the reprinted version. [Compiler's note.]

itivist and realist elements. And as regards individual and social life we see the exaggerated importance of sport, the cult of the physical body and of its power and skills. A boxer can now command hundreds of thousands of pounds for one fight and a football match can attract more than one hundred spectators!

Even popular uprisings calling for national and social reform, though often inspired by lofty ideals, have been marked by demonstrations of physical force: they have been aggressive and violent, they have been mass movements, they have reaffirmed what are nothing more than earthly values, such as attachment to land and race, and they have placed political, economic and organizational problems at the centre of the stage.

This brief summary will demonstrate that I have no illusions and no idealized view of the present century. But it is not enough to list such phenomena, and it helps even less to criticize and deplore them.

Every student and observer of life has a duty to understand what he sees, and in order to understand phenomena he must not stop at the level of their outward manifestation or consider them in isolation—and more importantly he should not take up an ill-considered position either for or against them. One needs to get rid of prejudices and to put aside one's normal reactions and personal preferences.

If we attempt this for the twentieth century it takes on a very different complexion: behind its pained, twisted features we glimpse a new soul, and we see a new light shining in its eyes.

First of all we need to see the twentieth century in the context of the nineteenth century from which it followed on. We will remember that, particularly during the last few decades of the 1800s, it was far from spiritual beneath the humanist veneer and behind the idealism to which it gave verbal assent. The life of society was dominated by a bourgeois outlook. Philosophically it was materialist, positivist or skeptic. In terms of literature it was realist, sensual, romantic and decadent. In general culture was intellectual, and intellectualism is not spiritual, indeed it is one of the most insidious hindrances to spirituality. In other words the nineteenth century had lost contact with the forces of life, both natural and spiritual, and had found its way into a blind alley.

The 'revolt of the earthly forces' then, as Keyserling aptly describes them, the reawakening of instinctive, primitive, irrational forces, which were nevertheless wholesome and life-giving, came as a reaction, a return to our origins—and this was necessary if man was to escape from the cul-de-sac he found himself in, and if civilization was to be rescued from a dangerous decadence and decay.

But this is an inadequate justification for assessing the contribution of the twentieth century. We need to ask ourselves some searching questions about it. Are there any clear signs of spirituality alongside the phenomena we have already listed? Is it possible to spiritualize the earthly forces that have been unleashed? And how?

Before answering these questions, however, we need to make sure we know what we mean by the word 'spirit'. As the Chinese sages of old rightly said, and as the new science of semantics is reaffirming, before any serious study, any exchange of ideas and any productive discussion, there must first be an agreement about the terminology to be used, i.e. we must state what we mean when we use certain words. How often we set out solemnly, lance poised, to tilt at windmills! And how often we unconsciously create a caricature, an unreal image of an adversary, a theory or an idea, and then claim a victory which is as easily won as it is futile!

If there is any word that lends itself readily to misunderstanding and confusion, it is this word 'spirit'. And this is not surprising; if we misunderstand and misuse other words, referring to more definite, more generally accessible facts and concepts, how much easier it will be for such mistakes to arise—as has and continues to happen—about a word that refers to so lofty a reality, so difficult a grasp and to experience, and almost impossible to define in rational terms. One only realizes how difficult this is when one comes to attempt an explanation or definition. Let us look first at what 'spirit' is not.

There is often confusion between spirit and intelligence, a confusion which is not helped by the ambiguity of the words *esprit* in French and *Geist* in German, which can be used to refer to these very different realities. In other circumstances the word spirit is used in the sense of psyche or the psychological side of our make-up. It is used, for instance, in the expression 'the spirit of the times', even when talking about times that are not at all spiritual!

In our attempt to accurately define the meaning of the word 'spirit', we need to make a clear distinction between what is in essence its ultimate reality, and what are its various manifestations, i.e. the characteristics by which it is revealed to us, the ways in which we perceive it and recognize it in ourselves, in others, in nature and in history.

In itself the Spirit is the Supreme Reality when looked at in transcendent terms. In other words it is absolute, free from any limitations and concrete definition. The Spirit, then, transcends every restriction of time and space, every material limitation. The Spirit is essentially eternal, infinite, free and universal. This supreme, absolute Reality cannot be perceived with the intellect because it transcends the human mind; it can, however, be postulated in rational terms, cultivated intuitively, and experienced mystically to a degree.

In light of the above let us now consider those manifestations of the Spirit that are more accessible to us and concern us more directly.

The Spirit is that element of transcendence, superiority, permanence, power, liberty, inner reality, creativity, harmony and synthesis in every manifestation, both individual and social. In man, therefore, the term 'spiritual' (to varying degrees) can be attributed to everything that compels him to transcend his selfish exclusivism, his fears, his inertia and his love of pleasure, everything that urges him to discipline, control and direct those untamed forces, instincts and emotions that seethe within him, everything that induces him to recognize a greater, superior reality, social or ideal in nature, and to become one with it, extending the limits of his own personality.

In this sense the following are—to an extent—spiritual manifestations:

— *courage*, in that it overcomes the self-preservation instinct;
— *love* and *devotion* to another human being, to one's family, country or to humanity in general, in that it overcomes selfishness;
— *the sense of responsibility*;

— *the sense of cooperation, social conscience, solidarity*;

— *disinterest*, and even more *devotion* and *sacrifice*;

— *the will* in its true sense, as the principle and power of self-control, choice, discipline and synthesis;

— *understanding*, i.e. the widening of our sphere of awareness, sympathetic identification with others, with other manifestations of the universal life—and above all an understanding of this universal life, a recognition of its meaning and purpose, recognition of an intelligent, wise and loving Will and Power from which the universe originates, by which its evolution is directed, and which is guiding it towards a glorious goal.

Not all these manifestations of the spirit have the same value, in other words, they are relative to the individual or group in which they are revealed. Thus what may represent transcendence, the overcoming of weaknesses or liberation for one individual or for one group of people, may only be a limitation, a barrier and a passive experience for another individual or group, so that it has nothing more than an anti-spiritual effect. It is not possible here to pin labels on people or to make absolute, unchanging judgements. We are dealing with an aspect of life which is characterized by marked differences, operating in time and space, expressing in a material world, and thus in an area where there are relationships, perspectives, scales of values, an area defined by hierarchy and development.

Thus the physical courage with which one faces dangers is a genuine expression of spirituality, but it is primitive and elementary when compared with moral courage. Love for one's family, which can take a man out of his selfish isolation, causing him to accept duties and responsibilities, is a valid form of spirituality, but it is somewhat limited when compared with a love, solidarity and devotion directed at a whole nation, with its millions of individuals, at a community, or even at the whole of humanity.

To avoid misunderstanding, however, it should be pointed out here that these ever wider spheres of spiritual life do not cancel or exclude the preceding ones, indeed they assume them. It is only by progressive stages that man is able to recognize and realize the various forms of spirituality.

Now that we have defined the main areas of spirituality, and allowing for the fact that we could only give a brief indication, we will now go on to consider whether any of these have been exercised in the twentieth century.

From this broader, more profound perspective, the twentieth century is seen in a very different light. We become aware that the release of the earthly forces, which occurred in the two world wars and in the various revolutions that have taken place since, gave rise to countless acts of valour and courage, both individual and collective, self-sacrifice, solidarity and altruism.

It is observed that for millions of primitive individuals physical courage, the disdain of danger, resistance to pain, the acceptance of hardships, solidarity and devotion have been the forms of spirituality most appropriate for the levels to which they could be expected to rise.

It is unfair—and reveals a lack of understanding, indeed a lack of spirituality—for others to claim forms and types of spirituality for which they lack the necessary maturity, and for which they even lack the necessary means and psycho-physical organs of expression.

Thus for millions of individuals those experiences, those basic acts, brought about a considerable acceleration of the development of their personality. One thinks of a peasant in 1914, locked up within narrow confines of his monotonous, uneventful life that was more of a vegetable existence than a human one, limited to the satisfaction of very few basic instincts and interests, the only highlights of his life being the close ties with the family. One then imagines this same peasant caught up and overwhelmed by the turmoil of war, trained in the various activities of military life, thrown together with fellow soldiers and officers, enemies and allies, exposed to bombings, enduring the hardships of the trenches, enjoying victories, suffering defeats, sworn to discipline and self-control, sick and wounded, in contact with a thousand different faces of life ... What a difference from the life he was used to! What an expansion of his experience of life, and what an expansion of his mind!

Let us move on to consider the mechanical and technical developments of our civilization. As we have already mentioned, it is outwardly materialistic. But we need first of all to consider the treasures of intelligence, tenacity and will-power, as well as the hardships, risks, and sacrifices endured by man in order to achieve his present dominion over matter. Then there is the raising of the general standard of living. Finally there are the great benefits to be had from this dominion over matter: the freeing of man from the most irksome and demeaning of tasks, the reduction in working hours, and the opportunity this provides to have time and energy for cultural, artistic and spiritual activities.

Another feature of the twentieth century which appears to be anti-spiritual, but which contains vital seeds and has actually already produced spiritual fruit, is the way the collective, social aspect of life is gaining ground over the individual aspect.

Here too appearances show us the worst side. The mass of humanity is primitive; their predominance seems to threaten the higher spiritual values. But we need dispel a great mistake in our thinking at this point: the amorphous mass of the crowd is one thing, but the organized, collective initiatives and the new forms of social life that are developing within the various national bodies are another. They are not only different, they are opposites.

The crowd is atomistic, indifferent, regressive and atavistic: the individual is lost or diminished in a crowd. It may give the illusion of liberty, but it is actually ruled over by demagogues. The organized collective is organic, finding its expression in ever broader-based, hierarchical groups, so the individuals in it are at one and the same time being directed and giving direction to others. They are on both the giving and receiving end of orders: they learn to obey and to command. They have clear-cut, effectively formulated duties, responsibilities and powers.

There are, however, mixed aspects to this new social life. There are many undeveloped, undistinguished individuals who bring to these new social groups the same old passive attitudes they had under the old system. But this is inevitable: they would have been like this in any case.

We need to openly recognize the danger of the excessive predominance of the collective, social element over the individual element. There must be a balance between the two, or better still what Keyserling calls a 'creative tension'.

Returning to the problem of the human masses, it is important that people be transferred as quickly and effectively as possible from the crowd, or 'flock', to the group. This is essentially a problem or task of individual and social education, a responsibility and clear duty of the more developed, spiritually aware groups.

This raises us to a higher, more distinguished level of spiritual life. And here we have to face the problem of the role and function of the élite, the 'spiritual aristocracy'. The tasks are great and pressing for all that. It is a matter of containing, controlling and disciplining the earthly forces so that they do not erupt into waves of destruction, of elevating and channelling people's elementary spirituality, that barely conscious spirituality of the masses, mixed with earthly concepts, and encouraging them to express it in ever more conscious, higher, purer, and more constructive ways. It is also a matter of creating a new form of art for the people, but not 'popular' art in the bad sense of the word.

These may seem very demanding tasks to perform, but we should remember how great the moulding, creative power of the spirit is. Moreover the crowds, because of their passivity, are very receptive and ready to be moulded. Carlyle and others have shown how heroes and geniuses have woven themselves into the fabric of a whole nation, culture or century, transforming them by their influence.

The new means of communication now available to us make it even easier and faster for us to exert such influence, and more extensively at that. The scarcity of these higher beings is compensated most remarkably by the single-minded, organized collaboration of groups of men of good will who are spiritually aware and active.

Moreover, even though it is true that heroes, sages and geniuses cannot be mass-produced, if we seek out those who are highly gifted and provide them with an appropriate form of education, it will be possible—using educational methods based on the new integrated psychosynthetic techniques—to greatly encourage the blossoming of the considerable latent potential of the superconscious and the spiritual Self.

It is essential then that such agreements and areas of joint activity be established among spiritual workers as quickly and as effectively as possible. But before speaking about the training of this elite, it would be helpful to consider other characteristics of twentieth century spirituality.

At the very beginning of this century there arose, in every aspect of our culture, a series of lively movements reacting against the materialist and positivist tendencies that held sway in the 1800s. In the biological sciences the mechanistic interpretation of Darwinian evolution was ousted by broader concepts. Great changes were taking place in medicine: the purely anatomical and pathological approach, which placed such great emphasis on external pathogenic agents (e.g. microbes) and on local lesions was giving way to a dynamic understanding of life as a whole, an approach which took account of the individual's overall make-up and of the effect of psychological and spiritual forces on the body.

The effect, indeed at times the supreme power, of mental and spiritual energies was studied and proven indisputably by the new science of parapsychology. Serious, rigorously carried out studies demonstrated the existence of para-normal and super-normal phenomena and powers. According to such eminent scientists as the physiologist Richet, the physicists Lodge, Barrett and several others, the survival of the individual psyche after death of the body was demonstrated with a high degree of probability.

However, the most triumphant and decisive offensive of the scientific front was perhaps in physics, which literally caused the 'matter' of the materialists to vanish before their astonished eyes—the matter to which they had attributed certain characteristics of mass, density and inertia.

Not only did the physicists resolve matter into energy, they even showed that all energy-related phenomena obey complex, well-defined mathematical formulae. This meant—and they freely confessed as much—that the basis of all those varied phenomena was nothing more than a thought process, since a mathematical formula is essentially thought, reason and spirit. This demonstrated the truth of the brilliant intuition of ancient philosophy when it stated: 'God performs in geometry.'

In the field of philosophy the metaphysics of the positivists and the rationalists was effectively countered by the various idealistic movements, by the spiritualist revivals and by the strong anti-intellectualist currents, whose attitude was most typical of the new generation.

One discipline in particular, which stands between the natural sciences and philosophy, i.e. psychology, has undergone a rapid and eventful development during this century. Having been subject initially to positivism, it is now rapidly freeing itself from such ties, and is heading in a broader, more spiritual direction.

In the area more specifically equated with spiritual and religious matters, the twentieth century has taken great strides forward in the development of its thinking. We can point out three main trends here and these are becoming more widespread and gaining strength.

1. The move towards expansion, universality and synthesis. Anti-intellectualism has affirmed itself here too in the form of anti-dogmatism and anti-formalism. There is now a growing recognition of the relative nature of every doctrinal formula and every formal systematization, as people's understanding of the indicative, symbolic nature of such teaching increases. Thus the former doctrines are not denied or suppressed, but put in their proper perspective.

A great spurt in this direction has been the increased knowledge, in depth or through general exposure, of the spiritual ideas of other peoples, particularly those of eastern philosophies, and most significantly those from India. One might say that a real cultural and spiritual synthesis has taken place between East and West, the extent and consequences of which may be very far-reaching: they may result in the unification of humanity, not so much formally and externally, but an essential, inner unification.

2. The second trend is that of inner awareness or direct spiritual experience. This manifests itself in the growing interest in mysticism and in the methods of inner discipline and conquest: concentration, meditation, yoga, etc.

3. The third trend is that of bringing spirituality into one's everyday life, be it at an individual level or at a more general level.

There are another two facts of fundamental importance:

1. People are moving towards an integrated form of spirituality which includes the *whole* man, without any water-tight compartments, any opposition between heart and mind, between body and soul, between inner life and the outward life—a spirituality which extends to the social life (we can call this spirituality psychosynthesis);

2. We are witnessing a growing number of human beings involved in the rapid increase of endeavour and research in the field of spiritual awakening. In most cases this may not be immediately apparent because we are dealing with inner matters that most people prefer to keep to themselves. But I can quote an important witness to this—the testimony of the psychologist and psychiatrist C.G. Jung who, in one of his books with the significant title *Modern Man in Search of a Soul*, makes the following statement:

> Over the last 30 years people have come to consult me from all corners of the earth. I have treated many hundreds of sick people ... Among those in the second half of their lives, that is to say those who were over 35 years old, there has not been one whose problem was not, in the final analysis, the question of finding a religious viewpoint on life.

We might well say that mankind as a whole is not only in the middle of an economic, political and social crisis, it is also in a profound spiritual turmoil, even though many are not willing to recognize this consciously. Indeed, many sick, troubled people are unaware of the deep cause of their illness until they are helped to understand it.

This inner turmoil or striving is the greatest sign of nobility in our times and represents, at the same time, the greatest hope and promise for the future.

As observers with the greatest insight see it, this is nothing less than the travail which will lead to the birth of a new type of civilization, the advent of a new era in man's history.

Against this general background we can understand the urgent needs of the hour and take determined steps to meet them. Let us make a close examination of the situation. The present time is a very difficult one. It is a period of transition.

Here, in summary form, are some of the problems and tasks to be tackled.

1. To *understand* what is going on. This is the essential starting point.
2. To *endure* and put up with the various kinds of hardships, reactions, knocks and inconveniences involved.
3. To *actively collaborate* in construction of the new civilization. In other words, to become *builders*.

As with any building, this cannot be achieved by isolated individuals. Hence the need, stated earlier, for the formation of an élite, or groups of 'spiritual workers'. These groups need to have new characteristics: they must be free, flexible and universal.

The union resulting from these groups will be entirely internal in nature, based on a common understanding, a common zeal and a common urge to serve humanity, but there must be complete freedom in terms of particular concepts, methods and the areas of activity. This union will have the nature of a deep friendship and a spiritual brotherhood, not that of an external organization. The function of this élite will be to provide guidelines, encourage initiatives, educate, enlighten and lift people up to a higher level in all areas of life and human activity. The scope here is immeasurable. This is what Hermann Keyserling has to say on the subject:

> The whole of the hereditary organism is disconnected and disturbed; the soul is opening up in a natural way; a remoulding is taking place in terms of the spiritual die which will give it its new form. It is precisely this tremendous potential, glimpsed and perceived by millions of people, when it comes down to it that feeds all the enthusiasm, all the zeal and all the sacrificial commitment we see at work in countries where revolution is happening. And the reason for this is that man—even if he is preoccupied with earthly matters and values—is essentially Spirit . . .
>
> There is clearly a unique possibility, at this stage in our history, for the Spirit to take a giant leap forward in its ongoing process of breaking into the earthly order of things. From this point on it will

all depend on the spiritual, and thus personal, initiative of men and women.

If this is the case—and there are a great many of us who are convinced it is so—it is our fervent wish and firm intent that all awakened souls, all enlightened minds and all generous hearts be worthy of the wonderful opportunity before us, so that the glorious new Era of the Spirit can be ushered in.

20

TRANSMUTATION AND SUBLIMATION OF EMOTIONAL AND SEXUAL ENERGIES

It will be useful, indeed necessary, to tackle the serious problems connected with love and to see how one can begin to resolve the many considerable difficulties presented in this area and to settle the disputes that so frequently arise within the human soul, causing so much inner suffering.

The conflicts that arise in the area of love are of various types: conflicts between instinctive urges and the thousands of circumstances and reasons that prevent those impulses from finding satisfaction, conflicts between sensual attractions and the aspirations of the heart, tensions between the desires aroused by passion or emotion and the sense of duty, responsibility and dignity, and conflicts between an emotional attachment to a given person and the claims or demands of a wider and higher love.

All these conflicts are often the cause of great soul-searching and keen suffering. They represent noble struggles and splendid victories, resulting in a person being purified and ennobled: indeed, they mark important stages in the soul's ascent.

These inner struggles, then, form part of the most vital of human experiences, and there is no value in trying to evade them. Anyone who, through false modesty, fear or ignorance, turns his back on his duty to tackle these problems head-on, is making a mistake and exposing himself as an easy target for failure. On the other hand, a person who has the courage to take a firm stance before the internal and external questions and situations of life, and examines them calmly in the light of the spirit, will go a long way towards dispelling confusion and disappointment, avoiding mistakes and guilt, saving himself and others unnecessary suffering, finding unexpected and welcome ways of bringing harmony to opposing energies, and discovering dignified, liberating ways of solving the problems he encounters in life.

Let us take a look at the various attitudes that may be and are being adopted to overcome the above conflicts.

Repression of the Lower Elements

Those who have a rigidly dualist and separatist understanding of the human psyche, and who regard instincts and passions as something fundamentally bad and impure, naturally tend to regard them with horror and disgust, and make every effort to repress and suppress them. But there are serious drawbacks to this attitude. Psychological observation has shown that there are forces within us that cannot be suppressed and cannot be killed.

The method of repression can only be used to prevent outward expression of such elements, paralysing them with an opposing force of the same intensity in order to balance them out. But this forced inhibition does not provide an adequate or satisfactory solution: it requires a great expenditure of energy, sapping a person's resources and detracting from other activities. It also produces great inner tension which may result in crises and disturbances of a nervous or psychological nature.

It is this in particular that some people interpret as evidence that sexual restraint is harmful to one's health. However, it is not chastity itself that one should blame for such disturbances, but the wrong methods employed to maintain that state.

Giving Free Reign to one's Instincts and Passions

This attitude has become very prevalent in recent times, either as a reaction against the excesses of imposed repression, or as a consequence of the weakening of religious and moral feeling, and the emphasis placed on individual rights as opposed to duties.

The return to nature propounded by Rousseau and his followers, the revival of the hedonistic and aesthetic ideals of ancient Greece, materialism and practical, philosophical positivism, the rigid Nordic individualism highlighted by Ibsen, in short all the main philosophical movements of the last century have contributed in their various ways to creating this cult of the personal 'I', and justifying the free expression of one's instincts and impulses, abandoning oneself to every passion and whim.

The results of this lifestyle—as we all know—are disastrous, both at the individual level and at the collective level. The expected satisfaction and happiness of those who have sold their spiritual birthright in this way have completely failed to materialize. Such excesses are inevitably followed by disgust and exhaustion. Often these passions cannot be satisfied because they are not reciprocated by other people, or because they are thwarted by opposing passions. The lack of any strong inner reference point makes man restless, unable to rely on himself, and enslaves him to every change within as well as to every change in his external world. Even in those who regard themselves as being quite free from any prejudice, therefore, enslavement to the lower nature results in a dull discontent, a continuous protest at the violated spiritual element present in each man. The voice of conscience gives no peace and it is in vain that some people try not to hear it, losing themselves in a state of continuous activity, or attempt to suffocate it by wallowing in ever greater excesses.

In other words, this second method of free expression and abandonment to one's instincts and passions not only goes against the higher moral principles, but fails to give any lasting satisfaction.

Fortunately there is a third way which does not have the drawbacks of the other two and can lead to liberation, satisfaction and peace.

The Transformation and Sublimation of our Instincts, Passions and Feelings

This method has long been known; moreover, since it is a good, 'natural' method in the highest sense of the word, that is to say it is in accordance with the true nature of man and with the ascendant path he is destined to follow, it is successfully employed by many people in an intuitive fashion, without their being aware of it, without their even knowing or wanting it consciously, as they follow the dictates and promptings of that inner Guide who can always be relied on by those who sincerely seek good.

This is the method behind alchemy, the true spiritual alchemy which used material symbols to express inner realities and processes.

The sulphur, salt and mercury referred to by alchemists represent the various elements of the human psyche. *Athanor*, the recipient in which they are placed, symbolizes man himself. The fire over which the recipient is placed has been given the very significant name *Incendium amoris* [the Fire of Love]: this is the heat, the transforming power of spiritual love. Substances subjected to this process pass through three transformations: in the first stage they become black—this is referred to as the decomposition stage and relates to the stage of purging or purification spoken of by mystics—then in the second stage they become white, being transformed into silver—this refers to the enlightenment of the soul. Finally, at the third stage, which is the highest, they become red, and are transformed into gold, the spiritual gold—this marks completion of the *Magnum Opus*, and corresponds to the glorious state of unity referred to by mystics.

The method of sublimation has also been perceived and referred to, explicitly or implicitly, by the better, well-balanced Christian mystics. For instance, St John of the Cross said, 'Only higher love can overcome lower love' and 'It is from the passions and appetites that virtues are born when those passions are brought under control...' But to come right up to date in the form of a more explicit exposition I will quote from an unexpected source, namely a positivist scientist. In studying the sexual and emotional life of his patients, Sigmund Freud was able to ascertain at first hand the amazing possibilities of transformation and sublimation. This is what he had to say on the basis of his observations:

> The very elements of the sexual instinct are characterised by their potential for sublimation, exchanging their sexual goal with a more distant, and more socially valuable goal. It is very likely that we owe the highest products of culture to the sum of the energies thus gained by our mental endeavours.

The English writer Edward Carpenter, who studied in great depth the characteristics and laws of sexual life, stated even more explicitly:

> Do we not perhaps have grounds for stating that there exists a kind of continuously realized and realizable transformation in man? Sensuality and love—Aphrodite Pandemos and Aphrodite Ouranios—can be subtly exchanged. It is an accepted fact of common experience that the unchecked expression of purely physical desires robs human nature of its highest energies for love; whereas if physical satisfaction is denied, the body is overwhelmed by waves of emotions which can often reach excessive and dangerous proportions. But even this emotional love can be transformed, as one checks or stops its expression, into the subtle all-pervading influence of spiritual love.

Lastly I will give the testimony of the great German philosopher Schopenhauer:

> On those days and in those hours when the inclination towards pleasure is at its strongest ... that is precisely the time when the highest spiritual energies are ready for maximum activity, though they remain hidden once the conscious mind is taken up with its longings. However, it takes only a determined effort to focus the direction of one's conscious attention away from those miserable, desperate, tormenting yearnings and to let it become occupied with the more noble activities of the higher spiritual energies.

Using this and countless other observations, we can define the process as the *transformation of the various manifestations of love from one level to another*, that is to say:

1. Transformation of the instinctive sexual energies into emotions and feelings.
2. The sublimation of the emotions and personal feelings into spiritual love of God and of the souls of men.

This sublimation of human love into a religious love is evident in the lives of many mystics and many saints.

We must sound a warning note here about pseudo-sublimation, however. I am speaking of masquerades and substitutions for true human love. But there are many stages in between, where one begins with substitution and eventually achieves a more or less full sublimation.

There are certain characteristics which enable us to distinguish between true sublimation and pseudo-sublimation. In the former love assumes an increasingly impersonal, universal and disinterested nature. It is generous and radiant, free from possessiveness and sentimentality. This type of sublimation is generally linked with the *transformation and sublimation of emotional and sexual energies into creative and benevolent works.*

This has happened quite clearly in the lives of many artists and writers: one need only think of Dante, Wagner, and in more contemporary times Fogazzaro. The same could be said for a host of philanthropists, educators and social workers. In these one can often see a sublimation of maternal or paternal love, a true spiritual maternal or paternal instinct which expresses itself in caring for bodies and souls (doctors, nurses, nuns, educators, social workers, spiritual guides).

It is not necessary to think that one must be some sort of genius or a person of exceptional qualities to achieve such sublimation. Each of us can do this to some measure. We must, however, sound a warning note against pseudo-sublimation, which is only a covering and a substitution for personal love.

The first requirement is the aspiration to achieve it, followed by a serious intent, a decision of the will, and affirmation of what one is aspiring to. This acts as an effective spur, an order the psychological energies obey.

One must then move on resolutely to external action, throwing oneself into the new activities which are likely to draw to one the energies for transformation, immersing oneself in those activities with a lively interest, with zeal and with enthusiastic commitment. It is then that all our energies flow in. The important thing is not to repress or try to suppress the lower energies in a separatist, hostile fashion, but to bring them under control with a calm firmness, at the same time giving free reign to expression of the higher energies. *It is not a question of loving less, but of loving better.*

Modern man often makes the mistake of desensitizing himself

through intellectualism, sterile activism, ambition and selfishness. He thus severs the links that exist between the various aspects of love.

One needs, rather, to love without fear: to love people, ideals, noble social causes—national and human—to love what is beautiful, what is best. The radiant, ascendant power of this kind of love will attract to itself and absorb the sexual, passionate and emotional energies.

Loving in this way, one must give and create. Give and create in different ways, depending on the circumstances and on one's own capacity, but always pouring out, giving oneself, radiating and expending one's energies.

This way of tackling the problem of love is rather different from the usual way, but I hope I have shown that it is based on well-substantiated facts and laws of life, that it is the widest, noblest, all-embracing and at the same time the most practical form of love, and that it offers the only true solution for bringing together those inner tensions in a creative, harmonious synthesis.

MONEY AND THE SPIRITUAL LIFE

There are still so many preconceived ideas and so much misunderstanding about spirituality that it would not at all surprise me if some readers were taken aback by the title of this chapter. It would not come amiss, therefore, if we restated the fact that spirituality does not consist of theories and abstractions, in other words it is not a form of idealism separate from life itself.

More than anything else spirituality is concerned with considering life's problems from a higher, enlightened, synthetic point of view, testing everything on the basis of true values, endeavouring to reach the essence of every fact, neither allowing oneself to stop at external appearances nor be taken in by traditionally accepted views, by the way the world at large looks at things, or by our own inclinations, emotions and preconceived ideas.

To do this is not at all easy—indeed it would be quite presumptuous to imagine one had fully succeeded. But to attempt it is not only permissible, it is also a clear duty, because when spiritual light is focused on the most complex of individual or collective problems it produces solutions and reveals ways in which we can avoid many dangers and errors, sparing us much suffering and thus bestowing incalculable benefits on our lives.

The spiritual view of life and of its various manifestations—far from being theoretical and unpractical—is extremely revolutionary, dynamic and creative.

It is revolutionary because in the light of the spirit one's ordinary value system and the practical way this works itself out in our behaviour is shown to be fundamentally wrong. It is only to be expected that this should be the case, because those value systems and behaviour patterns are self-centred and separatist, and because of the false perspective on which they are based, they distort reality and set up artificial barriers in what is actually a single life. The spiritual point of view, then, brings about a series of 'Copernican revolutions', replacing man-centred, individualist views with a spiritual 'heliocentric' viewpoint which places facts, problems and above all ourselves in their proper perspective.

Spirituality is dynamic and creative because the changes of perspective, the turning upside-down of values, the clearing away of illusions, and the transformation of the world and of life in general which this new light makes possible produces great changes within us, awakening new and powerful forces, expanding the field of our influence on other people, and greatly altering the quality of that influence.

The radical review now being attempted by some of the most enlightened and committed souls, in all areas of human life, is therefore of the greatest significance.

These spiritual reviews involve two areas of activity: first of all there is the clear understanding and confident reaffirmation of the eternal principles and values of the spirit; then there is the application of these principles and values to the real problems of modern life, both personal and social.

In every age and in each individual these problems take a different form. It is not only that new events, new conditions and new energies are encountered on life's stage, particularly in modern times, but also that the numerous facts already in existence come together in ever more varied combinations, creating new forms. Thus the spiritual solutions, although they always start out from the same point, need to be flexible and, in a certain sense, continually new and original if they are to meet the needs of that ever-changing reality and make a practical contribution.

Among the many problems assailing mankind there are two which have to do with its most central interests, the strongest spurs to action in our individual and corporate lives. These problems therefore require examination in the light of the spirit, and the insight it alone can give.

These are our attitudes to love (taken in its widest sense, including sexuality, but not limited to this area) and to money. I have dealt with the first of these elsewhere.[1] With the assistance of others who have also tackled this subject, I will now attempt a brief consideration of the second.

If we examine ourselves with that courageous openness which is a prerequisite for any authentic spiritual life, we will recognize that the thought of money strikes a deep, intense chord within us, a confusion of obscure emotions and impassioned reactions, showing that the 'idea of this metal' touches very sensitive parts of our personality.

There is a need for this chaos to be brought out into the open, to allow it to surface in our conscious minds, laying aside any form of censure and any of those attitudes rising from the depths of our unconscious. What emerges is a turgid gush of mixed currents—currents of fear, desire, greed and attachment—and feelings of guilt, envy and resentment.

Let us attempt to go back to the source of these forces with the help of Hermann Keyserling who, better than anyone else, I believe, made a study of the hidden, earthly roots of those aspects of the human personality which have developed from the bottom level—the animal, vegetable and mineral aspects of man's nature. But let us do so without falling into the error committed by other explorers of the depths, namely the failure to recognize things that have a higher level of origin, and one that is completely independent of the rest: what he so aptly refers to as the 'breaking through of the Spirit'.

In his *Meditations Sud-Americaines*, which is perhaps his most profound work, and then in his compilation *Intimate Ways*, Keyserling clearly shows that there are two primordial tendencies at the very roots of life. The first is Original Fear, about which he says something very significant: 'This Original Fear does not refer to death, but to want.' By this he means the fear of not having enough food, the fear of hunger. He says:

> It is likely that behind this fear is an obscure, yet intense memory of the pressing search for food, an all-consuming concern of

[1] See the previous chapter.

primitive man. As a safeguard against this Original Fear the safety instinct is the first active impulse of every living being.

It is from this safety instinct, he continues, that the instinct of ownership or possession has evolved.

The other basic tendency rising up from the depths of the unconscious, as a dynamic opposite of the first, is what Keyserling calls Original Hunger, though in order to avoid confusion it would be better to call it Original Greed. According to Keyserling:

> This is the primary motive of all growth. Now growth, by its very nature, is a quest for the infinite; from the outset it recognizes no boundary as fixed. As a result this initial Hunger is basically aggressive and insatiable. It is opposed, by nature, to any safety instinct; risk is its element; at any given moment it strives for what is infinite and unlimited. This produces a fundamental conflict with all that belongs to the order of Ownership and Law. In the depths of the unconscious there is an ongoing battle between Hunger and Fear; there can be no lasting, harmonious balance.

It is not difficult to see how in our own materialistic civilization both these tendencies manifest themselves in the frenzy to acquire and keep the largest possible amount of money and material goods. The power of these impulses, despite the thousands of years that have passed and despite the way human life has been refined to a certain extent, is still so strong that it usually prevails—either in the form of violent confrontations, or in less direct, underhand ways, covered up by hypocritical justifications—over any other urge or higher restraint, indeed it can often overcome the self-preservation instinct.

If we only knew how many crimes, betrayals, thefts, how much bullying, physical and moral prostitution, and how many base deeds of every kind are committed daily by mankind, overtly or in secret, out of the hateful greed for money, we would be deeply disturbed, indeed terrified. And if we were then to take an honest look at ourselves in this area, I am afraid we might be in for an unpleasant surprise.

This was clearly understood by those higher Beings who have

come down to tackle the demanding task of raising man's moral consciousness and awakening him spiritually, in order to release him from his enslavement to passions.

Thus Buddha renounced wealth and every earthly possession, firstly so that he might seek Truth, and then, once he had received enlightenment, in order to help other people to find liberation from pain, the fruit of desire. Indeed many centuries before Buddha came onto the scene there were those in India who had reached a certain spiritual level and would then renounce all worldly goods and become sannyasin, living as beggars.

Jesus often used strong words to warn people about the serious obstacle riches could be to the spiritual life, and his most energetic, aggressive action, from what we know, was when he used a whip to chase out the money-changers whose greed led them to desecrate the Temple with their dubious trade.

This attitude against money continued through the centuries of Christianity until it culminated in the dramatic, sublime gesture of St Francis, who rid himself of every possession, even the clothes he stood up in, and then celebrated his mystical marriage to Lady Poverty. These attitudes and the ways of life derived from them, cannot help but cause us to ask two questions:

1. Are such attitudes right and necessary from the spiritual point of view? Is it necessary to condemn money if one wants to live a spiritual life?
2. And if the answer to the first question is yes, is it feasible to live in this way in our present age?

The answer to the second question is easy. It was not many decades after the death of St Francis that the Franciscan Communities realized that for normal monastery life to continue it was almost impossible to do without money and some form of buildings and land. This gave rise to serious differences of opinion between the rigorous observers of the original rule and those who wanted to adapt it to meet the demands of everyday life. The latter group won the day, and Franciscans now use every means the modern world provides:

printing, postal services, and travel by rail, by car and by air, paying in the normal way for their use. If this is what the sons of St Francis do, how can any more be expected of us, the laity, caught up as we are in the very fabric of economic, family and social life, and intimately involved—not out of necessity, but by conscious choice—in the life of our times, convinced that any transformation of that life, in the spiritual sense, will not come about from outside, by our estranging ourselves from it, but only as we act as yeast from within?

Now let us tackle the first, and most difficult of the two questions.

Firstly we need to be on our guard against the all too easy hypocritical attitudes that the disregard for money can lead to. It can become a comfortable mask for laziness, weakness and cowardice; it can result in individual and collective parasitism. This was often the case in India where the climate, the living conditions and the prevalent outlook on life made this an easy way out.

But there is a more fundamental objection to the attitude to money expressed above, and this takes the form of a completely opposite view, also inspired by religious principles. According to this view, the view expressed throughout the Old Testament, riches and prosperity are to be regarded as tangible signs of God's favour, and as rewards for correct and fair behaviour. Accordingly poverty and adversity are seen as the effects of divine punishment, or at least as the result of mistakes in thinking, attitude and conduct, either individually or collectively.

This idea has been picked up again in certain modern religious systems, and it is this, consciously or not, that characterizes the American outlook. In that system practical success and personal worth are equated: the former is the proof of the latter.

Let us discover what elements of truth this theory contains. If God is good, the advocates of this school of thought would say, if God is love, if He wants man's good and wants man to have a full, joyful, 'rich' life, how could He not want man to make the fullest possible use of the worldly goods nature provides in such abundance?

If there is a hierarchy in the kingdoms of nature—and this

would appear to be the case—it is in the natural and divine order of things that the lower kingdoms are there to serve the higher kingdoms. In the sub-human kingdoms this takes place spontaneously: the mineral kingdom makes possible the life of the vegetable kingdom by providing it with the building blocks it needs, and the contribution, or 'sacrifice' of both those kingdoms is necessary for the existence of animal life.

There is the same sort of relationship between the sub-human kingdoms and man himself. Human life requires a considerable contribution from the other three kingdoms. Man's excesses and abuse of those kingdoms does not justify the spiritual condemnation and practical renunciation of their *correct use*.

But this is not all: by using them correctly, man not only obtains benefit from the other kingdoms or, to use a more realistic expression, exploits them, he also gives much back to them in exchange, lifting them up and refining them in many different ways. Might one not perhaps say that man glorifies and exalts mineral matter when he releases from the darkness of the earth the gems that were imprisoned in its crooked veins and transforms them into glistening diamonds, rubies, topazes and shining sapphires? Is he not in a sense imitating the power of God when he transforms the raw, lifeless lump of metal into the most delicate of objects that pulsate with life, objects brought to life by his skill, and when he harnesses and transforms the subtlest of energies in the ether?

But man's most significant area of beneficent action is in the vegetable and animal kingdoms. How much progress he has made in developing plants and how he has refined them, transforming wild bushes with small, sour fruit into plants that provide us with sumptuous gifts, bringing health and joy with them.

Even more obvious is the effect a part of mankind—not the whole race, unfortunately—has had on the animal kingdom. The domestication of animals itself, that is to say their breeding by man—even if for practical purposes—invariably results in a refining of those animal species, and in the manifestation of such germs of intelligence as their instincts are able to develop.

Thus we have the affectionate, understanding relationship between the rider and his horse, between man and his elephant or dog—relationships which almost have a humanizing effect on those animals. Not to mention certain prodigies in the animal kingdom: instances of animals undergoing intense teaching and demonstrating unusual intelligence are sometimes disputed, but they cannot be wholly discounted.

All this serves to show the positive side of man's use of material resources, a use that requires some form of possession and active exchange of those resources between men— exchanges which, in turn, require a fast, easy means of transaction, and of these money, if not the only, is certainly the most practical means. Given the circumstances in which we have to operate today, it is essential.

Another element of truth in this favourable attitude towards possessions is that in many cases the attaining of such benefits is actually the fruit of hard work, careful planning, saving, discipline and other moral virtues. Conversely poverty and the absence of success can quite often be traced back to the opposite defects or vices: laziness, carelessness, wastefulness and lack of self-control.

This is not always the case, of course. The accumulation of riches is often the result of greed, hardness of heart, the absence of scruples, and sometimes clever fraud and legal subterfuge.

We can therefore see that it is a one-sided view, and a view that is often at variance with the facts, to equate divine favour, moral merit and economic success. A typical, I would even say an unconsciously satirical, expression of this view being the way people will sometimes say, 'That man is worth a million dollars.'

Clearly our examination so far of the relationships between money and spirituality have not brought us to any firm conclusion—indeed, it may have left us even more confused. But this cannot be helped because the problem as we have stated it so far—and as it is usually stated—has not been stated in the right terms. In other words, we have attempted an objective appreciation of money and tried to give it the label 'good' or 'bad', blessing or curse, but this objective, external assessment, as with any others of this kind (such as the assessments made by certain systems of formalistic ethics), is fundamentally wrong in that it is based on an error and is therefore unreal.[1] Let us

[1] In saying this it is certainly not our intention to criticize or detract from the

dispense with this approach, then, and start all over again in a completely different way. Let us begin by defining what it is we are talking about.

What do we mean by money? It is a convention created by men to facilitate the exchange of goods and to make this possible on a large scale, in the complex ways and at the increasing speed required by life in today's world. Thus money is an instrument, it symbolizes material goods. In itself, then, it deserves *ni cet excès d'honneur, ni cette indignité* [neither this great honour, nor this ill repute].

Thus the vehement condemnations launched against money are misdirected, and it is only right that the 'sorting office', i.e. ethics, return them 'to sender', i.e. man. It is in the heart of man that we find truth and error, good and evil, merit and guilt. And if we look at the problem from this more accurate and less superficial point of view we will see that man's errors and guilt with respect to money are essentially of two types: one related specifically to money itself, and the other related to material goods in general.

The first misunderstanding, and the wrong conduct it results in, is based on man's tendency to exchange the means for the end, identifying the instrument with what that instrument is meant to produce and, in a more general sense, mistaking the symbol for the reality it represents, form for life.

We are always coming up against what are often comic examples of this type of error. It manifests itself in all those forms of collecting that have become an end in themselves: bibliomania, for instance, which causes a person to reach the stage where he prefers almost illegible editions of books, provided they are old and rare, to excellently printed modern versions. Thus a book fanatic will not hesitate to cry out exultantly (as it says in the epigram of Pons de Verdun):

sublime act of St Francis, which was indeed heroic and had an incalculable positive effect as an example to others, providing us with a practical lesson in detachment and constituting one of the most powerful blows that have ever been inflicted on the idol Mammon. The renunciation of all worldly goods is thus appreciated for its true value by way of an exception. Our intention was only to show that this way cannot provide us with a generally applicable solution in our everyday lives.

This is it! God, what a stroke of luck!
Yes, it's the good edition;
Look, there are pages twelve and sixteen,
The two mistakes the printers missed
In the bad edition.

In the case of money, however, we are not dealing with a harmless, somewhat ridiculous mania: what we are faced with are sordid manifestations of greed which, speaking symbolically, can cause a person to 'lose his soul'. We are dealing with violent covetousness, with an avarice that will stop at nothing, stooping to the basest of crimes: bloody murder and the more refined, damaging, despicable forms of theft, such as that practised by the manufacturers and sellers of weapons who, in order to sell more of their wares, do all they can to create hostility between different groups of people, by those who illegally produce and sell drugs, and those who organize prostitution and exploit interest in sex by publishing and distributing 'suggestive', pornographic pictures and articles, not to mention those who produce semi-pornographic materials under the pretext of literature or art.

Thus the first spiritual act we need to perform is to free ourselves from this tendency to place too much value on the means, or on the instrument whereby worldly goods are acquired and exchanged: money. Let us be determined in our refusal to offer any further sacrifices on the altar of this false god, let us free ourselves from the fascination this idol has for us and, with an unclouded vision and a calm indifference, reduce it to what it actually is: a mere instrument, a useful device, a practical convention.

Having thus got rid of the first obstacle we can then go on to tackle the real problem: our relationship with material things in general, of which money is only a symbol or a temporary substitute.

We have seen that material goods—be they food, clothing, homes, machines, objects of beauty—are essentially made up of materials from the three kingdoms of nature, being used either in their natural state or, more often, after they have undergone some process to make them more useful to man. They do not therefore contain any intrinsic evil. From the naturalist point of view they are things; from the religious point of view they are gifts of God. Thus their significance to us, and the positive or negative effect they have on us, depend on our inner attitude to them and on the use we choose to make of them.

Understanding this basic fact clarifies a number of spiritual and practical issues of great importance. In the first place it is quite clear that the absence of external possessions does not in any way resolve the problem. Apart from all the limitations and the slavery that poverty brings with it in today's world, if a poor man has a passionate desire for material goods, if he is always thinking of how he can obtain them, and if he is bitter and twisted inside because of his resentment against those who have such possessions, he will still—psychologically—be their slave.

This does not of course mean that he is not entitled to actively endeavour to better his lot, indeed it is his duty to do so. But he can do it without allowing it to totally absorb and obsess him, maintaining his own inner liberty and dignity.

On the other hand a rich man who is morally detached from his possessions and who feels free from them in his spirit, will not be spiritually diminished by them in any way; psychologically he is 'poor in spirit'.

But even this 'inner poverty' does not solve the problem completely. Once man has settled matters with his own conscience and, to a certain extent, with God, he must then come to terms with his fellows, people with whom his life is inextricably bound up in a number of different relationships, in both moral and practical terms. Thus inner liberation must be followed by the correct use of one's possessions. This in turn raises two problems:

1. correct use at the individual level;
2. correct use at the collective level.

The basis for correct individual use lies in the concept of possession itself as a personal right. Legal ownership is purely a human invention, but one that is justified psychologically and practically in view of the limited level of moral development man has reached. The desire to possess is a primordial force that cannot be discounted: it cannot be killed or forcibly repressed. In spiritual terms, however, ownership has a very different aspect and significance. No longer is it a personal right, but a *responsibility* towards God and man.

If one accepts a religious view of life, one must recognize that everything comes from God, that everything is given by Him and is therefore actually His. He alone is the true universal 'owner'.

A person who adheres to the more metaphysical view that life is indissolubly one, that only the Supreme, Absolute Being has any real existence and that all individual manifestations are but passing appearances (as maintained in the Vedanta philosophy, for instance), must also recognize that personal ownership has no spiritual basis.

From the spiritual point of view, then, man may only consider himself a trustee, guardian or administrator of the material goods for which he has obtained legal ownership. Those goods are for him a real test, a test he must submit to. They are a social, moral and spiritual responsibility, and one that requires great effort to fulfil worthily.

This type of language is seldom encountered in our modern times and it may seem like the expression of an impractical idealism. I believe however I can show that it has an immediate value, and a greater value than may at first sight seem the case.

First of all those with a fairly well developed moral sensitivity come to the above conclusion spontaneously. One remembers, for instance, the noble qualms that troubled Antonio Fogazzaro when he came into possession of inherited wealth. This has been discussed by Gallarati Scotti in his *Life of Antonio Fogazzaro*. One also remembers the inner turmoil Tolstoy went through for most of his life.

But the idea of being merely trustees of wealth, or of being 'social servants'—either in the acquisition of that wealth through the production of useful goods for the community at large, or in the subsequent distribution of that wealth in the form of donations for humanitarian purposes—has been adopted or, more importantly, put into effect by certain of the most practical, realistic and productive men of our age. We are all familiar with the examples of disinterested giving, frugality in one's personal life and hard work inspired by the ideal of social service, which we see in such men as Edison and Ford.

But even among those who in the first part of their lives were merely businessmen, intent on accumulating wealth, often fighting tough battles against their competitors, there have been those who, at a certain moment, felt compelled (probably for various, mixed motives that it would be difficult and indiscreet to inquire into) to use or earmark a large proportion of their wealth for humanitarian and cultural purposes.

The most typical example of this kind is that of John Rockefeller. After becoming perhaps the richest man in the world, as the 'oil king', he founded and financed the Rockefeller Foundation at the enormous cost of hundreds of millions of dollars. This Institute promotes scientific study and research—particularly in the area of medicine—and uses its findings in practical applications on a vast scale. Among other things it eliminated yellow fever which claimed thousands of victims among the working people in the Panama Canal area, and financed a worldwide campaign against malaria.

Another example, also well known, is that of Carnegie, the 'king of steel', who created a vast network of public libraries, first in America and then in other parts of the world. Who can begin to calculate the intellectual and moral benefits that have been, are now being and will continue to be enjoyed by the countless number of readers of the hundreds of thousands of books in those libraries? Later on the nephew of Ford, Henry Ford II, created the Ford Foundation, endowing it with hundreds of millions of dollars, for humanitarian, cultural and educational reasons. More specifically spiritual reasons moved Eli Lilly to realize the project of Doctor Pitirim A. Sorokin, namely the Harvard Research Center in Creative Altruism at the University of Harvard. This centre has published several books by Doctor Sorokin and his fellow workers.

Nor is Europe short of examples of its own of this kind, some of them here in Italy. We will mention, among others, the cultural and social efforts by Olivetti, the Cini Foundation, the Marzotto cultural prizes and the Motta prizes, etc.

There is an important reason why these initiatives should not remain the exception, why they should not be perceived as a rare gesture, but instead should multiply rapidly in all areas. The human masses are in an agitated state of impatience and rebellion against the individualistic concept of property as an unconditional right, characterized by an irresponsible attitude to the collective good, and against any system that upholds that right. For this reason the people are not content with aid and financial assistance in the form of 'charity' or paternalistic benevolence, implying a superiority and a magnanimity in the one donating the funds and an obligation of appreciation and gratitude in the one who receives such benefits.

Now until the social changes I will be saying more about later have been put into effect, it is necessary—in order to restrain the impatience of the masses—that those in possession of material goods do not cling to them as an unconditional right, but show that they are willing and able to make worthy use of their wealth for the benefit of all. This needs to be done in two ways.

The first—which may be regarded as somewhat negative in nature—consists of limiting, or rather eliminating, the selfish waste, the lives of luxury, the ostentatious display of costly objects and other manifestations of this kind that irritate and indeed exasperate those who lack what is necessary, or what as time passes is regarded as necessary, for a less wretched standard of living, i.e. those basic essentials that are in accordance with the dignity every human being should have.

It might be useful here to reveal a false argument or pretext that many use, often in good faith, to justify a life of luxury. They say that by living in this way they are stimulating the circulation of money and enabling many working people to make a living. To this one can and should raise the objection, first and foremost, that too rapid a circulation of money is a hindrance to the long-term investment in production necessary for the collective good, and secondly that money spent on a luxury item could be used more humanely to meet the urgent needs of those who lack the bare necessities.

If this social and ethical conversion of the rich were to reach such amazing, though not very likely, proportions that companies producing luxury items went out of business, this would be swallowed up by the normal changes in employment that are always taking place due to technical changes and changes in fashion. But it would not be difficult to make provision for such redundant workers to be found new jobs.

The second way of making good use of one's wealth is to invest it in companies that produce goods that are of real use to other people, and then to devote as large a proportion of the profits as possible to humanitarian works.

In this connection, without wanting to detract from those who have and continue to contribute to raising the standard of living and health of other people, we would have to say that the most beneficial use one can make of wealth is to use it to educate people morally and spiritually.

This use of wealth is valuable on two counts: firstly, by way of prevention, it tackles the deep causes and roots of the many different ills that so overwhelm mankind. Each person who has undergone a moral regeneration represents one less danger and one more force for good in society. Secondly, and this is more direct and immediate, it has the effect of giving men the most noble and lasting of riches, the sort of riches that produce the highest and most substantial form of comfort and the purest and most life-enhancing form of joy.

There are countless simple ways in which a spiritually awakened rich person of good will can use his wealth for the moral and spiritual good of mankind. Here are some of them.

One way is the publication and distribution of good books. These are real sources of spiritual energy; they have what one might almost call a 'magical' power to bring us into fellowship with the highest spirits of humanity, outside of the limitations of space and time, so that we can receive their life-giving messages. There are some books which have significantly affected the course of history. One need only think of the work of the encyclopaedists who prepared the ground for the French Revolution. In Italy there was the book of Silvio Pellico *Le mie prigioni* [My Prisons] about which G. Pallavicino, in a report addressed to the Austrian Government in 1837, said, 'This could do your Government more harm than the loss of ten battles.'

Who can quantify the spiritual effect exerted over the centuries and many different countries by booklets such as *The Little Flowers of St Francis* or the *Imitation of Christ*? To mention but one example among many others, the reading of a pamphlet by

Gandhi led one young Englishwoman, the daughter of an admiral, to leave her home and family and go to Gandhi in India, becoming first his disciple, then his active co-worker. In recent times the healing effect of good books has been recognized and appreciated, and this has led to their use as a method in psychotherapy: the doctor's contribution to this so-called 'book therapy' consists of 'giving the right person the right book at the right time'.

It is often the case, however, that the best, most helpful books are difficult to find. Some editions are sold out and not reprinted, and they are not always translated into other languages. In this area 'enlightened' rich people could do incalculable good with fairly modest sums. For the price of a house, a yacht or some jewels, one could establish and set in motion a publishing firm that would print series of 'uplifting' books at low prices. And for the price of a car, a fur coat or an antique, one could publish a book that would bring light, comfort and encouragement to thousands of people. For much less, one could give libraries or private individuals copies of a book that has been of benefit to us and to others.[1]

The same can be said about the publication of newspapers. In this area we might mention the modern newspaper the *Christian Science Monitor*, which contains full coverage of world events, but leaves out descriptions of crimes and suicides, accounts of lawsuits, and any other form of concentration on the negative, baser aspects of life.

Apart from the press, one can produce and distribute messages of great moral and spiritual value through various modern means of communication, for example the cinema, radio and television. There have been some (alas too few!) uplifting films—apart from those in the category of specifically educational films—but one can imagine how much good could be done by an enlightened producer who financed a film that, in additional to its human interest and artistic value (which alone would make it successful in practical terms), could provide the

---

[1]Anyone can give a good book as a present instead of some other object, making the gift more personal with an appropriate dedication, if necessary enhancing the gift with an artistic binding.

spiritual messages people so desperately need to hear and for which, unconsciously, they are hungry.

Then there is the potential for setting up and developing institutions to act as centres for psychological and spiritual help: child-rearing consultants for parents, pre- and post-marriage consultants, centres for psychological prophylaxis and psychotherapy, organizations to help potential suicides, and institutes to help precocious and highly gifted children and young people. Some of these centres already exist and do useful work, but they are few in number and their sphere of influence is inadequate when one considers the immensity and urgency of the need.[1]

Then there is the training and use of spiritual workers or 'servants'. These need to have a special vocation and special qualities that are difficult to find. Therefore those who have them should be sought out and valued as precious instruments for good, and they should be given access to all the necessary means for achieving the best possible results so that they can carry out their mission in the fullest and most effective way. The need in this area is for these 'humanitarian, spiritual experts' to receive all the resources they need, just as experts in the various branches of technology are provided with the necessary resources as a matter of course.

We must now take a brief look at the collective, i.e. national, social and worldwide, aspects of the use of money and material goods in general.

Even if the majority of rich people decided to do what we have been talking about, regarding themselves simply as managers or

[1] One might at this point study the work carried out by the Churches and by specifically religious institutions. I have not done this because it would require greater space than I can afford for the purposes of this article. Moreover those who are sincerely religious have no need of external encouragement: they feel a spontaneous urge to 'give' or to respond voluntarily to appeals addressed to them. I will only say that Churches and religious institutions also have the problem of distributing and using the money available in a way that will be of the greatest use for the true, highest good of its beneficiaries—in other words, what proportion should they give to corporate worship (buildings, furnishings and fittings, etc.), to material aid and to direct moral and spiritual help? But this difficult problem is one that the heads of the ecclesiastic hierarchy must tackle themselves.

administrators of the benefits bestowed on mankind by God—and no one is naïve enough to think for a moment that they will—this would still not fully solve the problem. In the complexity of modern living, individual action is not enough. There are great problems in the areas of production and distribution, work and organization, not to mention economy and finance, and these can only be solved if action is taken on a very wide scale, through national, international and worldwide bodies.

The basic principles for the spiritual use of money and the goods it is able to purchase are those of true social justice and the fair distribution of natural resources among all peoples of the world. These principles are now rapidly gaining recognition and being asserted: in all directions, and in various forms, we are witnessing an intense, dramatic struggle between those who are demanding action (often in violent, fanatical ways, taking no account of the gradual process needed) and those who oppose it, openly or behind the scenes, because of their blinkered vision, their attachment to the possessions and privileges they enjoy, or their lack of fellow feeling.

I cannot of course deal with this vast subject here: it is too complex—and too thorny an issue—given its inevitable political repercussions. I will only refer to the important international organizations which, under the auspices of the United Nations, are intent on the implementation of such principles on a worldwide scale: the FAO (the Food and Agriculture Organization), the World Health Organization, the International Bank, etc. Nor should we forget the immense sums given in aid by rich nations, particularly the United States, to poorer nations. Again there is no need for us to engage in a psychological analysis of motives—it is enough to show due appreciation for the benefits received in this form.

It is in this way, and this way alone, that the serious dangers threatening humanity can be eliminated: the bloody, social revolutions, the violent rebellion of the masses in Africa and Asia, or another world war which could destroy a vast section of the human race.

The responsibility, urgency, and importance of this large-scale work in the material realm should not, however, dwarf the equally necessary urgent work in the ethical and spiritual realm.

Those who in their preoccupation with the ideology of historical materialism only take account of 'economic man', ignore the profound truth—psychological at least, if not moral and religious—contained in the warning: 'Man shall not live by bread alone.' He also needs cultural and spiritual feeding, and is therefore entitled to receive it.

But this is not all: not only is economic well-being insufficient, it can also produce drawbacks and dangers. It can have harmful effects on those who lack the necessary moral qualities to make good use of such material benefits. There are many well-known examples of this, but because the vast majority (if not the totality) of the human race ignores or forgets them in its blind greed and in its desperate race to achieve material wealth, it would not come amiss to mention some of these examples.

We are familiar with the way the sons of millionaires and multi-millionaires often abandon their father's business, leading a profligate existence in full gaze of the public eye. We are all too aware of the scandals that frequently take place in so-called 'high society'. Even among very rich people who are free from such degenerate behaviour, there are cases of suicide. Moreover research carried out by journalists in various countries has shown quite conclusively that in many cases the hundreds of thousands won in lotteries, on the pools or at the races do not bring happiness—these sums are often squandered in a short space of time, sometimes resulting in serious family crises.

A lesser-known, and less obvious, fact—though one that deserves our attention—is that even moderate, justifiable well-being, economic security, and freedom from the fear of want can, and do, have their disadvantages.

An example of this is the Scandinavian countries, particularly Sweden, where the extensive social security system guarantees citizens pensions and help in times of need. It has been observed in these countries that the lack of incentives and the lack of risks induce a sense of monotony and boredom with life, indeed statistics show that the suicide rate there is higher than elsewhere. The Swedish Minister of Home Affairs, speaking about 'Teddy Boys', actually referred to them as the 'criminal face of well-being'.[1]

There are other causes of this phenomenon, of course, but this shows that economic well-being does not solve problems, nor give happiness, nor even give a sense of peace. This does not mean that the answer is to take away such provisions for social security—such systems are deeply humanitarian and they eliminate many ills and much suffering. The real answer is to make adequate provision for people's psychological and spiritual needs.

Such provision is also necessary and urgent for another reason. Rapid technological development, the industrial revolution now ushering in automation, and the use of nuclear energy on a vast scale will result in a great reduction of labour and working hours, once the inevitable crises of adjustment have been overcome, and there will then be even greater economic well-being. People will have more time, more energy and more money at their disposal as a result. But if they are not taught to use these resources well in a constructive way, in a way that would actually enhance the quality of their lives, these apparent benefits could all too easily become a trap and a source of danger.

In this regard we need to show the greatest admiration and give every possible moral and material support to UNESCO (the United Nations Educational Scientific Cultural Organization) which is already engaged in education and cultural activities on a vast scale. One thing it is doing is to wage a campaign against illiteracy, and it is also giving substantial support to the development of higher forms of culture, in particular subsidizing young people who show great promise to make the best use of their talents.

There is one more aspect of this subject that we need to clarify. In order to prevent any sense of inferiority or noble frustration on the part of those who are not in a position to make financial contributions, we would do well to remember that this form of giving is by no means the only one, nor is it the highest form— there are many ways of serving mankind. Even the simplest and most humble of activities, such as making copies of articles,

[1]Quoted from an article by C. Savonuzzi entitled 'The Too Affluent Youth of Sweden turns to Crime' (*La Nazione*, 25 September 1959).

writing addresses, etc., have a real value and a spiritual dignity when done out of humanitarian motives and in the service of some spiritual endeavour.

One type of service which combines both material and moral assistance in a natural way is Voluntary Service Overseas. It is encouraging to see a growing number of young people giving themselves to such activities with great enthusiasm, cheerfully bearing the hard work and discomfort involved. Moreover they themselves testify to having been amply rewarded for their efforts in the form of the precious lessons the experience teaches them, the spiritual development it causes them to undergo, and the brotherly relationships that come out of it.

In fact the various forms and means of service are complementary and need to go hand in hand. The work of those who give their time and energy requires the material means for that work to go ahead. Similarly, the greater the number of givers, and the more generous they are, means that there needs to be a greater number of people able to make the best, most productive use of the resources provided. Thus the central, pressing task we face is to establish the new élite, the teams of pioneers of the New Age who will build a new and better civilization, with a new, superior culture.

From all that has been said above it seems to me that the problem of money and material goods is essentially a spiritual one, in other words it is a problem that can only be solved in the light of the spirit. Indeed spirit and matter, which appear to be 'enemies' in relative terms, can and must be united harmoniously in a dynamic synthesis, in the unity of life itself.

22

MARTHA AND MARY: THE ACTIVE LIFE—THE CONTEMPLATIVE LIFE

As Jesus and his disciples were on their way, he came to a village where a woman named Martha opened her home to him. She had a sister called Mary, who sat at the Lord's feet listening to what he said. But Martha was distracted by all the preparations that had to be made. She came to him and asked, 'Lord, don't you care that my sister has left me to do the work by myself? Tell her to help me!'

'Martha, Martha,' the Lord answered, 'you are worried and upset about many things, but only one thing is needed. Mary has chosen what is better, and it will not be taken away from her.'

Luke 10:38—-42
[English translation: The New International Version]

The gospel has been referred to as the 'unread book'. It is certainly a book that is generally not understood or put into practice. If the sublime precepts it contains were truly understood and put into effect, people's lives would look very different.

In the current awakening of spiritual aspirations—aspirations that are fervent and sincere, albeit somewhat confused, erratic and uncertain about the best directions to go in and what exactly the goals are—people often ask whether the gospel can fully satisfy the needs of the modern human soul, or whether some alternative food is required. On the one hand there are those who advocate an honest, straightforward 'return to the gospel' as the only antidote to the religious, moral and social ills of our day, and on the other hand there are those who bluntly ask whether the gospel (to use an expression that comes so readily to the lips of certain contemporary philosophers) has been 'superceded'.

The fact that the ethical and spiritual values we see affirmed and exemplified in the gospel are universal and eternal in nature, that they respond to the deepest ongoing needs of the human soul, and that they cannot therefore be superceded, seems so obvious that it does not even need to be demonstrated. However, closer and fuller attention needs to be given to the question whether the gospel is able to meet all the needs of modern man, and whether it can satisfy all the hunger and thirst in his soul.

There are a number of people who think it appropriate, indeed necessary, to integrate the gospel with other forms of knowledge and spiritual activity—some of which are to be found in the experiences of ancient, distant civilizations and in the teachings of other philosophical and religious traditions, and some of which are the contribution of the latest developments and achievements in man's study of the modern soul. Such an integration could succeed in creating a great synthesis the richness and universality of which has never been seen in our history, but to enter into a discussion of it is not my present purpose.

I have hinted at this, however, both to suggest it as one of the fundamental areas that need to be considered by all those engaged in problems of the spirit, and to point out that even those who feel that the type of integration referred to above is necessary also feel a deep need to go back to the gospel with an open mind, interpreting it in the light of our new knowledge in order to discover how it applies to problems of today, and in particular to endeavour to make its lofty principles an everyday reality in a less imperfect fashion than has been the case until now.

The passage we have chosen contains a teaching that is perhaps less understood, appreciated and acted upon than all the others in the gospel. It therefore deserves a closer, more careful study because it has the potential for offering greater benefits than other passages.

In order to better understand the deep significance of Jesus' warning, let us pause a moment to recreate the scene in this house in Bethany. The unexpected arrival of Jesus was bound to have a considerable effect on the two sisters, but the way each of them reacted psychologically to the event was very different. Both of them felt a fervent desire rising within them to show honour to their guest, but they chose to do so in very different ways!

Martha, with her middle-class mentality, was concerned to show the proper respect and devotion by preparing a lavish meal, spreading the table with the best produce they had. She was thus honouring the body, the external personality, of Jesus.

Mary, on the other hand, by a spontaneous act from within her being, honoured his Spirit, and whereas to outward appearances she was doing and giving nothing, apart from listening, enraptured by the words of light that flowed from Jesus' lips, she was actually offering him the thing he prized most of all, perhaps the thing he desired most intently, something which only men and women could give him: an understanding of his divine message, and complete dedication to the ideal of which he was the living incarnation.

How often his heart overflowing with love must have bled as he came up against the hard, closed hearts of men, how often his soul must have suffered from man's skepticism, hardness, lethargy and wickedness—not only from the Scribes and Pharisees but, even more painfully, from those closest and dearest to him, those who called themselves his followers! Their frequent misunderstanding of his words, their falling asleep during his hours of agony in the Garden of Gethsemane, Peter's triple denial—not to mention his betrayal by Judas—show quite clearly the great distance that separated Jesus from men, and his acute awareness of his isolation from them must have been the most intimate, hidden, and perhaps the most painful, aspect of his passion.

How Jesus' heart must have warmed, then, to the unwonted tenderness of understanding and the intimate spiritual communion showed him by Mary in her rapt stillness and in her ecstatic silence. Jesus nevertheless recognized that the solicitous Martha was also honouring him in the best way she could, and accepting her prosaic homage he was prepared to enjoy the lavish meal his bustling hostess was in the process of creating. He allowed her to get on with her preparations without requiring her to listen to what he had to say—teachings she could not have understood.

However Martha lacked the very tact that Jesus himself was showing her. Not content with acting as she saw fit, she wanted her sister to do the same—indeed she even reproved Jesus indirectly for not telling Mary to follow her example: 'Lord, don't you care that my sister has left me to do the work by myself? Tell her to help me!'

This aggressive attitude of the interfering, bustling hostess forced Jesus out of his indulgent restraint to admonish her in calm, yet serious and effective words, words full of deep, universal significance: 'Martha, Martha, you are worried and upset about many things, but only one thing is needed. Mary has chosen what is better, and it will not be taken away from her'.

What does Jesus' admonition have to say to us today? I believe it has many, far-reaching implications, but before we can implement them we need to clearly understand the true nature and the various forms of what we call action.

Martha and Mary are generally regarded as symbols of action and inaction. This interpretation would be true if one accepted the ordinary, limited definition of action as an external activity, but it does not in fact reveal to us the intimate nature of the contrasting functions of activity. It has therefore led to error and to wrong conclusions in practice. The fact is that the problem of action is much more difficult and complex than it seems at first sight. This was fully appreciated by the ancient sages of India who went into this subject in some depth. The unknown author of the Baghavad Gita, the great philosophical religious poem contained in the *Mahabharata*, says:

What is action, and what is inaction? Even the sages are puzzled about this ... The nature of action is difficult to understand. He who is able to see inaction in action and action in inaction is among the wisest of men and will be devout in whatever he does.

Let us examine this apparent paradox. The criteria by which ordinary man judges any form of action are completely external, quantifiable and mechanical. By this definition the man of action is someone who produces tangible, visible results, someone who earns a lot of money, someone who erects large buildings, or someone who controls many other people.

As the man in the street sees it, meditation and contemplation are synonymous with useless dreams, inertia and the failure to produce anything of value. He regards those engaged in meditation and mysticism as being on a par with the poet in Carducci's verse:

> . . . an idler
> who goes around
> bumping his head against corners,
> his nose in the air,
> his eyes for ever tracing
> the flights of angels and swifts.

This is a widely held view. We must therefore show how fundamentally wrong it is. Anyone prepared to make a thorough examination of the true nature of what passes as activity today, without allowing himself to be taken in by appearances, will soon become aware that much of it is tinsel rather than gold; it is busy-ness, bustle, strain, agitation and activity for activity's sake, rather than true action.

The essential characteristics of true action—as nature itself reveals—are harmony, organic unity, rhythm and above all productivity. How sadly lacking these characteristics are from much of our activity! How often our activity is nothing but a sham, a vain expenditure of energy. How similar our activity is to the feet in Tagore's perceptive poem, 'raising dust, but having no effect on the fertility of the land'.

Think of the businessman who is already rich, caught up in a life of frantic activity in order to accumulate more riches which he will not only have no noble, productive use for, but will not even have the time to enjoy selfishly, think of the politician, eaten up by ambition, who relentlessly does everything he can to climb onto the unstable pedestal of public office, getting involved in endless intrigues and turning a blind eye to underhand practices, or think of the worldly woman hurrying from a reception to a tea party, from a dinner to a theatre trip, always preoccupied with her appearance and her jewels, for nothing but the futile accolades of vanity. Can we say that any of them is truly active? Or is it not simply the case that their incessant agitation within the limited confines of their paltry preoccupations is more like the ridiculous obstinacy with which some dogs will run round in circles trying to catch their own tails?

But this is not the worst of it: there are activities which are decidedly harmful and destructive in nature, acts that offend against the sacred nature of life, acts that mutilate the body, as well as those that wound and pervert the soul. There is the whole sad gamut of transgressions and crimes—those that are recognized and condemned by codes of law, and those that escape human punishment but not the infallible jurisdiction of moral law.

In all these manifestations, I repeat, man is not truly *active*. By behaving in such ways he is allowing himself passively to be governed by his instincts and passions; he is deceived by mirages, prompted by suggestion and habit.

One particularly strong influence to which people are often prey is that of suggestion, be it individual or collective: so often we think mistakenly that we are acting independently when we are actually being carried along, without our realizing it, by a powerful force outside of ourselves.

I will relate a minor incident from real life, which clearly demonstrates the unconscious force of imitation. A friend of mine who had just arrived in New York and had nothing in particular to do left his hotel with the intention of taking a stroll around the city. After a few minutes he noticed that he was hurrying along, out of breath. Surprised by this he started to walk more slowly, but it was not long before he again found himself hurrying along! Everyone around him was in a great hurry and he had succumbed, against his will, to the unspoken yet compelling suggestion of their example.

In contrast with this, the true activity of one's deepest being is often hidden beneath apparent inactivity, in the heart of silence. As in the world of nature, so in man every creative act, every original initiative and impulse, and every surge of life is produced in darkness, in quietness and in apparent immobility. Seeds germinate in the darkness, covered by two layers of dark brown soil and unspoilt snow, spring waters gush from the earth, living and pure, while deep down under the ground is the vein that feeds them. Thus in man the deep, hidden work through which he forms himself and develops his powers, the demanding task of processing and assimilating the building bricks of experience collected in his outward life, the hard work that lies behind every productive inspiration, indeed every truly productive and creative act takes place in a collected mind, in silence, in the inner regions of the soul.

Modern man, whose attention is always focused on the outside world, continually distracted by the illusory images of outward appearances, does not even suspect the reality, the substance or the richness of that inner world, the power of the forces acting in it, or the importance of the events that take place there. Far from being a world of inertia, full of dreams, it is actually the world of effective causes, and every external, visible manifestation is simply the result and effect of those causes.

It is true, of course, that the inner world also harbours the region of vain dreams, enervating nostalgia, plaintive laments, morbid sentimentalism, and the region of pointless criticism, faint-hearted doubts, spineless laziness and shameful lethargy. But this is not the true inner world: it is an intermediate zone, the place of refuge for the weak, the barren, the cowards and all those who do not know how or want to brave either the difficulties of life in today's world or the equally great difficulties of the true life within. Indeed, the difficulties of the inner life require just as much toughness, effort and commitment.

Within the vast world of the soul there are the glorious peaks of spiritual contemplation where all sense of effort melts away and where man abandons himself completely to the influence of the Spirit, but in order to reach these heights he must first tread a long, weary path—to achieve the state in which pure contemplation is possible requires a tough, methodical work of purification, self-discipline and ascent.

In order to highlight and state more clearly the various relationships that operate between external activity and internal activity, we will make a brief examination of the two opposing types of anomaly and aberration that we come across in the area of action, and the methods for correcting them. One of these anomalies takes the form of impulsiveness and the other that of loss of will-power.

Impulsive, violent and restless people are those in whom the central inhibiting force is unable to properly discipline and control the forces of the instincts and the passions, either because the latter are too intense or because the inhibiting force is intrinsically too weak. They therefore either feel compelled to undertake all sorts of actions, but rarely complete them, or else they commit aggressive, destructive acts. These are the sort of people we referred to earlier, who raise a lot of dust but do not create anything of real value.

Quite clearly the highest and truest action such impulsive people need to engage in would be to appear not to act at all, to continuously and strictly control their impulses, to perform a series of acts of will aimed at disciplining their unruly energies, forcing those energies to come under a form of central control and to be brought into harmony with one another so that they might be purified and ennobled, until such time as they are able to express themselves externally in constructive works. This is a clear example of how a reduction in outward activity can serve as an indication of intensified inner action.

An examination of those who have lost their will-power, who are weak, half-hearted and unable to act, will bring us to the same conclusions. Indeed it is pointless trying to get a person suffering from aboulia to act, for if he were able to act he would not be in the condition he is. In order to get such a person to act, or to cure him of his aboulia, we must first discover the underlying causes and deal with those. These causes are more varied and complex than one might imagine and would require a special study of their own, so for our present purpose I will only refer to some of the main problem areas.

Aboulia is often not related to true weakness, but to the inhibiting effect of intense impressions and experiences from as far back as early childhood, things the person concerned does not usually even remember. Or it can be related to a conflict between two conscious or unconscious forces which, being opposite extremes and having more or less the same intensity, sap a person's mental energies in a futile struggle from which there is no escape. In other cases aboulia is attributable to an excessive sensitivity and malleability, which means that the individual in question is continuously being affected by a whole host of contrasting influences in his surroundings and becomes like a weathercock that changes direction with the wind. In yet other cases aboulia is the product of an exaggerated intellectual activity of a critical or analytical nature, and this blocks the flow of energy from deep within. In all these cases release from aboulia and the acquisition of normal power for action require a complex, long drawn out period of adjustment, reconstruction and inner strengthening. While this lasts there will be no outward manifestation, but it will nevertheless be true action and the source of all activity in the future.

What is true for the extreme cases of those gripped by impulsiveness or aboulia is just as true for all people, for each one of us. Too often we forget that it is not the amount of work that counts, but the quality of that action, and that even where others are concerned, and for their good, our first and most urgent duty is to improve ourselves.

'Every soul that is lifted up will in turn lift up the world,' said the modern mystic Elisabetta Leseur. Every passion brought under control, every error corrected, means one less danger for everyone; every new light of wisdom that shines within us, every newly developed moral force, and every higher sentiment awakened within us will just as inevitably be a benefit for humanity as a whole.

These spiritual treasures can permeate the world around us in a thousand different ways, without any conscious effort, even without our knowledge, showing themselves in every word spoken or written, in every act, and revealing an invisible yet powerful radiance. We often neglect this basic duty, however, and in our presumption, impatience or carelessness we set out on our mission unhesitatingly to tackle the demanding task of improving ... others. As soon as we have some small change we are at pains to act as benefactors and philanthropists, without considering the smallness of our gift, the inner debts we still have to pay and without remembering, as Tagore says in one of his telling aphorisms, that 'He who is too involved in doing good will not have the time to be good.'

Indeed, if we examine our motives with all sincerity we often discover that the reasons for our preoccupation with helping

others are not as pure and noble as we thought. We begin to
realize that the shining alloy, mixed with gold, also contains the
base metal of vanity, presumption, proselytism and—most
subtle and concealed of all—the desire to appease our conscience
so that we will have some excuse for not undertaking the hard
work of inner purification.

Yet even when these baser motives are not present, even when
our motives are pure, we can commit the error referred to above,
out of weakness, out of condescension, out of ignorance, or out
of too narrow and external a view of duty.

Maurice Maeterlinck warns us in an illuminating image:

Let us avoid acting like the lighthouse keeper in the legend who gave
away to the poor people in the nearby hovels the oil for the
lighthouse lamp which was intended for giving light to the ocean.
Every soul, deep within, is the keeper of a lighthouse, and these
lighthouses are all necessary to varying degrees. The most humble
mother who allows herself to become saddened, absorbed and
completely destroyed by her narrow duties as a mother is giving her
oil to the poor, leaving her children to suffer for the rest of their lives
because their mother's soul was not as bright as it might have been.
The intangible power that shines in our heart must first of all shine
for itself. Only in this way will it be able to shine for others.
However small your lamp, never give away the oil that feeds it—give
the flame that is its crown.

If we give careful consideration to the lives of those who have
benefitted mankind most, bringing help not only to the body
but also to the soul, we will discover that their period of service
was also preceded by long periods of silence and apparent
inaction, during which their spiritual energies were awakened
and powerfully concentrated—energies which would then burst
forth and spread out irresistibly, *ex plenitudine contemplationis* [out
of the fullness of contemplation], to use the beautiful expression
of St Thomas, producing amazing effects.

The life of Jesus provides us with a clear example of this. It is
significant that we know nothing about his life between the ages
of 12 and 30. Various theories have been put forward to fill this
gap in our knowledge: some have spoken about a period of
instruction and initiation in the secret schools of the Essenes,

others have wondered whether he went on journeys to other regions and came into contact with other currents of spiritual wisdom. Whether or not such theories are true, we are left with the fact that for 18 years Jesus was out of the public eye and that, in one way or another, alone or in some community, he was engaged in a silent work of inner preparation, the visible effects of which were only seen by men for three years—but which had such power that they continue today, after some 2,000 years.

The most important mystics followed the same course. St Catherine of Siena, for instance, lived for a number of years in a tiny room in her father's house, but when she came out, she tirelessly covered the length and breadth of Italy and France, warning and castigating prince and pope alike for their striving after material well-being, arousing fierce opposition and bringing new life to countless souls.

This calm inner silence, conscious reflection, meditation, prayer and contemplation—in short, all those essential elements of a work deep within—are not only the necessary preparation for external action, they continue to be indispensable for inspiration and renewal. They are an ongoing source of nourishment.

Even this great law is clearly evidenced in the life of Jesus. There is explicit mention of this in the gospel. 'Having dismissed the crowd,' Matthew writes, 'Jesus withdrew to the mountain to pray.' Mark tells us that 'In the morning, a great while before dawn, Jesus got up and went out to a solitary place in order to pray.' Luke confirms this and tells us that before performing the most important actions in his life he would go off to pray for many hours. Thus before choosing the 12 apostles from among his disciples and preaching the Sermon on the Mount, 'He went out to a mountainside to pray, and spent the whole night praying to God.' Again in Gethsemane, the night of his betrayal, Jesus drew strength from prayer, from communion with his Father, receiving the superhuman strength he needed to freely and consciously go forward towards his crucifixion, the strength that supported him through his passion. The same method was employed by his greatest 'imitators', the most active apostles, from St Paul to St Teresa, from St Francis of Sales to St Vincent of Paoli.

That such close links of integration and alternation between the inner life and the external life are universal in nature, representing a necessary condition for a harmonious, fruitful human existence, is confirmed by the fact that they have also been discovered in distant civilizations very different from our own. We need only look at the clear way in which the Bhagavad Gita poses and resolves the problem of action to see how the ancient sages of India had reached the same conclusions as the Christian saints. We also find practical confirmation and a noble example of this in the life of the greatest of India's sons, Gautama Buddha. After his revelation of universal pain had forced him to leave his father's home in search of liberating truth, he devoted himself tirelessly, for many years, to the inner life. After various unsuccessful attempts, and having tried the methods of asceticism to no avail, it was through purely internal self-discipline, using a method of attainment and development of ever higher states of meditation and contemplation that he eventually discovered the Supreme Light. In the period of active service which followed, lasting half a century, travelling throughout India and converting millions, he taught and advocated with particular insistence the practice of those inner activities.

It is only in our present civilization that these universal principles have been ignored and looked down on. We alone hold Martha up as an example to be admired, while Mary is ignored or despised. I hope, however, that I have succeeded in showing that such an attitude is wrong and has harmful consequences, as well as showing that many of the most serious shortcomings and evils of our contemporary world can be traced back to this cause.

Everything follows a rhythm, be it the outward expression of nature or the inner nature, and just as there is summer and winter, day and night, a waking state and sleep, every ordered, harmonious life should also be characterized by the alternation between contemplative silence and external action. There is no need for this rhythm of silence followed by external action to follow the same rigid patterns as the cycles to which natural phenomena are confined: it is free to adapt, in a flexible, appropriate fashion, to the various conditions and practical demands of human life in all its complexity. Anyone who truly wants to apply this principle will be able to do so. Let us remember the wise distribution of time employed in the past: two periods of quiet each day—the morning for meditation and preparation for practical activity and the evening for reflection—once a week, then, after six days devoted to Caesar, a day given mostly to God, and once a year at least a longer retreat in which a person had the time to engage in a more effective, systematic work of inner improvement.

So far it will have been fairly easy to gain the ready agreement of anyone with an open mind on this subject—a mind, that is, with aspirations for what is good. But now we must tackle a question on which such agreement will be more difficult to achieve. This has to do with the way we look at those who lead a purely contemplative life, i.e. those who, having abandoned the ordinary way of life, never return to the 'world', but remain in monasteries, convents or hermitages. It might seem that they have infringed the law of rhythmic balance between the external life and the inner life we have just been talking about, and it might be suspected that this represents nothing other than an exaggeration or a degeneration of mysticism. It might be thought that these contemplatives do not know how to strike a right balance, that they are weak, the victims of shipwreck, or deserters from the human scene. As an impartial observer I have to admit that in some cases this is to an extent true, but having expressed this reservation one can confidently state that true mystics, the great contemplatives, have a real and effective function to perform in the life of humanity as a whole, that they are in fact active—indeed when they are successful in achieving the highest goals of their vocation they acquire the ability to perform a type of activity that requires the most intense and continuous concentration of mental energies, the most direct control over matter by the spirit, and this can result in the most powerful and far-reaching of benefits.

So ingrained is the extroverted, materialistic mentality of our civilization that even those who call themselves spiritualists do not even appreciate or understand this special form of human activity. Within the Churches themselves the contemplative life has attracted fewer and fewer followers in modern times, yet there is convincing evidence of the effectiveness of the spiritual forces radiated by superior souls in whom the fire of contemplation burns brightly. Such evidence may escape the eye of the superficial observer or of those with preconceived ideas, but it is quite clear when considered carefully and impartially. The countless supporting testimonies to this power that we find in the history of different civilizations cannot be ignored.

The radiating effect of silent prayer, the many extraordinary healings, the conversions that have taken place over great distances, the influence of a person deep in prayer as perceived by those to whom that prayer was consciously directed, and sometimes the feeling that the persons were actually present, are facts which may cause great surprise, but they must not be rejected out of hand on the basis of doctrinaire preconceptions or stamped with the sentence of impossibility.

It is even less valid to do this now when the material sciences, with their most recent discoveries, are rapidly changing our understanding of the universe, providing valid evidence in support of spiritual concepts. The facts of telepathy, telekinesis and ideo-plasty, which some men of science have now confidently established, show that psychical forces can act outside of the confines of the physical body, having a direct effect on matter at a distance and causing it to vibrate or change its form. Now that it has been shown that such powers exist, who has the right to predetermine new limits? What arguments can a person use to deny the effectiveness of the spiritual acts performed by contemplatives and mystics?

This effect is also confirmed in other ways. Every day we come up against instances of mental activity being more powerful than muscular effort alone in changing the external world. The temporary mental effort required to invent a machine and direct its construction provides us with a means of saving vast amounts of muscular energy—it can even enable us to produce effects no amount of muscular effort could achieve. There is much factual evidence for recognizing a similar relationship between mental energy and spiritual energy, and for supposing that the latter is just as superior to the former as the former is to physical force. For these and other reasons one might wish to put forward, I believe we need no longer doubt the effectiveness of direct spiritual radiation, but should instead come to the point of recognizing that its power is immeasurable. This is a real revelation, and one that opens up limitless possibilities for the hidden powers for good within the human soul, revealing the way in which divine action itself is expressed, and it gives us a view of life and of the world which is very different from the prevailing view. This view has not yet gained general acceptance and the contemplative life is rarely paid any serious attention, even by today's spiritualists. But we are not without those who even today proclaim the value and excellence of the hidden action of the contemplatives.

The powerful spiritual radiation of these contemplatives, then, is the purest and highest form of action, the form that comes closest to the *modus operandi* of God Himself, in other words it is the apotheosis of Mary. But precisely because it is such a high, almost superhuman calling it is an exceptional activity, one that transcends the capacity of ordinary man. It is therefore an activity to which only those with a vocation for it should devote themselves, those who feel they have all the necessary inner resources for fully expressing it. Everyone else 'needs to make another journey'. For their consolation—now that we have recognized the essential value and superiority of Mary—we can also give due credit to Martha, a Martha who has heeded Jesus' admonition, a Martha who has been reconciled to Mary and then humbly and willingly continues her useful work.

There are many advantages in external activity when it is kept within its proper limits and is illuminated by the light of the spirit. Apart from its immediate use, it is a way—especially for the young—of putting their exuberant energies to work, a fertile field of experience, a training-ground where the virtues produced by inner discipline can be put to the test, or a forge on which the steel of the will undergoes a more thorough toughening process. But this is not all: the spiritual significance and inner effects of any action depend primarily on the underlying motive that inspired it. This is what is at the heart of the action. This simple, self-evident principle, though one that is often forgotten, provides us with great scope. If we perform an action, however humble and menial it may be, with a soul that is free from any personal attachment or interest, and if we offer it as a pure act of love in service to God and men, then we are performing a spiritual action. This is the precious compensation, the great comfort of all those who, though hungry for silent contemplation and peace, are forced by the harsh realities of life or by inescapable family and social responsibilities to lead a life of gruelling hard work. When they discover that by their inner attitude they can infuse each action with spiritual significance, that each circumstance of their external lives can be used as an opportunity for expressing inner virtues, in other words that each gesture can become a rite, their lives are transformed, and from being miserable, barren and hateful, they become, as if by magic, rich, fertile and joyful.

In this way it is possible to ascend, step by step, a peak which is just as high and glorious as that reached through contemplation; indeed one can reach a state in which external action no longer hampers the inner life of the soul and in which the latter does not detract from the effectiveness of the former, but supports, guides and empowers it. In this state man almost has a double consciousness which enables him to express his essential spiritual unity to the full. He is both actor and spectator at one and the same time: simultaneously he experiences the joy of productive work and the joy of free spiritual insight. This exalted achievement has been recognized, pursued and advocated both in the East and in the West.

This high ideal is particularly suited to life in today's world because it neither imposes limitations on our necessary external activities, nor compels us to abandon any task or neglect any duty. The transformation required is wholly an internal one. It takes hard work to achieve this, but the great spirits of the past affirm that it is possible and invite us to aim for the same goal. The waves of a glorious harmony come down to our ears from that glorious height: it is the union of two very pure notes, the spiritual embrace of Martha and Mary.

23

THE SPIRITUAL ELEMENTS IN OUR PERSONALITY: BEAUTY

We will now turn to the spiritual elements that come down like rays of sunlight into the human personality—into our personal consciousness—and form a link between our ordinary human personality and the spiritual 'I', the spiritual Reality. They are like rays of light pouring down, taking on various shades of colour and dispersing, depending on the permeability or the transparency of our personal consciousness.

We have referred elsewhere to the moral sense as one of the aspects in which spiritual reality and the personal human consciousness are revealed. We have therefore dealt with the rational and intuitive mental consciousness as a means of contact between the personal consciousness and the spiritual reality of man.[1] We will now look at a third element that comes down from above to illuminate, enrich and animate human life. This is the sense of Beauty.

In order to fully understand the nature and power of beauty we need to remember the spiritual concept which states that everything that exists externally, in concrete form and individually is the manifestation, effect and reflection of a higher, transcendent, spiritual Reality. It is the great principle of involution or emanation. From a basic, original absolute reality, a series of levels of life, intellect, feeling and material life has developed, through gradual differentiation, to the point of inorganic matter. Thus every quality or attribute of the external world, of matter itself, and of the countless different creatures, is but a pale, obscure reflection of a quality or attribute

[1] See Bibliographical Notes, page 292. [Compiler's Note.]

of the spiritual Reality, the Divine Being. This is particularly true when it comes to Beauty.

The fact that beauty is the essential attribute of the Supreme, Divine Being has been recognized and proclaimed by thinkers since the dawn of history, and by the great mystics and by the most gifted artists of all ages. This has been affirmed particularly in the West by Plato, Plotinus and, in the Christian world, by the unknown mystic of the fifth and sixth centuries whose works have been attributed to Dionyges Areopagita. He wrote, 'The Infinite One is known by the name of Beauty', and defined God as 'The One who is essentially beautiful.'

Thus in all that has been created there must be some vestige, some trace of this essential attribute of the Prime Creator. Indeed, according to this same Areopagita, everything that exists, since it derives its very existence from the One who is essentially Beautiful, retains in the arrangement of its parts some vestige of intelligible beauty.

But if we now move on to study the effects of the perception of beauty as manifested in mankind in general, we find ourselves faced with a certain paradox, an apparent contradiction. On the one hand we can say that among the attributes of God beauty is the most easily recognizable because it is the one first manifested in ancient times, the most tangible attribute, one that left its imprint in concrete, material forms, and the attribute that struck the senses and the imagination more directly than any other. On the other hand it is clearly the most dangerous attribute, one that more than any other ties man to matter and form, and one which more than any other produces in him the desire for sensory pleasure, the sense of selfish, separate ownership, an attribute that more than any other blinds and deceives man, enveloping him in the iridescent veils of maya— those of the Great Illusion—and thus the attribute which most distances him and keeps him separate from God, the deep Reality of Truth.

How can we explain this paradox? It is not difficult. Precisely because beauty is the divine quality that has assumed the most concrete expression, has been made tangible and manifested itself in matter, it is the one man can most readily abuse, without recognizing its noble origin. The quality of beauty is no longer related to its source, rather it has come to be regarded as a quality that resides in matter itself and in its concrete forms.

But there is another reason. It is the very intensity of the power and fascination that beauty exerts which produces overwhelming desires, unchecked passions and the lust for exclusive possession in a man who has not yet been purified or become master of himself. What can be done to correct this undesirable state? How can we prevent the nectar of beauty from becoming a mortal poison for man, and allow it instead to be or become what it ought in essence to be—the water of life, the elixir of immortality? There are two ways.

The first is that of negation, recognition of *maya*, or illusion, a firm detachment, and a suppression of any activity of the senses. It is the way that is sometimes referred to, somewhat inappropriately, as asceticism. The word asceticism has acquired what I would regard as rather pejorative connotations, because of certain excesses on the part of certain ascetics, but etymologically it has a better, wider meaning than this. In Greek it simply means 'exercise, discipline, training', yet it has become associated with harsh imposition and privation. This is the way that some orientals have chosen, the more rigid Buddhists in particular, and it is also the way of certain ascetic Christian mystics, from the anchorites of Thebaid to St Bernard who, when travelling through Switzerland, would shut his eyes so that the beauty of the lakes and the mountains would not distract him from his meditations, and all the way down to the curate who had qualms about smelling a rose.

This is a way that very readily arouses our criticism and rebellion—it seems isolationist, inhuman, almost blasphemous. If we consider it impartially it can be a considerable short-cut, a violent yet powerful means of reaching the Supreme Being, having firmly severed all ties. Moreover it may be a necessary stage, or at least a useful one, along the path to detachment for those who are too easily allured by the desires of the senses, and for those who are enslaved to them and want to be released. But having said this it needs to be recognized that this way is not without serious drawbacks and that it is only suitable for a limited number of people.

There is another easier, more harmonious and gradual way,

however, and it too reaches the same noble goal. This is the way that leads to overcoming of exclusive, sensory attachment to beautiful things. It takes two forms: through the enlargement or inclusion, on the horizontal plane, of all forms of beauty, without showing exclusive or separatist preferences; and through elevation or sublimation, on the vertical plane, which raises one's eyes from the effect to the cause, from the expression to the essence, from the manifestation to the invisible source. This was admirably stated with clarity and precision by Plato in his *Banquet*.

> One needs to progress from love of a beautiful form to love of all beautiful forms and of physical beauty in general, then from love of beautiful bodies to love of beautiful souls, beautiful actions and beautiful thoughts.
>
> As one ascends through moral beauty one will reach the point where a marvellous eternal beauty appears, free from any corruption, absolutely beautiful. This beauty does not consist of a beautiful face, a beautiful body, a thought or any particular science or art. It resides in no other being than itself, neither in heaven nor on earth, it simply exists in itself in eternity and exists for itself in absolute, perfect unity.

This ascendant way has been used and described by various Christian mystics, St Francis in particular (one need only think of his *Canticle of the Creatures* in which 'the Sun refers to God'), who also expressed it in delightful detail and gave orders that flowers be grown in the monastery so that all who saw them would be reminded of the Eternal Gentleness. It was also the way of St Rosa of Lima for whom the song of a bird or the sight of a flower had the immediate effect of lifting her soul to God, and St Francis of Sales was also a master of the art of transforming every natural, beautiful phenomenon into some form of reference to God, an analogy and a symbol of spiritual truth.

This indeed is the secret: to recognize that external things have no true value, significance or reality of their own, that they only serve to highlight or represent inner realities and spiritual qualities. This secret is expressed so incisively by Goethe at the end of *Faust* in a statement that sums up the whole meaning of the poem: 'Everything transitory is but a symbol.'

Now let us take a closer, more practical look at the different steps on the Platonic scale or ladder, and the ways in which one can rise from one step to the next.

The first, as we saw, is the transition from love of a beautiful form to love of all beautiful forms. By this expansion in a horizontal direction one gradually overcomes exclusive attachment, that jealous longing for the material possession of one particular form, of a single isolated creature. In one sense we can call this discovering the beauty of the world. Again this can be done in two ways. First of all it can be done directly in nature itself, by learning to notice the infinite variety and beauty of natural phenomena and learning to really see them. For this we need a detached attitude, a forgetting of one's own personality, the separate 'I' with its selfish preoccupations, we need to immerse ourselves in the object being observed and admired until we almost merge with it and become one with it. This is the simplest way of opening a crack or a chink in the tough skin of the separate 'I'. It is a fairly easy way because all it requires is that we take one step towards an object and the intrinsic beauty of that object responds and attracts us—and the more it attracts us the closer to it we move and the more beauty we discover. Thus, little by little, we actually reach the point of coming out of ourselves, in search of communion between subject and object, and we reach that aesthetic contemplation which, as Schopenhauer puts it, has a 'liberating effect', a form of contemplation he considered to be the greatest consolation available to suffering humanity.

First of all there are those natural objects which, because of their very obvious beauty, their attractiveness or grandeur, draw us to them and help us in our quest. One of the natural objects that is of great benefit in this connection is the sky. Here are some of the beautiful things expressed by one of the men who have seen the beauty of world to varying degrees: Ruskin.

It is strange how unfamiliar people are with the sky. It is the part of creation in which nature, better than anywhere else, has expressed its desire to recreate man, to speak to his spirit and educate him. It is this educational aspect we know least about. Anyone, whatever his situation, and however far he is from any other source of attraction or beauty, has the sky, at least at some point. The noblest of earth's wonders may only be seen and known by a handful of people, no one can live amongst them continuously; he would cease to notice them if they were always before his eyes. But the sky is for everyone. The sky is eminently suited, in all its aspects, to comfort and uplift the heart, to soothe it and free it from its impurities. Sometimes it is soft and gentle, at other times it can be capricious or even sad—it is never the same from one moment to the next, always human in its passions, always spiritual in its tenderness, always divine in its infinity and grandeur. Its appeal to what is immortal in us is quite clear, and it performs the necessary task of chastening or wounding whatever is mortal in us.

The first step in our communion with nature, then, is with certain 'wonders' that attract us most. One then moves on to a general communion which is less individualistic: seeing that element of beauty in everything, in humble, everyday things—a blade of grass, a flower—even in things which at first glance seem to have no beauty.

It is this relationship, this solidarity, this unity which shines through the variety and multiplicity of things, giving them a sense of nobility and referring back to their origin. Some men have had the divine gift of seeing this hidden beauty in greater measure than others. It is as if things became transparent, illuminated from within—they are like thin veils which allow our eyes to glimpse and perceive something of the divine glory, a glory we would otherwise fail to see.

Already we have these different steps in the contemplation of nature: admiration of a particular object, some beautiful aspect of nature, followed by the first step out of ourselves, communion between subject and object, a sense of the beauty of all natural objects, then that perception of their profound unity, and lastly a revelation of the consequences of beauty in nature.

Another area is that of art. This is the true function and goal of art: to reveal the hidden beauty or the divine imprint in all things. The artist in a sense accentuates, draws out and reveals this beauty, so that those who would not otherwise notice it in nature by themselves are helped to do so through the eyes of the artist. The soul of the artist which experiences this beauty and expresses it in a new beauty, helps us to recognize the divine seal. And this is the touchstone—the difference between minor art, pseudo-art composed of external, artificial elements, and truly great art.

I will limit myself to these few comments on the matter, otherwise it would require a much fuller treatment, but I will, however, mention that this horizontal form of expansion, this revelation and manifestation of beauty in nature and in art has its limits and its dangers. One of the dangers is that of aestheticism which, however refined, always contains a degree of hedonism, a hint of sensuality, as though beauty were an end in itself, which takes too much delight and finds too exclusive an enjoyment in this aesthetic contemplation, and thus unjustifiably neglects the other aspects, the other qualities and attributes of the Divine that we need to discover and incorporate into our lives in order to achieve a full, all encompassing understanding of the Divine nature. There is also a limitation in terms of the formal, external aspects of beauty.

We must therefore move on to the step of inner beauty. In the case of beauty as perceived by the senses, this is clearly dependent on our attitude. An object can be a step, and thus a means of help for us to overcome an obstacle that is holding us back. The merit or lack of merit does not reside within the object, but within ourselves, in our inner attitude to that object.

Inner beauty, moral beauty, the beauty of sublime, harmonious thoughts, noble, generous sentiments and heroic deeds has been well described by Maurice Maeterlinck. Here are some quotes from the chapter entitled 'Inner Beauty' from his book *The Treasure of the Humble*, perhaps the most profound and exalted of his works.

Nothing is more eager for beauty than the soul, nor more susceptible of becoming beautiful ... A beautiful thought shut up within you, which you do not express though you perceive it, illuminates you like a flame inside a transparent vase.

Plotinus, having spoken of intelligible beauty in Chapter VIII of the fifth book of his *Enneads*, concludes:

We are beautiful when we belong to ourselves; we cease to be beautiful when we sink to the level of our lower nature. We are beautiful when we know ourselves; we cease to be beautiful when we do not know ourselves.

I do not in fact believe the nature and essence of moral beauty, of fine thoughts, noble sentiments and generous actions could be expressed better than at the level of what is individual and distinguishes one person from another.

It was Plato who revealed the third step to us: transition to the essential beauty which is above any form of beauty. A sense of the sublime helps us at this point.

Credit for having analysed this state of mind goes to Immanuel Kant. Whereas with normal beauty imagination and intellect act in agreement, when we come to the sublime they are opposed. Indeed the object is not sublime because it strikes our senses—the senses and the imagination feel powerless to reach it, as though it were something infinitely beyond the sphere of the senses. In the face of the sublime the savage flees, yet he cannot escape a sense of anxiety because the sublime impresses its material power on him. The emotion associated initially with the sublime is therefore depression, but the primitive sense of terror is followed by a deep satisfaction because the sublime arouses in us a sense of our moral greatness. Our feelings therefore change from depression to exaltation, from anxiety to enthusiasm.

There are two forms the sublime can take: the mathematical, what one might call the quantitative, expressed by its greatness in the form of expansion, and the dynamic, which reveals itself to us in the miracle of power. But as one moves deeper into an analysis of the sublime one in a sense comes into contact with the exalted, majestic, almost frightening aspect of divinity. This aspect has been clearly described by the deeply religious spirit of Rudolf Otto in his book *The Sacred*. He calls this aspect of the divine the 'numinous', which he defines in clear terms and places great emphasis on.

We have already referred to the two main aspects of divinity: immanence and transcendence. They are both real and necessary, but taken individually they are one-sided: they need to be integrated or merged. When the aspect of immanence is given the upper hand there is the danger of diminishing or debasing the idea of the Divine and all its manifestations. Thus in the aesthetic field, when this aspect of expression and form prevails we have the graceful, the pleasant, the elegant and the cold perfection of the Parnassians and the Neo-classicists. In the religious field we have the sentimental mysticism and the personal love of God become man: too much man. In the area of thought we have the deification of man as man, as it is expressed in certain idealistic trends. When there is an exclusive emphasis on the transcendent aspect, on the other hand, there is too great a dualism: nature and God are placed in opposite corners and an artificial opposition is created between them— between creation and Creator. There is then too wide a gap between man and God.

What is needed, as I said earlier, is integration—a synthesis between the two, and in order to achieve this in practical terms we must accentuate the aspect which is most needed in ourselves or in the age in which we live. The prevailing tendency today is clearly on the side of immanence. It is the age of science, an age which to all outward appearances gives us an expandable sense of the sublime.

As the prevailing trends are extroversion and the search for truth and beauty, as well as for power, both in the external world and in nature, the need today therefore is to accentuate the other aspect: both we personally and mankind in general need to be called back to a sense of the transcendent, to feel again that shiver caused by mystery and by a sense of the infinite.

Here too I would recommend *The Treasure of the Humble* by Maeterlinck. The chapter on silence helps us to re-evaluate and stand back from the pettiness and bustle of the outward-facing lives almost all of us are caught up in. A renewed and long overdue sense of transcendence will take us straight to the great Reality; it will enable us to perceive the beauty that is above all forms, the beauty of which Plato spoke in his matchless prose—that eternal Beauty which exists eternally within itself, in its own absolute and perfect unity.

THE SPIRITUAL ELEMENTS IN OUR PERSONALITY: LOVE

In our examination of the 'spiritual rays of light' that pour down into our personality we have so far spoken about beauty. We will now speak about another extremely important element: love.

Love is one of the most widespread aspects of life, one of the most universal of feelings and actions. Yet it is perhaps the least understood, and there is a great deal of confusion and misunderstanding about it, as a result of which very serious mistakes are made. It is therefore helpful, indeed necessary, to understand what love is so that we will be able to love well.

We will not be too surprised at the existing confusion and the mistakes it leads to if we remind ourselves that love is cosmic by nature, having a cosmic origin and cosmic functions, and that it is often an overwhelming feeling that dominates and overcomes an individual, manifesting itself internally and externally in very different and apparently contradictory ways. There is physical love and spiritual love, there is the love that desires, attracts to itself and absorbs, and there is a love that limits and enslaves, as well as a love that enhances and liberates. Then there is the sort of love in which the individual seems to lose himself, and a sort of love in which he finds himself. In order that we might bring some order and clarity to this confusion and to these contrasting descriptions of love and its effects, we need to place love in the great spiritual framework of life we have already referred to. Only then will be able to begin to penetrate the mystery.

As we consider the subject of love we need to bear this overall spiritual framework in mind. First of all we have the original unity, free from any form of differentiation, i.e. the Absolute, Transcendent, Unmanifested. It is from this that we have obtained the manifestation or differentiation we might regard as the projection, emanation or self-expression of the Supreme. This great cosmic process has various stages. The first is that of duality: the One becomes two. The first fundamental difference has been introduced: spirit and matter, the subjective aspect and the objective aspect, energy and resistance, activity and passivity, a positive pole and a negative pole, a male aspect and a female aspect. So far we have only spoken about the objective aspect of matter, something undifferentiated, we have not spoken about matter already differentiated as we know it. This is the primordial stage which we can call the relationship between the two.

These two great aspects of being do not remain separate, as though they were indifferent to one another, but exchanges take place—there is action and reaction—and the effect of this vital attraction is the creation or the manifestation of the universe as we know it, this fully developed, concrete universe. It did not reach its present form in a moment: there were successive stages of differentiation at the heart of creation. There was the expression of ever more concrete and material planes or levels of life, and ever more limited states of consciousness. And at each level countless new, successive differentiations until we reach the present highly divided state of separateness and difference between creatures in the widest sense of the word.

This then is the framework, or the stage on which we must come to terms with an understanding of love. Beneath the present state of division, difference and separation, in their various ways, and to different extents, these creatures have a distant, dim recollection of their original unity, a vague sense of common origin and an unconscious, though powerful, longing to return to that origin. Every creature, every separate being, feels incomplete, inadequate, unsatisfied; it lacks peace and searches for something, though it does not know what that something is. As it searches it makes mistakes and suffers one disappointment after another, but it cannot help continuing to search. It is spurred on relentlessly, and its thirst is never quenched. Indeed there is no alternative because this urge, this yearning, is an expression of the great law of evolution.

This gives us a glimpse of the secret of nature and the function of love. This earnest desire to be made complete, to become one, to merge with something else or with someone other than ourselves, is the very essence of love. And this union, this creative, productive merging, gives rise to something else. Just as One (the Spirit) and two (matter) make three (the differentiated manifestation), so the positive and the negative give rise to something else, something different, depending on the nature of the elements that come together. To state this in scientific terms we can say that the universe is based on the principle of polarity and operates in accordance with a law of attraction and a series of acts of reproduction. These principles, these basic laws, are to be found in all manifestations of love, however different and contrasting they may appear at first sight.

We see this quite clearly in inorganic matter. In the atom we have the positive charge of the nucleus and the negative charges of the electrons: these together make up the life and special quality of the atom. We find something similar with electricity, where the positive charge and the negative charge, if correctly combined, produce the spark that gives light and heat. With chemical elements, love, or the law of attraction and union, shows itself in the form of chemical affinity. For example there are the acids and the bases which come together to form salts.

In the realm of biology, in both vegetable and animal life, there is the attraction and merging of cells. In the most basic of organisms, i.e. single-celled organisms, two join together and produce other cells. In higher organisms, made up of many cells, there are differentiated male and female characteristics through which sexual reproduction takes place.

Now the subjective, psychological aspect of this sexual function is the powerful sense of physical attraction and the instincts aroused by the stimuli received via the senses. In this sense man is a participant in the life of the senses, but in man's case there are other levels at which love can be manifested. There is the emotional level, where it takes the form of sentimental, emotional attraction and the need for psychological completion—this covers a wide range of feelings, from a basic passion to possess to the noblest feelings aroused by the communion of souls—then there is the intellectual level where intellectual communion and the exchange of ideas result in a mutual enriching, and finally there is the spiritual level where other elements come into play. We shall speak about these later.

So far we have mentioned the most straightforward type of love: the tendency towards union, the law of attraction, or the relationship and complementary effect of two elements and beings of different poles or sexes. But there are variations, complications and refinements of the way in which love is manifested. To begin with there are those cases where, instead of a rigid or fixed polarity—as is the case with electricity or with physical gender—there is an alternation. Thus in the area of feelings or intellect, for example, the same individual may alternate between being negative and positive, active and passive, giving and receiving. There is greater flexibility, greater freedom of action, and thus greater choice.

Another complication or development of love takes place when there is a merging of several elements or individuals instead of just two. These even occur in the world of matter, of course, where there are complicated chemical combinations made up of three or more elements. Almost all organic compounds are of this nature: complex molecules containing carbon, hydrogen, oxygen, nitrogen and other elements. In the realm of biology there are cells in the form of primordial elements, then groups of cells and groups of groups of cells which form the organs, each consisting of a coherent group, carefully connected to other organs to make up a whole organism, carrying out their functions in harmony, in a system of mutual support: one might almost say in love.

In the world of human beings we also find various groupings that are held together, unified and created by strong bonds of affection. The first of these, what we might call the human cell, is the family. Clearly in many cases the family is a true unit, forming a small group that can almost be isolated from the rest, a group held together by strong bonds of the same love, the same ideal and the same inclinations. Another grouping is the community. The word community means union, a unit of various elements. Thus there are groupings and communities that are political, religious, social and even intellectual in nature; then there are the groupings of a few hundred people scattered around the world, such as, for example, astronomers, who speak a language which is partly unintelligible to others. This too is a form of union, or love.

In all these groups we find the same basic characteristics we spoke of with regard to love: a feeling of affection, a sense of union and completion, group activity and a level of productivity that is sometimes greater and different from what would be possible for individuals acting alone. But this is not all. We are only halfway through our examination.

All the relations based on polarity and union that we have considered so far are carried out on the same plane and are, so to speak, horizontal: they spread out and extend over a horizontal surface. The various chemical affinities we see operating in the realm of chemistry, the emotional human relationships we see in the area of the affections, and the relationships of the mind in the intellectual field are all examples of this. But there are other relationships and structures that we might call vertical, and these in fact are the most necessary ones. The horizontal structures are inadequate: they can only give temporary, partial satisfaction. In physical love and in passionate individual love there is always a sense of dissatisfaction. Many poets and writers have spoken about what takes place in the hearts of two people who are in love: a thirst for the eternal, for the infinite, a deep longing to make the present moment stand still so that this small human love might be made complete and perfect. Such a longing cannot be satisfied, of course. It is impossible to put into effect, and the result is pain. This can lead to a desire for annihilation or destruction, which is seen as the only way to render eternal what is intrinsically fleeting, and in some cases this is even taken to the point of suicide.

This happens for the reason indicated above: the sense of original unity which has its origin on a different plane from the horizontal, in something higher and transcendent. When it is first noticed it comes as a surprise and tends to be misinterpreted, but the revelation becomes clearer as time passes. It is a longing for the Spirit, a love for the Deity as Supreme Reality, as the union of all things and all beings. This longing, this restlessness, is love, expressed so succinctly by St Augustine: 'My heart finds no rest until it rests in You!' I must repeat, however, that just as the revelation of this desire is slow and gradual, so too the ways in which it is manifested are gradual and different. There are various stages and they have very differing characteristics.

Before we can love and appreciate the Deity in His essence, in His inconceivable greatness, we have to learn to love His veiled, tangible, individual manifestations. Gradually our understanding broadens, and we can then begin to channel our love vertically upwards to the Spirit and to love human beings, but human beings on a higher plane than ourselves, people who are closer to the ideal, in other words people who to varying degrees display something divine and spiritual. These are the heroes of mankind, the geniuses, the saints, and the divine beings like Buddha and Christ. They are like bridges, and act as supports for who are as yet unable to reach the Supreme, the Universal.

Another aspect, another step towards love for the Supreme, is love for the Spirit within us—that desire and attraction the personality feels with regard to its own individuality, the spiritual centre, the Self.

Then there is love for God understood in personal terms. There are two great concepts of God and they are not mutually exclusive: God understood as a person or personality, a sublime person, but always with an element of differentiation or self-revelation, and then the other more strictly mystical love between the soul and God, in which the soul has a 'negative' aspect and attitude, and in which there are similarities to a human love relationship. Mystics speak about mystical weddings and mystical union. Even here we find the same characteristics of love: a thirst for being made complete, union and then projection. For these mystical souls do not remain passively enjoying that feeling of divine love alone, they feel compelled to work among people to bring this same love to everyone.

There is then a love directed at creatures, at nature and at other people—a love which is spiritual in nature in that it is not love for any particular creature or person, but a universal love based on the principle of unity with all creatures.

I trust I have shown how this overall view explains the unity and the great diversity of love in its various manifestations, in different beings and at various levels of life, above all in man because man is a complex being, ranging all the way from the physical and chemical reactions of his body to the possibility of spiritual consciousness and communion with the Supreme. We see therefore that the various manifestations of love co-exist and come together in man.

It is also important to note that these various levels do not remain in isolation, but there are continuous chains of action and reaction between them. This means that the activities at one level affect and act on the activities at another, and so on. One can easily see how such interaction will be a source of confusion, misunderstanding and error. But at the same time it is a source of great scope for transformation, regeneration and sublimation, having practical implications for our spiritual advancement and development.

THE SPIRITUAL ELEMENTS IN OUR PERSONALITY: JOY

Another precious effect of the spiritual life, shining down like a bright ray of light from the sun of the Spirit to illuminate and give life to the human personality is that of joy. The spiritual origin of joy is borne out by the fact that one of the essential characteristics of the Spirit is bliss.

Indeed the Supreme Being in his omnipotence, wisdom and love, the sum of all perfection, cannot have any weak link in the form of unawareness, suffering or desire. He cannot be conceived of as being anything other than perfectly content and in a state of supreme bliss. All spiritual viewpoints are in agreement on this, both in the East and in the West. For the Indians the three essential aspects of the Spirit are *Sat-Chit-Ananda*, that is to say, Being, Awareness and Bliss.

Other texts, such as the *Upanishad*, refer to *Atman Shivam-Advaitam*, or Peace, Bliss and Unity.

According to the Christian viewpoint the attribute of God most often proclaimed and celebrated is His glory, and glory implies bliss. This conscious bliss is pervaded by love, and is praised by Dante at the end of his 'Paradise':

> O eternal light, existing in yourself alone,
> Alone knowing yourself; and who, known to yourself
> And knowing, love and smile upon yourself!
> *Translation: C.H. Sisson, Pan Classics*

This divine bliss, manifesting itself in our spiritual individuality, in our higher 'I', takes on the nature of pure joy, a joy that gradually works its way down to the different levels of the personality, fading, refracting and combining with other elements. There are thus human joys and sources of satisfaction, and these take various forms, with varying degrees of intensity and value, all the way down to the level of the body, where joy manifests itself as physical well-being and the pleasure produced by the impressions of the senses and by the satisfaction of natural needs and instincts.

Unfortunately man, in his selfishness, in his greed and in his desire for attachment to people and things, has contaminated the purity and original naturalness of joy and pleasure, and has created a great many excesses, perversions and disharmonies which act as sources of evil and pain. Man has often brought about the drying up within himself of the sources of high and noble joy, of pure happiness, and has gone off in search of satisfaction and self-gratification by pursuing without restraint the pleasures that are most readily accessible: the pleasures of the senses, the pleasures of ambition, achievement and material victories. But he fails to find lasting fulfilment in any of these because these sources of satisfaction are passing, changing, uncertain and imperfect; they often lead to reactions of disgust, or they are shown to be mean and illusory.

The true higher nature of man may be sedated or paralyzed for a short while, but it cannot be destroyed; it writhes in its prison, being in its very nature and essence indestructible. It gives to those who forget or neglect it a sense of unease, restlessness and a subtle, yet insistent form of torment which man tries to silence by throwing himself into the external world, busying himself with one frantic activity after another ... but it is all in vain. Then begins the return and the ascent, at first tiring and demanding, but accompanied by ever higher and more intense joys. It is then that man begins to replace physical pleasures with *spiritual joy*.

Spiritual joy has characteristics of its own that clearly distinguish it from other joys. It is permeated by *peace*, security and a sense of complete fulfilment that are lacking from turbulent pleasures and violent excesses. Pleasures and selfish satisfaction are followed by a sense of tiredness and emptiness, but spiritual joy does not produce such reactions—it is life-giving and even rejuvenates the body.

Finally, whereas selfish pleasures tend to separate us from others, causing us to forget everything and leaving us locked into or absorbed in savouring our petty personal satisfactions, or taking the form of a 'selfishness for two', true joy is by its very nature expansive, it makes us kinder and more compassionate, and it inspires in us an ardent wish to draw others into that same joy.

Another characteristic which at first glance may seem paradoxical is the fact that spiritual joy can exist alongside pain. This can be explained if we bear in mind the complexity of human nature or of our inner make-up. I have already mentioned that we are complex beings, made up of many varied elements, but even if we take the simplest division—personality and individuality—it will be observed that in those who are at an intermediate stage of development, those in whom spiritual consciousness has been awakened but who still retain many elements from their ordinary personality, there will be a fairly marked duality about they way they feel and react. This helps us to understand how it can often be the case that while the personality is suffering in human terms, their individuality, or soul, is rejoicing in the light of the spirit. This coexistence of pain and joy has been nobly expressed by Soeur Blanche de la Charité in the following words: *'Souffrir et être malheureux ce n'est pas la même chose'* [Suffering and being unhappy are not the same thing].

Let us now turn to the educational value of joy. Some religious thinking has expressed the restricted, separatist view that pain is of paramount importance. To regard joy as something bad, or something to be distrusted, is a spiritual error that has caused serious harm, because it has prevented many men from drawing close to religion and spirituality due to their being presented in such an unattractive way. We actually need to do the opposite— though not, of course, concealing the serious and austere aspects of spiritual ascent. We need, however, to accentuate the joyous aspects and the great compensations it offers, showing that for each personal satisfaction one might have to, or choose to, relinquish there is a broader, more beautiful and more glorious joy which more than makes up for it. This shows spirituality in a new light and makes it more attractive to those who are just taking their first steps.

Spiritual joy is not only good, legitimate and noble, however. It is also a real and clear duty. The most effective propaganda or 'publicity' we can produce for spirituality is to show that we are joyful, serene and content. Tormented by countless fears and continual doubts, mankind is irresistibly attracted towards people who show by their lives, by the qualities they radiate, that they have attained a central point of calm, harmony and contentment. Once a person has seen the positive effects and recognized the value of spiritual life in a living example, he will then be prepared to pay the price. Only then will he realize how undeserving he is of such a treasure—a treasure that becomes ours for eternity. Joy, then, is a duty.

Dante writes in his *Convivio* [The Banquet]:

Virtue must be joyful, not sad, in all its operations. For if the gift is not joyfully given and received, it will not be characterized by the perfection of willing virtue.

Along the same lines St Francis said, 'It is inappropriate for the servant of God to appear sad and to have a gloomy face.'

It is not easy to be joyful. So let us take a look at the chief obstacles and learn the best ways to overcome them. The first take the form of pain and adversity, the hardships we come up against in our lives. Indeed there may even be a certain attachment to suffering. If we examine such obstacles with a sincere heart, and take a dispassionate view of them, we will realize that the greatest cause of suffering is our attitude, the way we react to those circumstances and facts, for the source of suffering is often rebellion, and rebellion only serves to make the pain more acute. Another frequently encountered niggardly attitude in the face of the small inconveniences and the tiny pinpricks of life is the way we so easily allow ourselves to become irritated by things.

Another obstacle to joy which also depends on ourselves is being too demanding. We demand too much of others or of circumstances, and this attitude then expresses itself in moaning and complaints, and in the grumbling we are all too familiar with. Yet another obstacle is taking things too seriously, dwelling too much on the tragic side of life. And finally, as an extension of the last mentioned obstacle, is taking *ourselves* too seriously, being attached to a certain kind of satisfaction or to a specific source of satisfaction. This only leads to pain when that particular source of happiness is removed. The common denominator of all these obstacles is selfishness, and the result is an unhealthy self-pity. But they are obstacles that can be removed, and it is not too difficult to do this if we are serious about it. Rebellion is replaced by acceptance, a grasping, demanding spirit is replaced by generosity, patience and serenity. Generosity flows from a sense of dignity: we need to have dignity not to allow the minor inconveniences of life to exasperate us. Acceptance and generosity lead to praise and gratitude for all that is good in life, mingled with the adversity and pain. These help the flower of joy to develop and bloom.

It is not too difficult to free ourselves from the tendency to place too great an importance on events and from a sense of the tragic nature of life: we need only take ourselves firmly in hand. We need to view ourselves from a higher vantage point and see how silly are some of our reactions, how unnecessary the mental contortions we get ourselves into, and then see things in their true perspective, in terms of their true significance. Once we have done this for ourselves we can begin to do it benevolently for others.

I will now refer directly to the cultivation of joy.

Spiritual joy is an affirmation of the spiritual view of life which enables us to give maximum attention to, and place maximum emphasis on, the glorious goal that gives purpose and meaning to life itself. Having an appreciation of this glorious goal, this higher, more real life, is the greatest, inexhaustible source of joy.

St Paul said, 'For I consider that the sufferings of this present time are not worth comparing with the glory that shall be revealed in us.'

And St Francis said, 'There is so much good in store for me that every pain is a delight.'

Other sources of joy are nature, which is always ready to help us, always accessible to everyone, art, which in a certain sense perfects nature in that man adds a spiritual element to it (I am referring, of course, to true artists, those in whom their own spiritual nature has been awakened), and the example of others. One cannot overestimate the creative, inspiring effect of a living example, and if we are not fortunate enough to know and be in contact with such examples of spirituality and joy, we can derive benefit from thinking about those who had these qualities in their lives, and from reading about them in good books.

Other sources of joy are spiritual communion found in love and friendship. I have already spoken about love, but the joy of friendship is no less important when it is based on an ardent, living, disinterested communion.

Yet another source of joy, if we are able to achieve it, is work or activity. Since in one form or another this occupies us for many hours of the day, we will appreciate how important it is to work serenely and joyfully. Even when engaged on some unpleasant, painful task we can find reason for spiritual joy, based on our ability to overcome circumstances. A person with the good fortune of being able to carry out activities that are not unpleasant or boring, activities that are well suited to his natural inclinations, will have a greater duty and greater scope for working joyfully.

Let every activity be permeated by joy.

Through all your mortal work your soul should sing to God.

Approach every task with a smiling face and your work will almost do itself, recompensing your smile with satisfaction.

Mary Baker Eddy spoke of the importance of adopting the right attitude in the morning:

When you open your eyes in the morning allow your thoughts to rise above the discord of your human nature and matter, until they meet the eternally present Father.

Greet the morning with the radiant joy of gratitude for every task that lies before you, regarding each task as a new, joyous occasion for relying on the unlimited divine power, and serving the children of God with a willing heart; work in order to love and love by working. Commit yourself to this and be ready to receive the ever present, infinite goodness. Listen to the Father's voice and with a song of thanks follow the way the Divine Mind shows you. Gratitude will then colour everything with gold and you will find yourself saying, 'Surely the Lord is in this place, and I knew it not.' This is the house of God, the doorway to heaven.

Spending oneself for others and serving mankind is one of the greatest sources of joy. The first benefit is that it causes us to forget ourselves, releasing us from the 'steel box' of our personality. The real sense of satisfaction derived from doing good to those around us is great, and no one can take it away.

But the most direct method of reaching spiritual joy is that of silence and meditation: this may lead to contemplation, communion and identification with the Supreme Being, Who is glory and bliss.

I can think of no better way to close this chapter than to quote two verses from Dante that are very well known, but verses we ought to repeat to ourselves daily:

> Oh joy! and, ah, ineffable jubilation!
> Oh life made up entirely of love and peace!
> Assured wealth, with no longing for anything!
> Intellectual light, full of love;
> Love of the true good, full of happiness;
> Happiness which transcends any sweetness.
> *Translation: C.H. Sisson, Pan Classics*

THE SPIRITUAL ELEMENTS IN OUR PERSONALITY: POWER AND WILL

We are left with one more individual ray of light that manifests itself in our personality, the last of the spiritual attributes we are going to examine. But the English phrase 'last but not least' is particularly relevant here—indeed, not only is this last attribute not less important than the others, but in certain respects it may be considered the first and the most essential.

If we attempt to discover the origin or the first manifestation of the divine nature in the soul of primitive man, we find that it consists of a sense of some dark, supernatural, frightening and incomprehensible power before which man feels weak, dependent, like a slave, as though he were about to be annihilated.

This aspect of divinity has been illustrated by Rudolf Otto in his book *The Sacred*. He speaks of the tremendous mystery of the divine nature for primitive man, the shudder of fear it produces in him, and the sense of super-power and majesty that almost overwhelms him.

He then quotes the saying of a Christian mystic:

Man founders and falls to pieces in his nothingness and in his smallness. The more the greatness of God impresses itself upon him in its stark reality, the more his own poverty is shown for what it is.

Thus in this primordial experience of the divine, we see an absolute dualism, an extreme transcendence. The Power or the Deity is perceived as something external, something in opposition to man.

But this stage needs to be overcome in order that we might move on to the second stage, the awakening of a sense of power in man himself. As man develops he gradually acquires a growing awareness of the powers that are within him. Urged on, indeed compelled, by the primordial needs of life (food, shelter, protection from attack by animals or by other human beings), little by little man's powers are developed. First there comes physical strength and skills, followed by ingenuity and then intelligence. He thus learns to make use of minerals—stone, bronze, iron. He begins to use fire, his technical skill continues to grow, and with it an increasing dominion over nature, which, as we are well aware, has grown very rapidly over the last century.

Alongside this man has developed his powers over other men. Thus, depending on the type of civilization, we see tribal chiefs, primitive kings, sovereigns, heads of communities, party leaders and leaders of the masses. This psychological power is very interesting. It is made up of various elements—personal charisma, confidence, resolve, courage, bravery and the ability to sway people with words.

We see in man, then, an increasing desire to dominate, characterized by ambition, the tendency to assert himself and a use of his own powers. These tendencies are so strong in some people that they become an overwhelming passion, causing the person concerned to face hardship and risk, and even to endanger his own life.

Where does this passion come from, this obscure, yet intense feeling that there are greater, hidden powers in man which he must bring into use, this 'divine discontent'?

To begin with, this tendency to assert one's inner powers manifests itself in the wrong way, and the fundamental error here is that of focusing exclusively on external things, in other words gaining dominion over nature and over other people. Man then discovers, however, that in order to control others he needs to be able to control himself: first his own body and its senses (there is thus a kind of asceticism about the ambitious man), then his passions, emotions, feelings and his mind itself.

He may in this way achieve a considerable degree of self-control. But there is the danger of a separate personal 'I' developing in him, and thus pride, etc. A man in this state is in opposition to the world and to others; this is what characterizes

Nietzsche's superman. When a person's interest in self-control gains the upper hand, he begins to lose interest in the outside world. This is the stage of stoicism where man withdraws into an inaccessible 'inner rock', finding his satisfaction or contentment within himself, but he is still possessed by feelings of pride and isolation from others.

Another interesting, but dangerous state is when a person discovers he has supernormal or magical powers. We need to pause on this subject for a moment.

We must state at the outset that the reality of such powers is beyond doubt—not only are they referred to in religious traditions, but their existence has also been substantiated scientifically in modern times. Doctor Osty, for instance, has stated that if all the psychic powers demonstrated by various people were to be brought together in one person, we would have a superhuman being, a great Being, an Initiate, on a par with the founders of religions. This explains the interest shown in this area, but it is, for all that, an insidious area, one in which we must tread very carefully.

In the first place a distinction needs to be made between abilities and powers. It is usually the case that people with these abilities are not in control of them; often in fact it is the people who are possessed by the powers, and this can have serious effects on their health and mental balance. But this is inevitable—it should be remembered that ordinary man is not even master of the normal forces of his personality. How much more difficult, then, will it be for him to control these other broader, more overwhelming forces. In other words, being a medium is a passive thing—it is the medium who is being controlled. Spiritual powers, on the other hand, are controlled powers: a person uses them when he chooses. This is the essential difference.

Thus the first step in gaining a healthy control over supernormal powers, and in eliminating the inherent dangers, is to gain control over the normal forces within us.

A distinction must also be made in terms of the purpose for which these powers are to be used, i.e. distinguishing between 'white magic' and 'black magic'. The former is used for good whereas the latter is used for personal ends, often to the detriment of other people. There is no doubt that so-called 'black magic' only has destructive effects—it harms everyone, including the person who practises it. It is a violation of the law of balance, a law that cannot be breached with impunity.

We can see quite clearly from this that one must take great care in this area and that it is not advisable for those who lack the appropriate spiritual preparation to try to develop these supernormal powers.

By way of exception I would say that it is legitimate to use these powers, or to have them exercised by people in whom they reside, for the purposes of scientific experimentation when it is for the good of humanity—this purpose may serve to counterbalance the evil suffered by the subject. But I would repeat what I said earlier: great care must be taken in this area.

Supernormal powers, on the other hand, develop spontaneously without any contrivance in those whose spiritual consciousness is being raised and who are discovering the Centre of their being. In this case the powers are given naturally, as a bonus, to those who have gained control over their lower nature, when there is a guarantee that they will use such powers for good.

What characterizes true, healthy spiritual development in its pure form is a sense of the unity of life, and a sense of the relationship between individual spirit and universal Spirit. It is overcoming what has been called 'the heresy of separateness'. Spirit is unity and universality.

Once this is realized, one will have a new attitude of dependence and obedience towards the Divine Being, very different from the attitude of primitive man. No longer is it a separate, external dependence and obedience, but now something within, in other words it is an obedience to the God within, to the Spirit inside us. It is a response of our personality to the deep Spirit which it recognizes as itself, as its true essence. This spiritual attitude has been clearly expressed in the Christian statement 'Thy will be done.'

This attitude must be correctly understood, however. It should not be regarded as dualist, implying a sad, passive resignation, but as unitarian in the sense of joyful compliance and identification of one's personal will with the Universal Will.

Above all else this unity gives us a sense of security, joy, bliss and peace.

I will mention in passing that a survey was carried out in America to discover people's favourite verse from Dante. This was found to be the line 'In His will is our Peace.'

It is in the context of this unity that the various powers of the soul are renewed and developed. These are indeed powers that can affect the world and people around us, but they are benevolent powers: rather than enslaving, they arouse, attract and awaken energies, and bring about good. Man then feels himself to be a willing, conscious co-worker in the wonderful divine plan which he now begins to understand in its beauty and goodness. He thus identifies himself with the will of God. It is in this way that man maintains his own highest individual dignity, but free from any sense of pride or ambition. Instead it is in perfect union with other spirits united in the One Spirit.

How is this state reached? How is this spiritual power awakened? The methods are the same as for any spiritual attainment: silence, contemplation, quietness and obedience of the personality, aspiration and inner communion, and then affirmation, a continuous reaffirmation that helps us be released from our personality and from the external world.

Once this is achieved, when spiritual power has been aroused, nothing else is required, because afterwards the spiritual power will function on its own.

This highlights the error of the activism of today which is demanding, exhausting, discordant, and often has adverse side-effects. The other method, in contrast, operates within. We can make a comparison here with a lamp and light: we have to prepare the lamp for burning, but then there is nothing further to do—the light shines out of its own accord.

Let us take note once and for all that having been so enslaved, particularly to ourselves, we can now exercise this sovereign power, a power that is impersonal and superpersonal. After this nothing will be impossible. It is a case of awakening the 'atmosphere' of power and always remaining in it, creating and maintaining a 'magnetic field'. We then do nothing through personal effort: we merely arouse the power so that it can begin to operate spontaneously, easily and irresistibly in us. For the power of the spirit is a source of spontaneous irradiation which by its very presence opens doors and takes control of circumstances. It has no need to do anything—it simply is, and in being it transforms everything.

And now one final point. We have spoken of various aspects or characteristics of the spirit. But since the spirit is synthesis and unity we must realize that no one of these elements can be developed perfectly and harmoniously in isolation from the others. The relationships between them are quite clear: the moral sense implies awareness and love, and it is the source of joy, power, etc. Thus each of the aspects is inextricably linked to the others.

In conclusion the spirit is the synthesis of all these characteristics and holds them all together in wonderful harmony. Just as rays of sunlight shine down and merge, so the characteristics of the spirit shine down and take on various hues, becoming opaque and limited, and diverging in such a way that they seem to be in opposition with one another (e.g. power may seem to oppose love, or beauty goodness, etc.). At their source in the spirit, however, these different characteristics are not in opposition: they are complementary and form a harmonious whole.

The spirit is all this, and more besides, because we do not yet know it in all its glory. So far we are only children in the world of the spirit; we do not know all its wonders, but there is a great sense of anticipation, and this spurs us on to climb from one degree of light to the next, or from 'one degree of glory to another'.

REFLECTIONS ON PEACE

It is quite likely that man has never been so without peace as he is now. We need only look around to realize how true this is. There are open and concealed struggles on all sides, alongside the repercussions of war and the threat of conflict in the future; there are struggles between nations, races, classes and parties; and this is no less the case when we consider the inner conflicts, agitation and storms within the human heart itself, which can take many forms: emotional, moral and religious crises, dissatisfaction with ourselves and with others, rebellion against society, against the family, against life and against God Himself.

In such a world the cultivation of peace is not so much a spiritual luxury as a daily necessity for those who want to maintain their inner integrity and not be overcome by the collective currents of agitation, panic and violence. This cultivation of peace is no less of a duty in our dealings with others. A person who is able to be a living centre of peace in today's world and who is able to radiate that peace powerfully, ceaselessly, will be in a position to give needy mankind the benefit it lacks most and is in greatest need of.

Let us see how this can be done most effectively.

We remember first of all how in the form of a warning or an encouragement all the great spiritual Masters have placed particular emphasis on peace. The religious Indian texts begin and end with the formula: *Om-shanti-shanti shanti* (Om-peace-peace-peace), or with the phrase: 'Peace to all beings.' Both in word and by example Buddha taught the sublime peace of the spirit. It is said of him: 'The Awakened One is peace in himself and brings peace to the whole world.' In the descriptions of the various levels of Buddhist contemplation one of the characteristics emphasized most is the serenity of the soul in meditation.

In early Christianity, and then in its highest manifestations over the intervening centuries, peace has often been a resounding note. 'Peace on earth to men of good will.' The figure of Christ is suffused with an aura of peace. He often performed peace-making actions: the calming of the storm, the continual soothing of the disciples' spirits when they were afraid or arguing about which of them would be the greatest, or when, as in Peter's case, they reacted violently. At the end he left them a message of spiritual peace which has profound significance: 'Peace I leave with you; my peace I give you. I do not give to you as the world gives.' (John 14:27.)

In Christian mysticism perfect inner peace is referred to as 'stillness' or 'prayer of stillness', and it represents a clear, elevated stage in the ascent of the soul to God. This peace, this inner silence, in which all thoughts and feelings within a person are silenced, is regarded as an essential preparation for mystical union, for full communion of the soul with God.

Let us remind ourselves of the fine description of peace given in the *Imitation of Christ*: 'Solid peace, imperturbable and secure peace, peace within and without, a peace that is constant in all circumstances.'

Let us try to understand the spiritual significance of peace. There are various errors and misunderstandings where peace is concerned. There is a true peace and a false peace. The term 'peace' is most often used to describe the false type, referring to a passive, static condition which shuns difficulties and turns away from any struggle, effort or opposition. This is synonymous with laziness (*tamas*); it is an illusory peace that never becomes the real thing. Real peace on the other hand is positive and spiritual.

We have already referred to the unbreakable bond that exists between the various characteristics of the spiritual life. Indeed, if they are isolated from one another they will be wanting, for they are meant to be seen as facets of a single prism. As we meditate on them in depth we see that there is a point at which they come together and merge in the Spirit.

Thus we can say:

> Peace is will, peace is power, peace is wisdom, peace is liberty, peace is joy, peace is harmony, peace is truth, peace is understanding, peace is light . . .

It is helpful to meditate on the solidarity of spiritual qualities, taking each in turn as a starting point. This is one way of moving on from multiplicity to unity, or synthesis.

We have seen how Christ clearly taught the distinction between true peace and false peace in the words: 'My peace I give to you. I do not give as the world gives.'

What is this real peace, then, and how do we obtain it?

There is a beautiful chant which contains the illuminating phrase: 'There is a peace that transcends all understanding. It resides in the hearts of those who live in eternity.' This tells us that peace is a spiritual experience that cannot be understood by the personal mind. It belongs to another plane, another sphere of reality: that of eternity.

It is therefore pointless to look for it in the ordinary world, in our personal lives that contain neither stability nor security. It is vain self-deception to earnestly seek it in that place. Peace is only to be found when it is deliberately sought in the higher spiritual world and when a person succeeds in firmly remaining at that level.

This sort of peace—far from leading to inertia, to a static tranquillity, or to impassive acceptance—gives new energy. It is a dynamic, creative peace. It is from this inner place of peace that we direct all our personal activities, provide them with strength, and make them effective and constructive, because they are then free from ambition, fear or any sense of attachment. In other words we are able to live as masters, and not as slaves.

The touchstone of this peace is our daily life, the way we react to life's continual struggles and adversities, the pinpricks, the countless irritations that come our way every day. Spiritual peace must be able to resist and stand firm against the daily onslaught from the outside world.

This *true* peace must stand firm in bad times, when a person is suffering physical pain, or in the midst of various kinds of attacks. It can co-exist with inner pain. It is not a state of full joy until we have allowed our personality to be completely regenerated, until that full peace is 'incarnate' in us and our whole being is permeated with peace and has actually become peace.

This is the goal, but we will be well on our way when we have established an unassailable 'centre' of peace within that is able to withstand any test, whatever the cost, for this centre will be an inner fortress from which we can direct the whole of our life. This peace is the possession of the Spectator within us. One Teacher has said, 'Learn to observe yourself with the calmness of an outsider.'

In the initial stages, before regeneration of the personality, the inner centre of peace allows a person to stand firm despite the raging battles of his human nature, during the period when the purifying flames are burning, and when pain is performing its work of purification and redemption. It is here that one becomes aware of the value and meaning of all such tests. Whether we are aware of it or not, there are things that produce bitterness, resentment, rebellion and fatigue inside us, and these can rob us of our joy and serenity. But in the peace of the soul all this is appeased, brought into harmony and illuminated: one is shown the meaning and value of life, both its tangible aspects and its unrevealed aspects, as well as the meaning and value of pain itself, which is then transfigured as a result and becomes bathed in joy. It is then that the cross 'becomes bright', and then—as Tagore said in one of his lyrics—'Your light shines in my tears.'

Let us see how we can meditate in order to make this peace a reality.

It is useful to begin with enlarging our inner horizon, turning our thoughts to the contemplation of infinity and eternity. We then remember and realize that we are spiritual beings and that our spiritual essence is indestructible.

This broadening of our perspective will help us to re-establish a true sense of proportion and to see the relative insignificance of so many of the little things that can preoccupy and upset us. In this way we will gradually begin to truly experience the peace of eternity, the peace of the spirit, the peace Christ referred to as 'my peace'.

For those who find such meditation difficult, we would suggest another method which is based on the use of images. However the two methods can be used in association, as appropriate, representing two stages in the same meditation process. Various images can be used for this purpose and, depending on different temperaments and different psychological types, one may be found more useful than another.

We might imagine a large expanse of water, a blue sky, a brightly shining sun, and on the tranquil surface of the water myriads of lotus flowers opening in response to the sun's rays.

Another useful image is that of the scene portrayed in the gospel of Mark when Jesus calmed the storm:

> That day when evening came, he said to his disciples, 'Let us go over to the other side.' Leaving the crowd behind, they took him along, just as he was, in the boat. There were also other boats with him. A furious squall came up, and the waves broke over the boat, so that it was nearly swamped. Jesus was in the stern, sleeping on a cushion. The disciples woke him and said to him, 'Teacher, don't you care if we drown?' He got up, rebuked the wind and said to the waves, 'Quiet! Be still!' Then the wind died down and it was completely calm.'
>
> [*English translation: New International Version.*]

A third useful image may be that of the globe of our earth in the vastness of infinite space, as evoked in the magnificent verse of Amiel, which by its calm, august rhythm is an excellent method for evoking peace:

> *Dans l'éternel azur de l'insondable espace*
> *s'enveloppe de Paix notre globe agité.*
> *Homme, enveloppe ainsi tes jours, rêve qui passe,*
> *du calme firmament de ton éternité.*
>
> [In the eternal blue of unfathomable space
> our troubled globe robes itself in Peace.
> Thus robe your days, like a fleeting dream, O man,
> in the calm firmament of your eternity.]

With the help of these images to lift our souls to the supreme, glorious Reality, we will come to feel this peace and let it become a reality in us.

Let us learn to live in peace and thus to give and radiate peace around us wherever we go. We would all like to be givers of peace, but to do so we must first be at peace ourselves, living our lives in that great peace, and actually becoming one with it.

It is permissible to seek the help of those who have gone ahead of us in the pursuit of peace and have themselves become one with it.

Such peace brings about a transformation, not only in us, but in all human and social relationships. Only in this way—from top to bottom, from within man to the outside world—is it possible to bring about profound changes in our world, so that wars can be eliminated, and so that the dangers and threats that now darken man's life can be removed. Let us always remember that these problems cannot be resolved by treaties or cleverly devised plans, nor will they be resolved by yet more violent struggles. They need to be lifted up to a place where they will resolve themselves, where they will be 'liquidated', so to speak, and finally vanish altogether.

Appendix 1

THE SPIRITUAL ELEMENTS IN OUR PERSONALITY: THE MORAL SENSE

(Unrevised Notes)

The awareness of what is correct, right, good, manifesting itself as:

The voice of conscience. Sense of responsibility. Sense of justice. (The latter even in children and in primitive peoples.)

Gradual development, from the bottom upwards. Such development is awakened by external action, relationships with others, authority, external standards, moral codes, recognition of others' rights, justice, solidarity, transgression and penalties, guilt and punishment, punishment, acceptance, recognition that it is right. Within, introversion of the law, autonomy, refining and development of the moral conscience.

> *O dignitosa coscienza e netta*
> *come t'e picciol fallo amaro morso.*
>
> [O pure, noble conscience,
> how bitter to your taste is one small
> mistake.]

Elements already present in the personality (inherited, automatic, environmental) and descending ray of light.

Higher aspects: solidarity between groups at a broader level, unity in life (horizontal); an ever more spiritual, internal, dynamic view. Union with perfection, the Spiritual 'I' (vertical).

PATHOLOGY IN THE MORAL REALM

Remaining at a primitive stage: retardation, degeneration, caricatures, exaggerations, perversions, repression.

Excessive fear of evil: restrictive morality, negative morals, limiting, repressive and static morals.

Phariseeism: pride in one's own morality.

Pretence: hypocrisy, formalism.

Immorality. Amorality. (Beyond good and evil.)

The transition from a restricted, fossilized, dead view of morality to a broader view. From the law of strict justice to the law of love. *Apparently* immoral Promethean spirits.

Christ and the Pharisees: Spinoza, etc. *Destroy in order to rebuild.*

Dangerous transitional crises; possibility of deviation, of lapsing back into immorality. Pseudo-prometheans. Nietzsche and his followers. See poetry by Luigi Valli: *Pitecantropo* [Pithecanthropus] (a caricature of the superman).

Yet these developmental crises are *necessary.* Understanding them in *ourselves and in others,* controlling them well.

Remorse. Inability to overcome guilt. Lady Macbeth: 'All the perfumes of Arabia will not sweeten this little hand.'

In the hands of the Super-ego illness often becomes a means for punishing the Ego, causing it to suffer. The sick man is then obliged to act like a guilty party who needs the sickness in order to expiate his crime.

(Freud)

Obvious Self-Punishment Syndromes and Hidden Self-Punishment Syndromes

Various manifestations: Fear of being arrested, accused. An obsession with washing. Patients who spend hour after hour washing themselves.

Maiming of an organ regarded as the cause of guilt. The old precept: if your eye has sinned, gouge it out; if your hand has sinned, cut it off. Paralysis. Extreme self-punishment: *suicide.*

Not all suicides are attributable to this, but a number are, without the person concerned being conscious of the fact.

Confirmation: the relief experienced by patients after the 'expiatory rite' (e.g. after washing).

. . . their most ingrained, enduring symptoms can disappear overnight when the patient accidentally falls victim to some physical, organic suffering (fever, pain, surgery), or to some mental suffering (loss of a job or money, some struggle). See book by R. Allendy: *La Justice Intérieure* [Inner Justice], which is based on this idea.

Curing self-punishment. Replacing self-punishment, as the condemnation and revenge of the Principle perceived as a strict, inflexible, punishing judge, with expiation (whereby the sinner undergoes a conversion and has [new] life), catharsis, purification. Freeing absolution, redemption. Replacing unproductive remorse with liberating repentence, punishment with compensation. The sense of guilt and imperfection becomes the stimulus for an active, ennobling work, giving the strength for self-denial and the necessary sacrifices for a higher, purer, more noble spiritual and moral life.

This is symbolized and made a social reality in Christianity in the rites of confession and absolution; it can and must become an individual, internal process.

This is the aim in psychological treatment (psychoanalysis, psychosynthesis): reconciliation, elimination of stultifying, wearing conflict; the unification of the inferior in the superior, its use and sublimation. The stage-to-stage transition towards the light, perfection, the inner sun; the unification of personality and individuality.

(Alignment, coordination between personality and Ego, through the higher 'I', the superconscious.)

Appendix 2

THE SPIRITUAL ELEMENTS IN OUR PERSONALITY: THE DESIRE TO KNOW AND THE CAPACITY FOR KNOWLEDGE

(*Undeveloped Notes*)

The thirst for knowledge is one of the clearest differences between man and animals. Animals only display the desire to know when it bears some direct relationship to their needs and instincts: the *search* for food, protection, etc. Only man has the desire to *know for the sake of knowing*. This tendency is already present in children. Educators must make wise use of children's many 'Why?' questions. Children should never be put down, discouraged or made fun of; they should not be given simplistic answers, because they are able to grasp and take in far more than one might suppose. Their minds are concrete and they must not be spoken to in abstract terms; they are free from mental blocks and preconceived ideas. It is useful to answer children's questions using symbols, analogies and parables.

THE DESIRE TO KNOW

1. *On the surface:*
   a) Knowledge of the external world. This is the first step (Ulysses); children, young people; explorers of the earth's surface, of the depths of the sea, the air, the stratosphere.
   b) Intimate knowledge of nature, of natural phenomena;

laws, scientists; noble passion; ascetics and heroes of science (Pasteur).

2. *In depth:* The desire to know the secret meaning of life. Why? What are we? Where do we come from? Why are we here? Where are we going to? The problem of pain. The problem of evil (included in that). The problem of creation. Philosophical research (philosophy means love, the search for Truth).

The desire to know and become acquainted with the external world first, then the laws that govern it, and lastly its origin. From this we move on to seek the primal cause, the invisible Reality that is behind everything else; the Power that has created everything, the Spirit, God.

Everyone, including the peasant, the worker, the uneducated woman, has some concept of life, even if it is an unconscious, ill-defined or rudimentary one.

The importance of this concept; the importance of recognizing it clearly in ourselves: it determines our actions, our most important decisions; it gives us faith and power, or skepticism and discouragement. Some pessimistic concepts have even led people to commit suicide.

THE PSYCHOLOGY OF KNOWLEDGE

Vain, personal, superficial curiosity about other people's affairs. Negation. Excessive doubt; avoiding research. Barren metaphysical imaginings. Fanaticism, intolerance, persecution; excessive confidence/certainty.

Theological, philosophical, scientific dogmatism: this brings us to speak about the *criticism of knowledge* (gnosiology).

Organs of knowledge. Their areas and limits.

Knowledge Through the Senses. Its Nature and Limitations

The five windows on the world (the five senses). Stimuli (vibrations); sensations; perception; apperception; mental reconstruction of data from the senses.

The limitation and relativity of data through the senses:

1. We only perceive a small proportion of the vibrations that actually exist (from 16—20 per second (sound), up to trillions of vibrations).
2. The qualifying relativity of perceptions via the senses. Our senses are designed to operate in certain specialized ways, but this is only *one* of the ways in which our senses can operate. It would be possible to see sounds, to hear lights. Instruments for transforming light into sound.

Rational and Intellectual Knowledge. Its Nature and Limitations

Concepts/ideas.

1. The secondary compilation of data on experiences.
2. Independent rational activity.

Preconceived categories and forms in which we place or insert our experiences: time, space, quality, quantity, causality, relation.

Subjectivity and Relativity of Rational Knowledge

Phenomenon and noumenon. Essence, 'a thing in itself'. This escapes the rational mind ... But there is a way out. Namely:

Higher Spiritual Knowledge

Conscious identification. Intuition. Enlightenment. 'Cosmic' consciousness. Realization. Orientals; Plotinus; Bergson; Carpenter; Bucke; Ouspensky.

Liberating Knowledge

Even in the scientific field. Knowing about gravity and its laws enables us to fly. Knowledge of freedom, power, dominion, satisfaction (Keyserling). The sense of freedom or liberation as defined by *maya* (illusion): East. Vedanta. Buddhism, Jnana Yoga, Vivekananda, Ramacharaka.

Dis-identification: realization of the true Self (Vedanta). Realization of the unity of the individual spirit with the Universal Spirit. Silence. Contemplation, Aspiration. Devotion. Raja Yoga. See: Vivekananda, Patanjali, A. Bailey, *From Intellect to Intuition*, etc.

This is a faculty which, like any other, develops with exercise, but it requires discipline, self-control, development, and a raising of the whole personality. Nevertheless it is worth it. We must not only do it with an effort from our 'lower nature'. If we create the necessary conditions (removing obstacles: see: *Patanjali Yoga Aphorisms*) in accordance with the Ray of the Spirit, the Truth will have an irresistible power; it drives out the shadows of ignorance, the mists and mirages. It is a sun that gives life, makes productive, and creates. In its light we are transfigured, and we see ourselves as we are in spirit and in truth: sons of God, an integral part of the Supreme One.

BIBLIOGRAPHICAL NOTES

Part One: The Study of the Superconscious

Chapter 1. *The Awakening and Development of Spiritual Consciousness.*

Undated writing. Since it makes no reference to Maslow among the students of the superconscious, we can place it before 1964 when Maslow published his first contributions to transpersonal psychology. This has reached us in its Italian version, though Assagioli probably wrote it in English.

Chapter 2. *The Superconscious.*

Lecture given at the Institute of Psychosynthesis, Florence, on 7 April 1973, with the title 'Psychosynthesis and Superconscious'.

Page 23. For an in-depth study of the psychosynthetic concept, see Roberto Assagioli, *Per l'armonia della vita*, [For Harmony in Life], Edizioni Mediterranée, Rome 1966 [English translation, *Psychosynthesis: A Manual of Principles and Techniques*, Crucible, Wellingborough, 1990]

Page 24. For further explanations of the concept of scientific method, see Roberto Assagioli, *Principi e metodi della psicosintesi terapeutica* [Principles and Methods of Therapeutic Psychosynthesis], Astrolabio, Rome, 1973, pp. 164–5.

Chapter 3. *Psychological Mountaineering.*

Lecture given at the Institute of Psychosynthesis, Florence, 1970.

Page 37. For the function of the 'external centre' in the process of self-realization, see *Principi e metodi della psicosintesi terapeutica*, pp. 31—2.

Chapter 4. *Expansion of Consciousness: Conquering and Exploring the Worlds Within.*
Lecture given at the Institute of Psychosynthesis, Florence, 12 February 1972.
Page 42. For an in-depth analysis of the nature of the various levels of the unconscious, see *Per l'armonia della vita*; for a synthetic definition of these levels, see *Principi e metodi della psicosintesi terapeutica*, pp. 23—4.
Page 44. For the relationship between the 'I' and the Self, see *Principi e metodi della psicosintesi terapeutica*, p. 26.

Chapter 5. *The Superconscious and Artistic Creation.*
Lecture given at the Institute of Psychosynthesis, Florence, 1969.

Chapter 6. *Transpersonal Inspiration.*
Lecture given at the Institute of Psychosynthesis, Florence, 1973.
Page 67. The book *La psicologia dell'alto e il Se* [Higher Psychology and the Self] was not completed. Some of the essays contained in this book would probably have formed part of it.

Chapter 7. *Vertical Telepathy.*
Undated writing, but presumably before 1930.
Page 82. The expression 'vertical telepathy' was taken up again in 'Psychological Mountaineering', (see Chapter 3, p. 32).

Chapter 8. *Symbols of Transpersonal Experience.*
Published under the title *'I simboli del supernormale'* [The Symbols of the Supernormal] in the magazine *Verso la luce* [Towards the Light], No. 9 (1965); the text containing this chapter probably belongs to an earlier period.
Page 91. See 'Jung and Psychosynthesis', the Institute of Psychosynthesis, Florence, 1966. Assagioli knew Jung personally, and exchanged letters with him.

Page 100. The term 'bio-psychosynthesis', in the sense of the organic, harmonious unity of all aspects of man, is the exact term for the process and practice which, for the sake of brevity, have been called 'psychosynthesis' (see *Per l'armonia della vita*, page 180) [p.123 of the English translation].

Page 101. For the exercise of dis-identification and self-identification, published for the first time in 1931, see *L'atto di volonta*, Astrolabio, Rome, 1973, pp. 156—62 [English translation *The Act of Will*, Crucible, Wellingborough, 1990, pp. 211—17].

Part Two: Spiritual Awakening

Chapter 9. *Stages and Crises in Spiritual Development.*

Undated writing, but presumably before 1930. Original title: *'Le crisi di crescenza spirituale'* [The Crisis of Spiritual Growth].

Chapter 10. *Spiritual Development and Neuro-Psychological Disturbances.*

Writing published in 1933 (Tipografia Giuntina, Florence) under the auspices of the Institute of Psychosynthesis, with its head office in Rome at Via Eufimiano, 9. Referred back to over many years by the author himself (see p. 28 of this volume); it was to become chapter 2 of *Principi e metodi della psicosintesi terapeutica*.

Page 126. For the difference between repression and control, see *L'atto di volonta*, p. 24 [pp. 22—4 of the English translation] and *Principi e metodi della psicosintesi terapeutica*, p. 33.

Page 130. For the transformation of psychological energies see *Per l'armonia della vita*, pp. 129—55 [pp. 177—91 of the English translation]; *Principi e metodi della psicosintesi terapeutica*, pp. 221—30; *L'atto di volonta*, pp. 52—4 [pp. 61—5 of the English translation].

Chapter 11. *Mysticism and Medicine.*

Published in *Ultra*, XIX, 1925, 1, pp. 1—6.

Bears the annotation 'Keep for collection of spiritual essays', in Ida Palombi's handwriting. She was Assagioli's co-worker and became President of the Institute on his death.

Page 134. For a psychosynthetic evaluation of psychoanalytical theories, see Roberto Assagioli, 'Psychoanalysis and Psychosynthesis', Institute of Psychosynthesis, Florence, 1963.

Chapter 12. *The Awakening of the Soul.*
Published in *Ultra*, XV, 1–2, 1921.
Page 150. For an evaluation of the art and personality of Tagore, whom Assagioli met in Italy in 1922, see Roberto Assagioli, 'Rabindranath Tagore, poet, mystic, educator', in *Rassegna italiana*, 18 (1926), pp. 684–94.

Chapter 13. *Purification of the Soul.*
Based on a lecture presumably given in the period 1930–2; published in *Alba spirituale* [Spiritual Dawn], 5 (1959).
Page 155. See the exercise based on the *Divine Comedy* in *Principi e Metodi della psicosintesi terapeutica*, p. 175.

Chapter 14. *The Science of Applied Purification.*
Undated writing, produced some time around 1973 the year in which the film referred to on p. 166 was produced.
Page 165. For the development and use of the imagination, see *Principi e metodi della psicosintesi terapeutica*, pp. 124–39.
Page 166. For a more in-depth analysis of the problem of 'psychological fog', and the means for neutralizing it, see *L'atto di volonta*, pp. 56–61 [pp. 75–84 of the English translation].

Chapter 15. *Obstacles to Spiritual Development: Fear.*
This formed part of the 'Course in Spiritual Psychosynthesis' of 1938. Marked 'undeveloped notes', it outlines the theme that was to be elaborated on in the lecture.
Page 171. For the technique for training the imagination, see *Principi e metodi della psicosintesi terapeutica*, pp. 186–7.

Chapter 16. *The Fear of Suffering: Reflections on Pain.*
Page 176. For the possibility of joy and pain existing alongside one another, see *L'atto di volonta*, p. 150 [p. 201 of the English translation].

Chapter 17. *Obstacles to Spiritual Development: Attachments.*

A writing that formed part of the 'Course in Spiritual Psychosynthesis' of 1938.

Page 182. See Roberto Assagioli, *'La vita come gioco e rappresentazione'*, the Institute of Psychosynthesis, Florence, 1967.

Chapter 18. *Emotional and Mental Obstacles: Aggression and Criticism.*

A writing that formed part of the 'Course in Spiritual Psychosynthesis' of 1938, parts of which would be included in Chapter 17 of *Per l'armonia della vita.*

Page 186. For a psychological evaluation of humour, see Roberto Assagioli, 'A Technique in Psychosynthesis: Cheerfulness', the Institute of Psychosynthesis, Florence, 1970.

Third Part: Spirituality in Everyday Life

Chapter 19. *Twentieth-Century Spirituality.*

Published under the auspices of the Institute in 1935, and then published in *La cultura del mondo*, Bologna, 1962, Year XVIII, No. 6.

Chapter 20. *Transmutation and Sublimation of Emotional and Sexual Energies.*

Published in the review *Il Loto* [The Lotus], Tipografia Giuntina, Florence, 1938, Year IX, No. 3.

Page 210. For the relationship between sublimation and mysticism, see *Principi e metodi della psicosintesi terapeutica*, p. 226.

Chapter 21. *Money and the Spiritual Life.*

A writing probably based on a conference of February 1937.

Page 215. For an evaluation of the work and life of H. Keyserling, with whom Assagioli had strong bonds of respect and friendship, see R. Assagioli, 'Hermann Keyserling, a Master of Life', the Institute of Psychosynthesis, Florence.

Chapter 22. *Martha and Mary: the Active Life—the Contemplative Life.*

Published in *Delta*, 1923, Year 1, No. 9, 10, 11.

Chapter 23. *Spiritual Elements in our Personality: Beauty.*

A writing which formed part of the 'Individual Psychology and Spiritual Development' course of 1932.

Page 250. The text of the lectures on the moral sense and on the capacity for knowledge has not survived in full, only in the form of undeveloped notes which are in too much of an outline form to be incorporated into the body of this book. In view of the importance of the subject matter they contain, they are included by way of an appendix for consultation.

Chapter 24. *Spiritual Elements in our Personality: Love.*

A writing which formed part of the 'Individual Psychology and Spiritual Development' course of 1932.

Page 262. For the various types of love, see *L'atto di volonta*, pp. 72–5 [pp. 91–5 of the English translation].

Chapter 25. *Spiritual Elements in our Personality: Joy.*

A writing which formed part of the 'Individual Psychology and Spiritual Development' course of 1932.

Page 270. 'By acceptance I do not mean a passive acceptance, or a submissive resignation; it is a question of starting by accepting and then doing whatever is possible—if and when this is applicable—to change the situation.' See Roberto Assagioli, 'Course of Lectures on Psychosynthesis', Year 1970, Lecture V.

Chapter 26. *Spiritual Elements in our Personality: Power and Will.*

This text relates to the lecture which concluded the 'Individual Psychology and Spiritual Development' course of 1932.

Page 274. For the role of the will in the self-training process, for its characteristics and different aspects, and for the physiology of the act of the will, see *L'atto di volonta*.

Chapter 27. *Reflections on Peace.*

This chapter includes the notes of 16 May 1936 and the article published in *L'attesa del regno* [Awaiting the Kingdom], 1964, Year II, No. 3.

Appendices

Appendix 1: *Spiritual Elements in our Personality: the Moral Sense.*

An outline relating to the eleventh lecture in the 'Individual Psychology and Spiritual Development' course of 1932. Marked 'Unrevised Notes', representing the theme that Assagioli was to develop in the lecture.

Page 285. For the levels and aspects of the moral conscience, see Roberto Assagioli, 'Moral Conflicts', the Institute of Psychosynthesis, Florence, 1964.

Page 286. For an evaluation of amoralist ideas, see Chapter 13 of this book.

Page 286. For the distinction between the Super-ego and the higher moral conscience, see *Principi e metodi della psicosintesi terapeutica*, p. 190.

Page 287. The personality is the most external part of us, a more or less coherent accumulation of psychological elements from different sources: inherited aspects, the influence of our environment (to varying degrees), the assimilation of individual characteristics. Individuality, on the other hand, is our spiritual centre, who we truly are deep within, unique and universal at one and the same time ('Individual Psychology and Spiritual Development', Roberto Assagioli, the Institute of Psychosynthesis, Rome, 1932).

Appendix 2: *Spiritual Elements in our Personality: the Desire to Know and the Capacity for Knowledge.*

This outline relates to the tenth lecture in the 'Individual Psychology and Spiritual Development' course of 1932. Marked 'Undeveloped Notes', it represents the theme that Assagioli was to develop in the lecture.

Page 289. For an examination of the nature and different aspects of rational knowledge, see Roberto Assagioli, 'Notes on Education', the Institute of Psychosynthesis, Florence, 1968.

Page 290. Spiritual identification is very different from emotional identification: the latter is blind, exclusive and demanding; the former, on the other hand, is far-seeing free from attachment, and disinterested (Roberto Assagioli, 'Understanding Others', the Institute of Psychosynthesis,

Florence, undated).

Page 290. Intuition is not irrational, but super-rational. The cooperation of the mind is nevertheless necessary for its correct use. The functions of the mind with respect to intuition are: first, recognizing intuition and its messages; second, interpreting them correctly; third, formulating them and expressing them (Roberto Assagioli, 'Signposts for the Psychology of the Future', the Institute of Psychosynthesis, Florence, undated).

Page 290. Dis-identification, which we can define as achieving discrimination between the self and the non-self, and is obtained in the consciousness as we consistently take an objective view of the successive, passing contents of consciousness itself, aims at identification with the higher 'I' or the Self. (Extract from 'Studying Oneself', Roberto Assagioli, the Institute of Psychosynthesis, Florence, 1932).

INDEX